Punished for Aging

Vulnerability, Rights, and Access to Justice in Canadian Penitentiaries

ADELINA IFTENE

UNIVERSITY OF TORONTO PRESS
Toronto Buffalo London

© University of Toronto Press 2019
Toronto Buffalo London
utorontopress.com

ISBN 978-1-4875-0216-4 (cloth)   ISBN 978-1-4875-2428-9 (paper)

Library and Archives Canada Cataloguing in Publication

Title: Punished for aging : vulnerability, rights, and access to justice in
    Canadian penitentiaries / Adelina Iftene.
Names: Iftene, Adelina, 1987– author.
Description: Includes bibliographical references and index.
Identifiers: Canadiana 20190103280 | ISBN 9781487524289 (paper) |
    ISBN 9781487502164 (cloth)
Subjects: LCSH: Older prisoners—Civil rights—Canada. |
    LCSH: Older prisoners—Legal status, laws, etc.—Canada. |
    LCSH: Prisons—Government policy—Canada. | LCSH: Justice,
    Administration of—Canada.
Classification: LCC HV9507 .I48 2019 | DDC 323.3/29270971—dc23

This book has been published with the help of a grant from the Federation
for the Humanities and Social Sciences, through the Awards to Scholarly
Publications Program, using funds provided by the Social Sciences and
Humanities Research Council of Canada.

University of Toronto Press acknowledges the financial assistance to its
publishing program of the Canada Council for the Arts and the Ontario
Arts Council, an agency of the Government of Ontario.

Canada Council   Conseil des Arts
for the Arts   du Canada

Funded by the   Financé par le
Government   gouvernement
of Canada   du Canada

To the 197 men interviewed for this book, whose lives have been so devastatingly impacted by incarceration

Contents

Acknowledgments

This book exists because of the unwavering support and guidance that I received from many people during some seven years of research and writing.

The original research for the book was completed during my doctoral studies at Queen's University Faculty of Law. I am extremely grateful for all the support I received from the faculty and staff there, especially those who guided, reviewed, and commented on my work. I am particularly grateful to my PhD supervisor, Professor Allan Manson, for teaching me everything I know about prison law, as well as to my doctoral committee: Professors Sharry Aiken, David Freedman, and Fiona Kay. I am indebted to Professor Don Stuart for all the conversations we had that shaped my views of the law, as reflected in this book. I will never be able to thank Professor Anthony Doob of the University of Toronto enough for his contribution to this work – from teaching me how to conduct quantitative research to reading my work and providing valuable feedback every step of the way.

The writing of this book took place while I was a postdoctoral research fellow at Osgoode Hall Law School, York University. I am grateful for the support I received from the law school towards completing this work, and I am particularly thankful for the support and guidance I received from my postdoctoral supervisor, Professor Ben Berger.

I would also like to thank those who provided feedback on various drafts of the book and whose comments substantially improved this work: Professor Sheila Wildeman of Dalhousie University's Schulich School of Law, Basil Alexander, Tom Harrison, and the two anonymous reviewers.

This work would not have been possible without the generous support of the Social Science and Humanities Research Council, which funded my doctoral studies through an Armand Bombardier Award, my postdoctoral work through a Postdoctoral Fellowship, and the publication of this book through an Award for Scholarly Publications.

Thank you to the incredible team at the University of Toronto Press for all the hard work they put into this manuscript. I am particularly grateful for the fantastic guidance and support from my editor, Daniel Quinlan – one of the most patient people I know!

This book would also not have happened without the 197 incarcerated individuals who took significant risks in order to talk to me about their experiences, without any direct benefit to them. The book is dedicated to them and to everyone in their lives who have been touched by the devastating experience of incarceration. I am hoping that this book will contribute, even a little bit, to raising awareness of the injustices that take place behind prison walls and of the vulnerabilities that are being abused, and to perhaps helping improve the status quo. If any of that happens, it is entirely because of the 197 individuals who spoke to me.

I am also grateful to the prison officials and prison workers who have supported this study. Numerous men and women in the correctional systems work hard every day to help prisoners and to improve the system. While this book is a criticism of the system and some of the practices employed and perpetuated, it is not a reflection of everyone working in the system. I acknowledge and am grateful for the many compassionate and caring people who work with prisoners and who make the system a little better.

Thank you to my family for their love and support – my mom, my brother, my dad, and my partner, Jas.

Thank you especially to my mom, who taught me to fight for the vulnerable and who installed in me, from an early age, the belief that has guided all my professional life – that where there is a will, there is a way.

PUNISHED FOR AGING

The Actors Enter the Stage

Next time you have a question, ask a person not an inmate.
(Correctional officer at Joyceville Penitentiary)

The Creep

December 2014. I was sitting in a little room in the "programs" building of Collins Bay Institution, a medium security penitentiary in Kingston administered by the Correctional Service of Canada (CSC), the agency in charge of the federal correctional system. It was my second day of interviews, and I was thrilled to be there. It had taken me a year and four months to receive approval to conduct research with older prisoners in federal penitentiaries as part of my doctoral work, and I was feeling a bit like David who had fought the Goliath of correctional bureaucracy and came out successful. How little did I know!

As I sat in the chair of the small interview room, entering the second half hour of waiting, I listened to four officers having a burping contest in the corridor, their way of combatting boredom. I also wondered how the next interview would unfold, especially since a staff member had informed me that my next person was "creepy" and that I should be careful. I positioned myself close to the door, my personal alarm system in hand, ready in case my interviewee turned over the desk in a cartoonish attempt to get to me. That's when John walked in.

John was a man who appeared to be about seventy-five years old and moved with considerable difficulty. He wore dirty kitchen clothes and smelled like food. He was a heavy man, breathing loudly, with an exhausted look on his face. He had spent the morning cooking, had been on his feet since 5 a.m. (it was 11 a.m. at that point), and was happy to have a seat. He was also happy to talk to someone. The last visit he had received was back in 2008, despite having a number of relatives (his mother, eight children, and eight grandchildren). "Miss, I am very happy to have the possibility to get out of my house and talk to someone." John was the first in a long list of people I heard refer to their prison cell as their "house."

As it turned out, John was not seventy-five. He had just turned fifty-nine and had been in prison for twenty-eight years. At the age of thirty-one, a first-time offender, he was found guilty of first degree murder and sentenced to life in prison without possibility of parole for twenty-five years. When I met him, John was well acquainted with the federal correctional system; he had spent time in most of the federal institutions in Ontario, at all levels of security. In 2008, John was in Frontenac, a minimum security institution (now called Collins Bay Minimum Security Institution). He applied and received day parole at that time. On day parole John was allowed to go out into the community for a number of hours at a time, after which he was to return to prison on his own. Being successful on day parole was an important first step towards receiving full parole. While John had a life sentence that would never end (formally referred to as "a warrant that would never expire"), he was entitled to apply to have the place where he served his sentence changed from prison to the community (called "full parole") after twenty-five years. Thus, if released, he would be outside with his family, while still under supervision for the rest of his life. John's first full parole eligibility date was in 2011, but he never made it that far. During his day parole period, John got into an argument with a correctional officer whom he pushed. His day parole was immediately revoked, any chances for a full parole on first eligibility date were shattered, and he was sent to Collins Bay Medium Security Institution, where he spent ninety days in solitary confinement.

In 2004, John's wife was diagnosed with a form of cancer, which reached the aggressive stage in 2010. He told me that "we had been battling her disease for most of the last decade. But it eventually won." He applied desperately for all forms of parole so he could be with her through what they understood was her last illness. But he was only again granted day parole in time for his wife's funeral in 2012. It took a while for John to tell me this story. He showed me a worn-out picture of his wife. He could not stop crying, and I was thinking of this brave woman who had raised eight children by herself and stood by her husband for twenty-six years of incarceration. She never got to see him redeemed, to see him on the outside as an accepted member of the community, as someone who had paid his due to society. This thought broke his heart.

John took comfort in the fact that he was at least able to go to her funeral. But that, as it turned out, cost him many more years in prison.

He said the events on the day of the funeral were somewhat blurry in his mind. He returned to prison in the evening. A few hours later, an officer discovered a $20 bill in his coat pocket. Prisoners are not allowed to have cash on them, and John was supposed to hand the bill over with his other personal effects when he was processed upon returning to the institution. "I had just buried my wife, who I was not allowed to see while still alive. I was not doing very well. The $20 bill was a slip." John was charged with contraband and sent to Joyceville Medium Security Institution, to solitary confinement. After that, he was sent back to Collins Bay Medium Security Institution, where he had been for one year at the time I met him. John was grateful he could work in the kitchen there. He enjoyed it, and it kept his grief at bay. After his wife passed, the CSC did not offer him counselling, and grief groups were not available. He said he worked his way through pain. He also said he did not care much for being bullied, which happened a lot: hitting, pushing, insults, ridicule, and cutting in line. The only thing he still minded was being called a "kiddie diddler." And so, from my second day of interviews I learned about ageism in prison: many of the older people are deemed paedophiles, the most hated and targeted prison group. The only chance of shaking that bias is if the individual grows old in the same prison and is known to everyone. That was not John's case; he had changed institutions every two years for the last decade.

I returned the next day to talk about health care and security with John. As he had a total of seventeen chronic illnesses, took thirty pills daily, needed six medical devices that he had to pay for himself, required insulin shots, and had a leg ulcer, this conversation turned out to be a long one.

The Dead Man Walking

Pittsburgh Institution (now called Joyceville Minimum Security Institution) was one of the places where I conducted my 197 interviews with men over fifty years old. Pittsburgh Institution is a minimum security prison just outside Kingston, where 70 per cent of the population is over fifty. It is considered one of the good institutions, with house-style independent living accommodations, fewer disciplinary incidents, many people benefiting from community escorts, and nicer staff and officers. However, I found out almost as soon as I stepped inside that the place is infamously known as the "dead men's camp" because of the high rate of natural death occurring on its premises.

> It's calmer, so it is one of the better institutions to be sent to die in. (JJ, 56, in prison 30 years)

I interviewed dozens of men there. When I began my interviews, I thought minimum security would be a place of hope from where individuals were most likely to be released. Pittsburgh was, in fact, a place of desperation, with burned-out individuals who had spent decades in prisons, whose families were dead or dying, and who had little to return to. For the age group I studied, it was a place of loneliness and disease.

Eric fit this description, despite having been sentenced to "only" five years in prison and having already served two. Eric was brought to the office where I was conducting the interviews by his assigned peer caregiver. Eric was in a wheelchair and had difficulty moving more than a hand here and there. He was soft spoken, and I needed him to repeat himself many times before I could make out his answers. The interview was clearly a very tiresome process for him. When I asked him something, he often took a long time to answer, while staring at me (or beyond me). I was not sure whether he was thinking or didn't understand the question. His eyes were watery most of the time, and his hands were shaking. He had spots on his face that I later found out were skin cancer. Between his advanced stage multiple sclerosis (MS), Parkinson's disease, skin cancer, congenital heart problem, osteoporosis, and disability, he took a lot of medication, especially painkillers.

Eric was seventy-four years old. Three years earlier, he had been tried for a crime he committed when he was nineteen. Since that crime, he had joined the military and worked for both the Royal Military College and the North Atlantic Treaty Organization (NATO). He had a long career before he retired in his late fifties. He was still married to his wife of forty-four years. He had never been in prison before, and the trial and subsequent incarceration caused his health to deteriorate considerably. His physical health was not the worst thing, he said – his anxiety and depression were. He was anxious about his health and about being in prison. He was afraid of taking a shower because he might slip, and there was no panic button in the bathroom. He had recently fallen, and he was not sure how much his bones could take. He was being threatened by younger prisoners all the time but kept to himself, and he didn't really think he was in danger. What kept him up at night was the depression he had been battling over the last couple of years. Eric was particularly worried about his wife, who was old and sick and had never been without him in forty-two years. They didn't have children, but they were the legal guardians of his wife's brother, who had a mental illness. Eric was worried because it was very difficult for an elderly woman to take care of a man with mental disabilities by herself. He teared up when he talked about her.

I asked Eric if he had applied for parole. Because he had a determinate sentence (that is, one that has a clear end date, when the warrant expires), he was entitled to apply for full parole once he had served one-third of his sentence, which had passed by my calculations. It turned out he had indeed applied but did not receive parole, and now he was waiting for his statutory release. Individuals with determinate sentences who do not get paroled have a semi-automatic right to be released and serve their remaining sentences in the community once they have served two-thirds of their sentence in prison. That amounted to just over another year in prison for Eric. It was surprising that Eric did not get parole – he was far from a threat, he had family who depended on him, he had a clean disciplinary record, he was very sick, he had been convicted for a historic crime (a crime committed over thirty years ago), and he had not offended since. However, he explained to me that, similar to the majority of the CSC prisoners, he had been assigned a correctional program to complete, and he was recommended to take some other additional programs. Eric explained that he had tried going to three or four of those programs in his wheelchair but he could not stay awake, so he was kicked out. Eric took twelve pills daily, in addition to liquid nitrogen for his skin cancer. Among these pills, some were mild sedatives to ease the pain caused by MS and cancer. Staying alert was a challenge even before incarceration, so it was not surprising he could not stay awake for programs now. He had come to terms with the fact that he would have to spend another year in prison, but that did not keep him from worrying about his wife. He was scared that he might be "detained." In a small number of cases, the CSC can recommend to the parole board that the individual not be released on his statutory release day. In these cases, the individual would have to serve the whole sentence in prison until their warrant expired, an action formally known as "being detained." This action generally occurs when the individual has a significant number of disciplinary incidents in prison – not applicable in Eric's case – and has been convicted for certain offences. Eric said that the staff were nice and encouraged him by asserting that they doubted the CSC would ever recommend detention for someone in his circumstances.

As Eric left the room, the next man entered. The new arrival looked at me, pointed to the door, and said, "I see you talked to the dead man."

John and Eric's stories are stories of aging, disease, loss, and death. All of us have or will at some point in our lives experience these things. Nonetheless, what makes their experiences peculiar is the environment in which they take place: an enclosed, bureaucratic, isolating space that modifies the experience of aging and loss beyond recognition. In turn, aging and loss modify the carceral environment in a manner overlooked by policy and lawmakers.

During the research for this book, I visited seven federal penitentiaries and interviewed 197 men who, by prison standards, are considered "older." The stories that I have heard are the starting point, the background, and the end game of an investigation into the institutional services, correctional policies, and access to justice for a vulnerable and understudied but growing group of prisoners: older individuals. This book tells the story of the interplay between aging and imprisonment through the eyes of those who have experienced it.

Thus, the book has three main aims: to inform, to challenge, and to start a conversation about reform. First, the reader is invited to witness the experiences of people living their "golden years" behind bars, at a point in time when the elderly portion of the prison population has grown at unprecedented rates. Second, I will examine how the unique set of problems aging brings into the prison space challenges our understanding of what punishment is from an institutional, policy, and legal standpoint. How do heighted needs shape the prison environment? How does the prison environment respond to these needs? What are the rights of incarcerated individuals with heightened needs? What are the options available to these individuals to challenge the potential denial of those rights when their needs are not met? The book is built around a study about aging in prison, and it engages with a vulnerable group of prisoners. However, the issues raised in this book, in terms of health care, conditions of confinement, and especially access to justice, are not specific to this group alone. Rather, they depict systemic problems that infiltrate the body of the federal correctional system and other institutions that engage with incarcerated individuals. Nonetheless, older prisoners are an interesting group through which to study these problems. While any prisoner likely suffers because of the shortcomings of the system, older prisoners, like other vulnerable groups, feel these limitations more intensely as their needs are higher. At the end of each section, I will offer recommendations that could be used as a starting point for creating an age-sensitive correctional environment, as well as an inclusive legal system, which does not treat prisoners, in particular vulnerable prisoners, as "outcasts from our system of rights."[1]

These recommendations are modest, and it will be up to policy and lawmakers to use the information in this book, and in other prison studies, to design and implement tools to bring about much-needed change. However, the set of recommendations that I provide is envisioned as a conversation starter, not only for government and legal actors but also

---

1 *Sauvé v Canada (Chief Electoral Officer)*, 2002 SCC 68, [2002] 3 SCR 519 at para 40.

for individuals from other disciplines involved in prison work, prison rights advocates, as well as for any individual concerned about the state of affairs behind prison walls. The stories in this book need to preoccupy our minds and haunt our dreams until we do something to challenge their ending. Over two hundred years ago, John Howard, an early English prison reformer, undertook an extensive review of the state of prisons in England. While the present study is more modest in size than Howard's, the underlying aim is the same. Hence, the words of caution to the reader, with which Howard opens his 1777 book, apply here:

> The journeys were not undertaken for the traveller's amusement, and the collections are not published for general entertainment; but for the perusal of those who have it in their power to give redress to the sufferers.[2]

---

2 John Howard, *The State of the Prisons in England and Wales: with Preliminary Observations, and an Account of Some Foreign Prisons* (Warrington: William Eyres, 1777) at 6, online: https://archive.org/details/stateofprisonsin00howa/page/6.

Chapter One

Some Context: The Canadian Federal Correctional System

The federal correctional system is a complex state apparatus that changes the lives of those who at one point or another get entangled in it. The first goal of this chapter is to offer a bird's eye view of the structure, operations, life, and law in this complex machinery in order to set the background for the issue at the heart of this book: the phenomena of aging in Canadian prisons and the ability of the system to understand and respond to it. This overview is by no means an exhaustive one. The complexities of imprisonment, and the legal, social, and ethical issues it raises, cannot be properly addressed in one chapter. Instead, I will focus here on the broad framework needed to understand the issue at hand, as well as on some specific prison problems that may have direct bearing on health and access to justice. Health and access to justice, as we shall see in later chapters, are the underlying challenges present in all aspects of older individuals' lives. The second goal of the chapter is to provide the reader with background information on the phenomena of aging in prison, abroad and in Canada. In addition, I will introduce the reader to the methodology used for the research study on which this book builds, as well as to the general aims of the book.

Inside the "House" of 15,000 People: Life and Law in the Federal Prison System

> Look ... I lived in here most of my adult life. There is nothing for me on the outside. I don't want to live on the outside. I don't know how to live on the outside. But I really don't want to die in here. (AA, 63, in prison 43 years)

Daily Operations, Security, and Health Care in Canadian Penitentiaries

Correctional issues are not uniformly regulated in Canada. In fact, there are several correctional systems in this country. The *Criminal Code*[1] specifies that people sentenced to imprisonment for less than two years will serve their time in provincial or territorial prisons. Every province and territory thus has its own correctional system, which is to a large extent regulated by provincial and territorial legislation. Aside from prisons, the provincial correctional systems include jails and detention centres. There are approximately 160 provincial and territorial facilities with different levels of security in Canada.[2] Jails and detention centres are the point of entry into the correctional systems and are classified as maximum security. They hold individuals awaiting their trial or sentencing (on remand), as well as sentenced people awaiting transfer to a federal institution. Some treatment centres (prison hospitals) are also available. As well, each province has its own probation service. The provincial systems are financed entirely by the provincial government. The funding and organization of non-custodial sentences are also provincial matters.

John and Eric, as well as all the people interviewed, were incarcerated in penitentiaries, which are federal prisons. They were all sentenced to two years or more of time to be served in custody, which, according to the *Criminal Code*,[3] places them under the federal correctional authority. John and Eric are two of the over 14,000 individuals[4] incarcerated in forty-three penitentiaries under federal jurisdiction. In addition, they are part of a group of prisoners, those aging behind bars, that has increased dramatically, even though the overall federal imprisonment rates have remained stable throughout the last fifty years.[5] In 2006, 2,069 of 13,171 or 15.7 per cent of the incarcerated population was aged fifty or over.[6]

---

1 *Criminal Code*, RSC, 1985, c C-46, s 743.1 [*CC*].
2 Curt T. Griffiths, *Canadian Criminal Justice* (Toronto: Nelson Education, 2011) at 268.
3 *CC*, *supra* note 1, s 743.1.
4 The number of federally incarcerated individuals for 2016–2017 was 14,159. See Public Safety Canada, *Corrections and Conditional Release Statistical Overview, 2017* (Ottawa: Public Works and Government Services Canada, 2018) at 36, Table C2, online: https://www.publicsafety.gc.ca/cnt/rsrcs/pblctns/ccrso-2017/ccrso-2017-en.pdf [PSC 2017].
5 Cheryl Marie Webster & Anthony N. Doob, "Penal Reform 'Canadian Style': Fiscal Responsibility and Decarceration in Alberta, Canada" (2014) 16:1 Punishment & Society 3 at 28, Figure 1.
6 Public Safety Canada, *Corrections and Conditional Release Statistical Overview, 2007* (Ottawa: Public Works and Government Services Canada, 2007) at 49–50, Figure C7 and Table C7, online: https://www.publicsafety.gc.ca/cnt/rsrcs/pblctns/ccrso-2007/2007-ccrs-eng.pdf.

In 2017, the percentage had risen to 25 per cent.[7] It has been pre-
dicted that the number of older incarcerated people will continue to
grow, especially given the number of people now serving life sentences
(one-quarter of incarcerated individuals) who will age in prison.[8] The
older individuals are spread across the forty-three penitentiaries and can
be encountered, in different proportions, at all levels of security and in
all regions in the country.

The forty-three penitentiaries are administered by a federal governmental agency, the Correctional Service of Canada (CSC). Aside from
penitentiaries, the CSC also administers fourteen community centres,
as well as ninety-two parole offices and sub-offices across the country.[9]
For administrative purposes, the country is divided into five regions
(Atlantic, Quebec, Ontario, Prairies, and Pacific), each with its own
headquarters. The CSC's national headquarters is in Ottawa, and the
agency is directed by its Commissioner of Corrections. All of the 197
men I interviewed were from institutions in the Ontario region. I chose
Ontario for my study partially because of the convenience of the location: I was previously based in Kingston, Ontario, which, at the time of
the study, was surrounded by several correctional institutions within a
one-hour drive. Also, Ontario, as the most populous region in the country, has the most correctional institutions at all levels of security and
incarcerates some of the most diverse – both in terms of age and race –
people from across the country.

The CSC institutions include penitentiaries for men and women, five
mental health treatment centres (one in each region), and Aboriginal
healing lodges. Each institution is designated minimum, medium, or
maximum security. There are also some multilevel institutions, as well
as one special handling unit (SHU), or "super-maximum" facility, for
prisoners of the highest level of risk (situated in Ste-Anne-des-Plaines,
Quebec).[10]

Look Miss, let me explain to you how this works. I spent many years in the
SHU. They don't care about us there because we are seen as the worst of

---

7 PSC 2017, *supra* note 4 at 48, Table C8.

8 Canada, Office of the Correctional Investigator, *Annual Report, 2010–2011* (Ottawa: OCI,
   2011) at 21, online: http://www.oci-bec.gc.ca/cnt/rpt/pdf/annrpt/annrpt20102011-eng
   .pdf [OCI 2010–2011].

9 These are the numbers as of 7 November 2018, available on the Correctional Service of
   Canada website. See Correctional Service of Canada, "Facilities and Security" (accessed
   7 November 2018), online: https://www.csc-scc.gc.ca/facilities-and-security/index-eng
   .shtml.

10 *Ibid.*

the worst. It goes like this ... people who cannot be handled in society get sent to prison. People who can't be handled in prison get sent to maximum security institutions. People who can't be handled in maximum security get sent to the SHU. It's not a happy place. Once there, you have to fight. It's really kill or be killed. In these circumstances, it is really hard to prove you are not a danger and you are deserving of being in a lower security institution. (MM, 50, maximum security, in prison 32 years)

Some institutions also have protective custody (PC) units. Certain groups of prisoners, such as sex offenders, are particularly at risk in the general population in some institutions, and thus they may be segregated and kept for twenty-three hours each day in their cells.

I signed up to be in PC. I know I placed a target on my back. I can never go into the gen pop [general population] in this institution, because there is the belief that all PCs are rapists. I signed up not because I am afraid. I signed up to stay out of trouble. For the last thirty-two years the lowest I went was Warkworth [a high medium security institution] and I was first incarcerated for auto theft. But I always get into trouble. I fight to survive. I can't be fighting anymore or I'll never get out of here. (MM, 50, maximum security, in prison 32 years)

Other forms of segregation, such as administrative or disciplinary segregation, are intended to be mainly used for unstable people or as a punishment for those who have committed disciplinary offences. Segregation or solitary confinement units only exist within medium, maximum, or super-maximum security institutions (the latter are essentially solitary confinement–based institutions).

At the time of the interview, John was serving time in the Collins Bay Institution, a medium security penitentiary inside the city of Kingston. At the time I visited, Collins Bay was solely a medium security institution with two types of accommodation: independent living units and regular cell-based blocks. Intended for lower-risk individuals who were close to being released, independent living units were single-person rooms in which prisoners were provided with food they could prepare themselves. Prisoners in this block had greater freedom because it was intended to help prepare them for reintegration into the community. The other blocks were regular cell-based blocks, where individuals were under a medium form of supervision. They would eat in the common room together, partake in programs and work, and were locked up in their cells the rest of the time. Because of overcrowding, 30 per cent of the cells at Collins Bay were double bunked (that is, two prisoners were essentially living in a single-person cell). This accommodation created discontent among individuals, especially when an older individual was paired with a younger, more rambunctious person.

> I am cold all the time. I have diabetes and my circulation is so bad. My Bunkie works out in the evening and then, when he returns to the room, he is hot and leaves the window open overnight in the dead of winter. I have a cold every second week, and I had pneumonia twice in the last five years. I know better than to say anything. He is twenty! (DD, 62, in prison 5 years)

John was "luckier." He had many health problems, including a leg ulcer and no bladder control, so he was by himself in a cell. He had been in the system for a very long time and had travelled between most of the institutions in Ontario. As we have already heard, John was sent back to Collins Bay from Pittsburgh Minimum Security Institution after being caught with a $20 bill upon returning from his wife's funeral. It is customary for the CSC to send an individual to segregation when sanctioned for a disciplinary offence, even if the offence is not violent. As mentioned, minimum security institutions do not have solitary confinement cells, so he was shipped to Collins Bay where he continued to serve time after his release from sixty days in segregation.

Transfers to a higher form of security are also a common form of punishment for a disciplinary offence. A person like John, who is serving life, would have to work his way down to minimum security before having a realistic chance of day or full parole. The gradual decrease in the form of security during a prisoner's stay in prison is seen as an essential part of the CSC's philosophy of reintegration and rehabilitation for prisoners, and it is sometimes referred to as "cascading down the security levels." With each security level descent, the individual receives more independence and is gradually readjusted to an independent, un-institutionalized life. For example, at lower security levels, individuals are reaccustomed to cooking their own meals and cleaning up after themselves. However, this type of transitioning is not always possible for individuals who are serving determinate sentences. Whatever type of institution (regardless of security level) individuals serving a determinate sentence find themselves in at the time of their statutory release (that is, when they have served two-thirds of their sentence),[11] they are released directly from there into the community. But for people like John, who are serving life

---

11 Types of imprisonment sentences and the manner in which parole eligibility is calculated can be found in the *Criminal Code*. See *CC, supra* note 1, ss 716–45.

sentences, there is no statutory release. Such individuals have, generally, spent longer periods of time in prison than those serving determinate sentences. Thus, they are seen as more "institutionalized" and more in need of a gradual community reintegration process.

Low security institutions are not reserved for those who have worked their way down from a more restrictive setting. Eric was serving his sentence in the Pittsburgh Institution (now called Joyceville Minimum Security Institution), and it was the only institution where he had ever served time. When incarcerated, all people are sent to an assessment unit for each correctional region (in Ontario, this unit is currently located in Joyceville, a medium security penitentiary). Their risk level is assessed based on the crime they committed, their offence history, and their psychological traits. The results of the assessment dictate the level of security and the institution where the individual will serve at least the first part of their sentence. In Eric's case, he was incarcerated for the first time in old age, was already very sick, and had committed his offence forty years earlier. Thus, he was assessed as low risk and placed in Pittsburgh. While for most prisoners minimum security institutions (colloquially called "camps" or "houses") are ideal, the level of independence may pose problems for individuals who are not independent even on the outside. Pittsburgh provides "house-based" living in which individuals are assigned to a room. Each house has a bathroom and a kitchen. The first difficulty for individuals like Eric is that, as a unit, prisoners in each house order food for their house and cook it themselves in the house kitchen. Because of his numerous medical conditions, Eric could not eat everything. The food orders were placed by the more vocal prisoners in the house, who were younger and healthier. Hence, little consideration was given to Eric's different nutritional needs. In addition, Eric could not cook for himself. The CSC assigned a peer cook for the houses where very sick people lived, which made life a little easier.

The second difficulty was that Pittsburgh is a large, open space compound, where people need to walk from one area to another (for example, from their house to the programs building). Eric had considerable difficulty moving around, so these distances were hard for him. Having to wheel himself through the yard to get places made Eric isolate himself and partake in few to no activities.

The third difficulty was that independent living did not mean single rooms; instead, two people slept in single rooms in side-by-side beds. Eric's wheelchair turned out to be an issue, as sharing a single room meant limited space. Finally, Eric was very concerned about using the bathroom and showering because there was no panic button in the whole house where he lived. Its absence is an anomaly: cell-based institutions have a panic button in each cell for emergency purposes (mainly because the prisoners cannot get out of the cell to seek help). Yet, this institution had no panic buttons, probably because prisoners were not confined to their rooms – completely ignoring the fact that some people were confined to the space by their own physical disabilities.

Regardless, the Pittsburgh Institution is seen as one of the "most comfortable" institutions in Ontario. Indeed, as the last institution I visited, the friendliness of the staff was apparent, peer caregivers were available, and the programs offered were more diverse. Seen as a "safer, quieter" place, the feeblest individuals are often sent here. More than 70 per cent of those incarcerated at Pittsburgh were over fifty years old, many of whom had severe disabilities. In lieu of a hospice or palliative care units, the CSC also used this prison to incarcerate a large proportion of the terminally ill from across the province.

Unlike health care in the community, health care in federal custody is not a provincial or territorial matter. The CSC is instead responsible for the health care of its prisoners, from sickness prevention to end-of-life care. Prisoners' health only becomes a province's responsibility upon release. According to CSC documents, four main types of health facilities are found within federal correctional settings: institutional health units (for example, ambulatory care centres), CSC regional hospitals, CSC reception centres, and CSC regional treatment centres (for mental health).[12] When an individual is evaluated after sentencing in the region's assessment unit, a health assessment is conducted in addition to the risk assessment. The health assessments included are mental health assessment, tuberculosis assessment, and comprehensive health assessment.[13] The purpose is to identify the medical needs of the individual and to place that individual in a prison that provides the services their needs demand.

At the institutional level, primary care is offered on-site, generally by nursing staff. Primary care is the most frequently used level of care in prison. In some institutions, but not all, a nurse is present twenty-four hours. The nurse makes assessments, provides counselling, dispenses medication, takes blood samples, gives immunization, and does blood pressure checks, among other things. When deemed appropriate, the nurse may set an appointment for the prisoner with the primary care prison physician. Other services such as X-rays, dental and vision

---

12 Correctional Service of Canada, "Health Services" (accessed June 2010), online: https://www.csc-scc.gc.ca/health/index-eng.shtml. Note that the 2010 document cited here and in notes 13, 14, and 15 has been removed from the website, so some details are no longer posted on the health services pages.

13 *Ibid.*

care, and psychotherapy are available at pre-arranged times of varying frequency. A range of specialist physicians also make regular visits to institutions depending on need, location, and availability. For major surgeries and specialized treatments, prisoners are transferred to community hospitals.[14]

Four of the five regions have regional hospitals. In the fifth, the Prairies, in-patients are instead sent to the chronic wing of the region's mental health treatment facility. The regional hospitals are intended to provide care for a mixture of acute and chronic patients, who generally stay there from four days to eighteen months. The care offered includes post-operative care (for example, following surgery in a community hospital); treatment and care for head injuries, overdoses/self-injuries, muscular-skeletal injuries/fractures, skin ulcers/infections, diabetes (for example, for control and education), respiratory illnesses (for example, asthma, pneumonia, and tuberculosis investigation), thrombosis, urinary tract infection, lung puncture, and stroke; and palliative care. However, the use of these services is severely limited by resources, space, and distance considerations.[15]

For mental health issues, prisoners may be sent to the in-patient regional treatment centre (RTC). In the Ontario region, after the closure of the Kingston Penitentiary, the RTC was moved to Millhaven Institution, the maximum security penitentiary for the region. In these centres, the CSC has a total number of 675 beds across all five regions, with 781 full-time equivalent staff positions. RTCs are hybrid facilities according to the *Corrections and Conditional Release Act* (the legislation governing the activity of the CSC): they constitute a penitentiary, but three of them also operate as a hospital under provincial mental health legislation. They are multilevel security facilities, and four of them are operating within other CSC institutions (aside from the Prairies). The average stay of a prisoner at these treatment centres is between 147 and 232 days.[16]

> The best care I got since I came to prison was at RTC back in Kingston Pen. It was safe, people were nice, and there were all sorts of programs. But that didn't last long. Before I knew it I was back in my cell doing nothing all day and going insane. (EE, 54, in prison 10 years)

The centres offer assessments and stabilization of acutely disordered prisoners (for example, those who are psychotic, suicidal, or have other

---

14 *Ibid.*
15 *Ibid.*
16 OCI 2010–2011, *supra* note 8 at 14.

serious mental illness symptoms), rehabilitation of prisoners with chronic conditions, and treatment for violent and sexual offenders. Some prisoners are also transferred to provincial mental health systems, but the transfer is subject to the approval of the provincial institution. However, the majority of prisoners with mental health problems, especially those with non-acute symptoms, remain in their own institutions where they receive pharmacological interventions if ordered by a physician. For example, Eric, who was affected by chronic depression, never set foot in the RTC. He was treated instead at Pittsburgh with antidepressants, initially prescribed by a psychiatrist and further renewed by the prison physician.

Law, Rights, and Change Behind Bars

If you don't like it you shouldn't have come to prison. (Correctional officer, often cited by participants as responding in this way to prisoners' complaints)

John has been in prison since the early 1980s and has witnessed the transformation of the Correctional Service of Canada:

Prison was gladiator school in the 80s: survival of the fittest. Guards in [maximum security] would make people fight each other. They didn't like you: they beat you up themselves. The food was crap. That's why I have diabetes now. Sure, prison is hard ... I am an old man and I am sick and I didn't get to be with my wife when she died. But these kids running around ... They don't know how good they've got it now.

For the longest time, courts would refuse to intervene in any way in prison administration or exercise any kind of judicial oversight over the decisions of prison administrators. Individuals used to be outside the scope of the law, and their rights were virtually non-existent once incarcerated. In his book *Justice Behind the Walls*, Michael Jackson, one of the first and most vehement prisoners' rights activists and scholars in Canada, describes the tedious reform the Correctional Service of Canada has undergone over the last half century and the legal path to recognizing prisoners as rights holders.[17] Only after the two *Martineau* cases[18]

---

17 Michael Jackson, *Justice Behind the Walls: Human Rights in Canadian Prisons* (Vancouver: Douglas & McIntyre, 2002) [Jackson, *Justice Behind the Walls*].
18 *Martineau v Matsqui Institution Inmate Disciplinary Board* (1977), [1978] 1 SCR 118; *Martineau v Matsqui Inmate Disciplinary Board* (1979), [1980] 1 SCR 602 [*Martineau No. 2*].

did the court finally recognize that the CSC has a duty to act fairly and thus expand the purpose of judicial review to allow for court oversight of prison decisions on this ground. As David Cole and Allan Manson, two legal scholars and prisoners' rights promoters, put it, "*Martineau (no 2)* opened the modern era of prison law in Canada and exposed internal parole and prison process to judicial scrutiny ... [D]ecision-makers have been compelled to revise their processes to conform with the notion of fairness."[19]

Further prisoner rights advancement was achieved with the entrenchment of the *Canadian Charter of Rights and Freedoms* (*Charter*) in the Canadian Constitution.[20] *Charter* rights apply to all individuals, including prisoners, and all prison legislation, regulations, and decisions have to conform to the *Charter*. The *Charter* brought about a host of protections to prisoners, particularly procedural protections against unreasonable search and seizure, and democratic rights.[21] Significantly, in 1992, under the influence of the *Charter*, a new framework was created for the federal correctional system. Penitentiaries are now regulated by the *Corrections and Conditional Release Act (CCRA)*[22] and its related regulation, the *Correctional and Conditional Release Regulations (CCRR)*.[23] Under the new statutory and constitutional protections, prisoners have tools available to ask for redress when officers treat them poorly, when their basic human rights are infringed, or when unfair decisions are made against them. Gone are the days when John watched officers beat prisoners with impunity or allowed them to starve by serving them rotten food.

Significantly, the *CCRA* opens with a statement establishing the purpose of the federal correctional system and the governing desired

---

19 David P. Cole & Allan Manson, *Release from Imprisonment: The Law of Sentencing, Parole and Judicial Review* (Toronto: Carswell, 1990) at 63.

20 *Canadian Charter of Rights and Freedoms*, Part I of the *Constitution Act, 1982*, being Schedule B to the *Canada Act, 1982* (UK), 1982, c 11 [*Charter*].

21 On the matter of the *Charter* protection of prisoners' rights, see Jackson, *Justice Behind the Walls*, *supra* note 17 at 58–62; Mary E. Campbell, "Revolution and Counter-Revolution in Canadian Prisoners' Rights" (1996) 2 Can Crim L Rev 285 [Campbell]; Debra Parkes, "A Prisoners' Charter? Reflections on Prisoner Litigation under the Canadian Charter of Rights and Freedoms" (2006) 40:2 UBC L Rev 629 [Parkes]; Lisa Kerr, "Contesting Expertise in Prison Law" (2014) 60:1 McGill LJ 43 at 51–6 [Kerr, "Contesting Expertise"]; Efrat Arbel, "Contesting Unmodulated Deprivation: Sauvé v Canada and the Normative Limits of Punishment" (2015) 4:1 Can J HR 121 [Arbel].

22 *Corrections and Conditional Release Act*, SC 1992, c 20 [*CCRA*].

23 *Corrections and Conditional Release Regulations*, SOR/92–620 [*CCRR*].

outcome for all actions taken for or against incarcerated people. The stated purpose of the federal correctional system is "to contribute to the maintenance of a just, peaceful and safe society by a) carrying out sentences imposed by courts through the *safe and humane custody* and supervision of offenders, and b) assisting the *rehabilitation* of offenders and their *reintegration* into the community as law-abiding citizens *through the provision of programs* in penitentiaries and in the community"[24] [emphasis added].

The *CCRA* (with the help of *CCRR)* further regulates all aspects of life in prison, regulations that should be furthering a safe, humane custody and supervision with the purpose of rehabilitating and reintegrating prisoners into the community. Thus, the *CCRA* regulates the risk assessment procedure, the determination of a parent institution (the institution where the individual will serve their time once assessed), prisoners' rights, transfers from one institution to another, anti-discrimination practices (for example, sections 4, 17, 88), health care entitlements (sections 85–8), environment and infrastructure (section 70), the programs and activities available to prisoners (section 76), disciplinary action, and prisoners' grievances, as well as oversight mechanisms, such as the Office of the Correctional Investigator (OCI; sections 157–98). Three aspects of this piece of legislation have been highlighted as significantly changing the landscape for prisoners' rights: the CSC is to use the least restrictive measure against prisoners; prisoners retain the rights and privileges of all members of society, unless the rights and privileges are incompatible with their sentence; and prison decisions need to be made fairly, with the prisoner having access to an effective grievance system.[25]

To aid with implementing the statutory provisions, the CSC utilizes directives and Standard Operating Practices, which are essentially guidelines and regulations for the main correctional issues. These directives and procedures do not constitute law, but they are of mandatory application to CSC institutions. Indeed, they are policy-creating documents, which are useful for understanding what the CSC standards are and how the CSC applies the law in areas such as health care, solitary confinement, accommodation for vulnerable groups (such as women, people with disabilities, Indigenous populations), disciplinary actions, and so on. Other documents of similar importance are sets of guidelines (for example, the *Palliative Care and End of*

---

24   *CCRA, supra* note 22, s 3.

25   *CCRA, supra* note 22, s 4(d)–(g). See Mary Campbell's discussion on their significance in Campbell, *supra* note 21 at 321.

Life Care in Canadian Federal Institutions Guideline)[26] and formularies, which exhaustively provide for the availability of certain products to prisoners. For example, all physicians working for the CSC are allowed to prescribe only the drugs approved and listed on the *CSC National Drug Formulary.*[27]

Thus, the advancements that have been made in the creation of a legal framework to protect prisoners as human beings and rights holders are considerable. For all this progress, however, persistent correctional problems and human rights violations have lingered over the decades. The CSC continues to administer in an enclosed environment, protected from public scrutiny, where, despite the best intentions of the drafters of the *CCRA*, law is seen as an obstacle to meeting security requirements.

Pervasive problems have long been signalled and received different degrees of societal attention. As we shall see later in the book, many of these outstanding issues are well illustrated by the experiences of older prisoners. Some of these issues include an internal system for prisoner grievances viewed as overly bureaucratic, ineffective, and lacking in independence;[28] courts that are deferential to prison administration and rarely exercise significant supervision over their decisions;[29] high rates of infectious diseases in prisons, partly due to a lack of needle-exchange programs;[30] programs that are not equally available in all institutions, with some prisons lacking opportunities for meaningful work or activities for prisoners;[31] an ineffective parole system that lacks well-established

---

26 Correctional Service of Canada, *Palliative Care and End of Life Care in Canadian Federal Institutions Guideline* (Ottawa: CSC, 2009). This document was obtained through an *Access to Information Act* request in April 2016.

27 Correctional Service of Canada, *National Drug Formulary* (Ottawa: CSC, 2013). This document was obtained through an *Access to Information Act* request in April 2016.

28 Canada, Office of the Correctional Investigator, *Annual Report, 2014–2015* (Ottawa: OCI, 2015) at 31, online: http://www.oci-bec.gc.ca/cnt/rpt/pdf/annrpt/annrpt20142015 -eng.pdf [OCI 2014–2015].

29 Parkes, *supra* note 21; Kerr, "Contesting Expertise," *supra* note 21; Lisa Kerr, "Easy Prison Cases" (2015) 71 SCLR (2d) 235 [Kerr, "Easy Prison Cases"].

30 Canadian HIV/AIDS Legal Network, *Prison Needle Exchange: Lessons from a Comprehensive Review of International Evidence and Experience*, 2nd ed (Toronto: Canadian HIV/ AIDS Legal Network, 2006); Canadian HIV/AIDS Legal Network, *On Point: Recommendations for Prison-Based Needle and Syringe Programs in Canada* (Toronto: Canadian HIV/ AIDS Legal Network, 2016).

31 Canada, Office of the Correctional Investigator, *Annual Report, 2015–2016* (Ottawa: OCI, 2016) at 52–4, online: http://www.oci-bec.gc.ca/cnt/rpt/pdf/annrpt/annrpt20152016 -eng.pdf [OCI 2015–2016].

criteria to make early release frequent and/or predictable;[32] and the overuse of solitary confinement.[33]

Contextualizing the Study: Background and Methods

> Nobody messed with me. I had a reputation. I used to make guys shit themselves. These days the best way to protect my reputation and myself is to lay low. Not give away how weak I have become. (JJ, 56, in prison 30 years)

Solitary confinement, mental illness, the treatment of women, and the disproportionate number of Aboriginal people are decades-old, unsolved issues within the prison system. Some people have made it their life's work to right these wrongs, bring substantial justice to these people, and visibility to their problems.[34] Despite their considerable efforts, we have yet to see the kind of change they have advocated for, which begs

---

32 Anthony N. Doob, Cheryl Marie Webster, & Allan Manson, "Zombie Parole: The Withering of Conditional Release in Canada" (2014) 61 Crim LQ 301; Ivan Zinger, "Conditional Release and Human Rights in Canada: A Commentary" (2012) 54:1 CJCCJ 117 at 119–20, https://doi.org/10.3138/cjccj.2011.E.19; Kelly Hannah-Moffatt & Caroline Yule, "Gaining Insight, Changing Attitudes and Managing 'Risk': Parole Release Decisions for Women Convicted of Violent Crimes" (2011) 13:2 Punishment & Society 149; Michael Jackson & Graham Stewart, *A Flawed Compass: A Human Rights Analysis of the Roadmap to Strengthening Public Safety* (2009) at 109–15, online: http://www.justicebehindthewalls.net/resources/news/flawed_Compass.pdf; Adelina Iftene, "The Case for a New Compassionate Release Statutory Provision" (2017) 54:4 Alta L Rev 929.

33 Louise Arbour, *Commission of Inquiry into Certain Events at the Prison for Women in Kingston* (Ottawa: Public Works and Government Services of Canada, 1996) ch 2.3 [Arbour Report]; Paul Gendreau & Jim Bonta, "Solitary Confinement Is Not Cruel and Unusual: People Sometimes Are!" (1984) 26 Can J Crim 467; Public Safety Canada, *Commitment to Legal Compliance, Fair Decision and Effective Results: Task Force Report Reviewing Administrative Segregation* (Ottawa: PSC, 1997); Ivan Zinger, Cherami Wichmann, & D.A. Andrews, "The Psychological Effects of 60 Days in Administrative Segregation" (2001) 43 Can J Crim 47; Michael Jackson, "The Litmus Test of Legitimacy: Independent Adjudication and Administrative Segregation" (2006) 48 CJCCJ 157; Diane Kelsall, "Cruel and Unusual Punishment: Solitary Confinement in Canadian Prisons" (2014) 186:18 CMAJ 1345; Lisa Coleen Kerr, "The Chronic Failure to Control Prisoner Isolation in US and Canadian Law" (2015) 40:2 Queen's LJ 483; Arbel, *supra* note 21; Debra Parkes, "Ending the Isolation: An Introduction to the Special Volume on Human Rights and Solitary Confinement" (2015) 4:1 Can J Human Rights vii–xiii; Canada, Office of the Correctional Investigator, *Administrative Segregation in Federal Corrections: 10 Year Trends* (Ottawa: OCI, 2015), online: http://www.oci-bec.gc.ca/cnt/rpt/oth-aut/oth-aut20150528-eng.aspx.

34 See, for example, the work of Michael Jackson, Allan Manson, Debra Parkes, Kim Pate, and Mary Campbell.

the question of what happens when novel issues that hamper the prison population go uninvestigated, remain invisible, and add to the already known correctional failures.

The phenomenon of aging in prison has been attributed to the aging of the baby boomers, as well as to tough-on-crime policies (for example, more people entering prison for the first time in old age, increases in the number of indeterminate and life sentences, parole received later in the sentence, and so on).[35] American, European, and Australian scholars have long identified aging as a problematic reality for prisons, and extensive studies that trace this issue have been conducted in these jurisdictions since the 1990s.[36] The aging of the prison population has been

---

35 OCI 2014–2015, *supra* note 28 at 14.

36 Patricia Colsher et al, "Health Status of Older Male Prisoners: A Comprehensive Survey" (1992) 82:6 Am J Public Health 881; Jason S. Ornduff, "Releasing the Elderly Inmate: A Solution to Prison Overcrowding" (1996) 4 Elder LJ 173; Laura Addison, Delores Craig-Molerand, & Connie L. Neely, "Addressing the Needs of Elderly Offenders" (1997) 59:5 Corrections Today 120; Nancy M. Mahon, "Introduction: Death and Dying Behind Bars – Cross-Cutting Themes and Policy Imperatives" (1999) 27 JL Med & Ethics 213; Stephan Ardnt, Carolyn L. Turvey, & Micahel Flaum, "Older Offenders, Substance Abuse and Treatment" (2002) 10:6 Am J Geriatr Psychiatry 733; S. Fazel, J. McMillan, & I. O'Donnell, "Dementia in Prison: Ethical and Legal Implications" (2002) 28:3 J Med Ethics 156 [Fazel, McMillan, & O'Donnell]; Ronald H. Aday, *Aging Prisoners* (Westport, CT: Greenwood Publishing Group, 2003) [Aday, *Aging Prisoners*]; Susan Franzel Levine, "Improving End-of-Life Care of Prisoners" (2005) 11 J Correct Health Care 317; Melvin Delgado & Denise Humm-Delgado, *Health and Health Care in the Nation's Prisons: Issues, Challenges, and Policies* (Lanham, MD: Rowman & Littlefield, 2009); Tina Maschi et al, "Forget Me Not: Dementia in Prison" (2012) 52:4 Gerontologist 441 [Maschi et al, "Forget Me Not"]; Elaine Crawley & Richard Sparks, "Older Men in Prison: Survival, Coping, and Identity" in Alison Liebling & Shadd Maruna, eds, *The Effects of Imprisonment* (London: Routledge, 2011) 343; John Kerbs & Jennifer M. Jolley, eds, *Seniors Behind Bars: Challenges for the Criminal Justice System* (London: Lynne Rienner, 2014) [Kerbs & Jolley, *Seniors Behind Bars*]; Adrian Hayes, "Aging Inside: Older Adults in Prison" in Bernice Elger, Catherine Ritter, & Hein Stover, eds, *Emerging Issues in Prison Health* (Dodrecht: Springer, 2017) 1–12 [Hayes]; Natalie Mann, "Older Age, Harder Time: Ageing and Imprisonment," in Yvonne Jewkes, Ben Crewe, & Jamie Bennett, *Handbook on Prisons*, 2nd ed (London: Routledge, 2016) 514–28 [Mann, "Older Age"]; Brie Williams et al, "Addressing the Aging Crisis in US Criminal Justice Healthcare" (2012) 60:6 J Am Geriatr Soc 1150, https://doi.org/10.1111/j.1532-5415.2012.03962.x [Williams et al]; Chris Trotter & Susan Baidawi, "Older Prisoners: Challenges for Inmates and Prison Management" (2015) 48:2 Austl & NZ J Crim 200 [Trotter & Baidawi]; Glenda Reimer, "The Graying of the Prison Population" (2008) 14:3 J Correct Health Care 202; Judith J. Regan, Ann Alderson, & William M. Regan, "Psychiatric Disorders in Aging Prisoners" (2008) 26:1–2 Clin Gerontol 117, https://doi.org/10.1300/J018v26n01_10; Tina Maschi, Deborah Viola, & Fei Sun, "The High Cost of the International Aging Prisoner Crisis: Well-Being as the Common

deemed a "crisis,"[37] while the older prisoner group has been labelled as "forgotten."[38]

A number of issues have been consistently flagged in the non-Canadian literature. For instance, scholars have agreed that individuals exposed to incarceration tend to age faster ("accelerated aging"), and thus an incarcerated individual presents the health problems of someone ten to fifteen years older in the community. This finding explains why, in prison research, the lower limit of seniority is placed between forty-five and fifty-five years of age.[39] The American literature shows that older individuals present an increased number of chronic health conditions in comparison to younger prisoners, which are often exacerbated by inadequate prison health care.[40] They suffer from improperly managed

Denominator for Action" (2013) 53:4 Gerontologist 453 [Maschi, Viola, & Sun, "High Cost"]; Nicolas Combalbert et al, "Mental Disorders and Cognitive Impairment in Ageing Offenders" (2016) 27:6 J Forens Psychiatry Psychol 853, https://doi.org/10 .1080/14789949.2016.1244277; Lisa C. Barry et al, "Disabilities in Prison Activities of Daily Living and Likelihood of Depression and Suicidal Ideation in Older Prisoners" (2017) 32:10 Int J Geriatr Psychiatry 1141.

37 Williams et al, *supra* note 36 at 1152; Hayes, *supra* note 36 at 1; Maschi, Viola, & Sun, "High Cost," *supra* note 36 at 543.

38 Trotter & Baidawi, *supra* note 36 at 215; Elaine Crawley & Richard Sparks, "Hidden Injuries? Researching the Experiences of Older Men in English Prisons" (2005) 44:4 Howard J 345 at 352–3 [Crawley & Sparks, "Hidden Injuries?"]; Maschi, Viola, & Sun, "High Cost," *supra* note 36 at 545.

39 Brie Williams & Rita Abraldes, "Growing Older: Challenges of Prison and Reentry for Aging Population" in Robert Greifinger, ed, *Public Health Behind Bars* (New York: Springer, 2007) 56; Elaine M. Gallagher, "Elders in Prison: Health and Well-Being of Older Inmates" (2001) 24 Int'l JL & Psychiatry 325 [Gallagher]; R.V. Rikard & Ed Rosenberg, "Aging Inmates: A Convergence of Trends in the US Criminal Justice System" (2007) 13:3 J Correct Health Care 150 at 151 [Rikard & Rosenberg]; Canadian Public Health Association, "A Health Care Needs Assessment of Federal Inmates in Canada" (2004) 95, suppl 1, Can J Public Health 1 [CPHA]; Australia, Corrections Victoria, *Growing Old in Prison: A Review of National and International Research on Ageing Offenders*, Corrections Research Paper Series 3, 2010 at 10 [Corrections Victoria]; Correctional Service of Canada, *Managing Older Offenders: Where Do We Stand* (Ottawa: CSC, 1998), online: https://www.csc-scc.gc.ca/research/ r70-eng.shtml [CSC 1998]; OCI 2010–2011, *supra* note 8 at 20; Human Rights Watch, *Old Behind Bars: The Aging Prison Population in the United States*, (New York: Human Rights Watch, 2012) at 17 [HRW]; Elaine Crawley, "Imprisonment in Old Age" in Yvonne Jewkes, ed, *Handbook on Prisons* (Cornwall: Willan Publishing, 2007) 224 at 225; Margaret E. Leigey, "The Bio-Psycho-Social Needs of Older Inmates" in Kerbs & Jolley, *Seniors Behind Bars*, *supra* note 36, 43 at 45.

40 Aday, *Aging Prisoners*, *supra* note 36 at 125; Susan J. Loeb, Darrell Steffensmeier, & Priscilla M. Myco, "In Their Own Words: Older Prisoners' Health Beliefs and Concerns for the Future" (2007) 28:5 Geriatric Nursing 319 at 320; Williams et al, *supra* note 36 at 1153; Mann, "Older Age," *supra* note 36 at 519; Natalie Mann, *Doing*

pain;[41] present numerous and severe physical disabilities,[42] worsen due to a lack of proper accommodation in prisons;[43] experience terminal illnesses in an environment completely unprepared to address these issues;[44] and present high rates of mental illness, especially chronic depression,[45] suicidal ideation,[46] dementia, and other significant cognitive impairment.[47] It also appears that older prisoners have fewer disciplinary problems,[48] while they are at a significantly higher risk of

---

Harder Time? The Experiences of an Ageing Male Prison Population in England and Wales (Farnham, UK: Ashgate, 2012) at 46–51 [Mann, *Doing Harder Time*].

41 Aday, *Aging Prisoners, supra* note 36 at 20–1; James T. Lin & Paul Matthew, "Cancer Pain Management in Prisons: A Survey of Primary Care Practitioners and Inmates" (2005) 29:5 J Pain Symptom Manage 466 at 472; Reimer, *supra* note 36 at 205.

42 Williams et al, *supra* note 36 at 1152; Delgado & Humm-Delgado, *supra* note 36 at 115–16; Ken Howse, *Growing Old in Prison* (Prison Reform Trust, 2008) at 15, online: http://www.prisonreformtrust.org.uk/uploads/documents/Growing.Old.Book_-_small.pdf; Trotter & Baidawi, *supra* note 36 at 208–9.

43 Trotter & Baidawi, *supra* note 36 at 209; Mann, "Older Age," *supra* note 36 at 516–17; Hayes, *supra* note 36 at 5; Cynthia Massie Mara, "Chronic Illness, Disability, and Long Term Care in the Prison Setting" in Paul Katz, Mathy Mezey, & Marshall Kapp, eds, *Vulnerable Populations in the Long Term Care Continuum*, vol 5 (New York: Springer, 2004) 39 at 44; Mann, *Doing Harder Time, supra* note 40 at 43–6.

44 Mary Beth Morrissey, Tina Maschi, & Junghee Han, "Developing Ethical and Palliative Responses Among Seriously Ill Aging Prisoners: Content Analysis Implications and Action Steps" in Be the Evidence Project White Paper, *Aging Prisoners: A Crisis in Need of Intervention* (New York: Fordham University Press, 2012) at 32–6; John F. Linder & Frederick J. Meyers, "Palliative Care for Inmates" (2007) 298:8 JAMA 894 at 895; Franzel Levine, *supra* note 36 at 324–5; Maschi, Viola, & Sun, "High Cost," *supra* note 36 at 545; Ami Harbin, "Prisons and Palliative Politics" in Geoffrey Adelsberg, Lisa Guenther, & Scott Zeman, eds, *Death and Other Penalties: Philosophy in a Time of Mass Incarceration* (New York: Fordham University Press, 2015) 158 at 162; Crawley, *supra* note 39 at 231.

45 Delagado & Humm-Delgado, *supra* note 36 at 94; Leigey, *supra* note 39 at 52; Corrections Victoria, *supra* note 39 at 14; Howse, *supra* note 42 at 19–20; Hayes, *supra* note 36 at 4.

46 Judith F. Cox & James E. Lawrence, "Planning Services for Elderly Inmates with Mental Illness" (2010) 72:3 Corrections Today 52 at 54.

47 Aday, *Aging Prisoners, supra* note 36 at 102–3; Fazel, McMillan, & O'Donnell, *supra* note 36 at 156; Tina Maschi et al, "Forget Me Not" *supra* note 36; Williams et al, *supra* note 36 at 1154–5.

48 Aday, *Aging Prisoners, supra* note 36 at 116; John J. Kerbs, "The Older Prisoner: Social, Psychological and Medical Considerations" in Max Rothman, Burton D. Dunlop, & Pamela Entzel, eds, *Elders, Crime, and the Criminal Justice System: Myths, Perceptions, and Reality in the 21st Century* (New York: Springer, 2000) 207 at 218; John J. Kerbs & Jennifer J. Jolley, "Inmate-on-Inmate Victimization Among Older Male Prisoners" (2007) 53 Crime Delinq 187 [Kerbs & Jolley, "Victimization"]; Marilyn D. McShane & Frank P. William III, "Old and Ornery: The Disciplinary Experiences of Elderly Prisoners" (1990) 34 Int J Offender Ther Comp Criminol 197 at 209–10.

victimization than their younger counterparts.[49] Improper living conditions, unsuitable programs, and increased vulnerability leads to isolation inside prisons of older prisoners, who have often already lost contact with their outside family and friends.[50]

As a result of this work, some positive modifications have occurred in certain US states, as well as in England and Australia. Some prison hospices have been created, often run by volunteers and healthier prisoners, where security is decreased and substantial specialized health care, social work, spiritual care, and other services are offered.[51] Assisted living units are increasingly common in the United States. Some of these units provide nursing home services, and most of them have specialized staff and a host of programs appropriate for the elderly.[52] Inside these units, and sometimes even outside the units in the general population, programs that target the needs of older prisoners have flourished: reminiscence groups, death education programs, property care, self-care, coping with loss, coping with aging, education on euthanasia and living wills, banking, welfare, and other similar programs.[53] Some of the

---

49 Joann Brown Morton, "Implications for Corrections of an Aging Prison Population" in Richard Tewksbury, ed, *Behind Bars: Readings on Prison Culture* (New Jersey: Pearson Prentice Hall, 2006) 78; Aday, *Aging Prisoners, supra* note 36 at 113; John J. Kerbs & Jennifer M. Jolley, "A Commentary on Age Segregation for Older Prisoners: Philosophical and Pragmatic Considerations for Correctional Systems" (2009) 34 Crim J Rev 119 at 126 [Kerbs & Jolley, "Age Segregation"]; Ornduff, *supra* note 36 at 175; CPHA, *supra* note 39; Andrew Tarbuck, "Health of Elderly Prisoners" (2001) 30:5 Age Ageing 369 at 369; Corrections Victoria, *supra* note 39 at 15; HRW, *supra* note 39 at 58; Leigey, *supra* note 39 at 57–8; Trotter & Baidawi, *supra* note 36 at 204–5; Maschi, Viola, & Sun, "High Cost," *supra* note 36 at 545.

50 Aday, *Aging Prisoners, supra* note 36 at 124; Leigey, *supra* note 39 at 59–60; Trotter & Baidawi, *supra* note 36 at 214; Natalie Mann, "Ageing Prisoners," in Carla Reeves, *Experiencing Imprisonment* (London: Routledge, 2016) 176 at 181–2; Maschi, Viola, & Sun, "High Costs," *supra* note 36 at 543.

51 See e.g. Angola Prison, Louisiana; Maryland Hospice Program; Federal Medical Center, Carswell Ft. Worth, Texas; Broward Correctional Institution, Florida; Oregon State Penitentiary; United States Medical Center for Federal Prisoners, Missouri; Vacaville State Prison, California; Michael Unit, Tennessee Colony, Texas; and Dixon Correctional Center, Illinois: Delgado & Humm-Delgado, *supra* note 36 at 147–9; Svetlana Yampolskaya & Norma Winston, "Hospice Care in Prison: General Principles and Outcomes" (2003) 20:4 Am J Hosp Palliat Care 290 at 292 [Yampolskaya & Winston].

52 See e.g. True Grit at the Nevada Correctional Centre; Ohio's Hocking Correctional Facility; Angola Prison, Louisiana; Pine Bluff, Arkansas; Whitworth Detention Center, Georgia; the Minnesota Correctional Facility Stillwater Seniors' Dormitory; Mississippi State Penitentiary; and Old Men's Colony, West Virginia: Yampolskaya & Winston, *supra* note 51 at 291; Delgado & Humm-Delgado, *supra* note 36 at 136; Kerbs & Jolley, *Seniors Behind Bars, supra* note 36 at 153–4; Rikard & Rosenberg, *supra* note 39 at 155.

53 Kerbs & Jolley, *Seniors Behind Bars, supra* note 36 at 87; Aday, *Aging Prisoners, supra* note 36 at 154–8; Rikard & Rosenberg, *supra* note 39 at 155.

most impressive programs are the ones that prepare older prisoners for successful release. These programs operate with the understanding that the place of sick and old individuals is not in prison, and they also recognize that the release preparation needed by people who have perhaps spent long periods of time in prison is different from the needs of their younger counterparts. Staff in these programs generally receive geriatric training, and they focus on helping prisoners find appropriate housing and employment, while teaching these prisoners about the welfare system, banking, social security, and other important aspects of life on the outside.[54]

Despite the rising number of people aging in the Canadian federal correctional system, similar initiatives are generally not available in this country. In fact, aging and associated problems have been the subject of very few studies, and the consequences are yet to be fully understood as a medical and legal carceral issue. That said, the OCI has reported on issues related to aging in prisons for almost a decade.[55] Since 2010, the CSC annual reports have raised regular concerns regarding the increasing number of people aging in prisons,[56] the prison infrastructure that is inappropriate for prisoners with disabilities,[57] the high vulnerability of individuals who are old and sick,[58] the overuse of segregation to ensure their security, and the lack of dedicated geriatric units.[59] The reports also pointed out the scarcity of relevant programs,[60] the lack of sufficient and appropriate medical care,[61] the unavailability or inadequacy of palliative care,[62] and the absence of a properly functioning compassionate release system.[63] More recently, the OCI has raised ethical and legal concerns

---

54 Such programs include the Hocking Correctional Facility in the United States and the UK programs Recoop and Restore 50, described in Maschi, Viola, & Sun, "High Cost," *supra* note 36 at 550–1.

55 Canada, Office of the Correctional Investigator, *Annual Report, 2017–2018* (Ottawa: OCI, 2018) at 25, online: http://www.oci-bec.gc.ca/cnt/rpt/pdf/annrpt/annrpt20172018-eng .pdf [OCI 2017–2018].

56 OCI 2010–2011, *supra* note 8 at 20–5; Canada, Office of the Correctional Investigator, *Annual Report, 2011–2012* (Ottawa: OCI, 2012) at 14, online: http://www.oci-bec.gc.ca/ cnt/rpt/pdf/annrpt/annrpt20112012-eng.pdf [OCI 2011–2012]; Canada, Office of the Correctional Investigator, *Annual Report, 2013–2014* (Ottawa: OCI, 2014) at 15, online: http://www.oci-bec.gc.ca/cnt/rpt/pdf/annrpt/annrpt20132014-eng.pdf [OCI 2013– 2014]; OCI 2014–2015, *supra* note 28 at 15; OCI 2015–2016, *supra* note 31 at 10–11.

57 OCI 2011–2012, *supra* note 56 at 20–1.

58 *Ibid* at 20–5.

59 *Ibid*; OCI 2014–2015, *supra* note 28 at 15.

60 OCI 2011–2012, *supra* note 56 at 20–5; OCI 2015–2016, *supra* note 31 at 12.

61 OCI 2013–2014, *supra* note 56 at 15.

62 *Ibid.*

63 *Ibid*; OCI 2015–2016, *supra* note 31 at 23–4.

resulting from the current implementation in federal corrections of medical assistance in dying.[64] In February 2019, the OCI together with the Canadian Human Rights Commission (CHRC) issued an investigative report detailing the issues that impact aging and dying prisoners and made a set of recommendations focused on conditions of confinement and release options for this category of individuals.[65]

Despite the OCI's calls for reform, the response of the CSC was, for the longest time, not positive. The CSC asserted that all of these initiatives were already in place and that it had no further immediate plans in this area.[66] The CSC has conducted two studies with older male prisoners[67] and three with older female prisoners.[68] The studies are brief, however, and mostly pertain to criminogenic factors in an older age group; all but one[69] are based solely on data from the CSC's administrative databases. Even the interview-based study focuses on the crimes committed by older female offenders and their age at incarceration. It states that "older women offenders demonstrated increased offending versatility and higher risk and need ratings over time, suggesting that these changes in the population could be considered in developing case

---

64   Canada, Office of the Correctional Investigator, *Annual Report, 2016–2017* (Ottawa: OCI, 2017) at 13–25, online: http://www.oci-bec.gc.ca/cnt/rpt/pdf/annrpt/ annrpt20162017-eng.pdf [OCI 2016–2017]. In 2017 medical assistance in dying (MAiD) became legal in Canada: Bill C-14, *An Act to amend the Criminal Code and to make related amendments to other Acts (medical assistance in dying)*, 1st Sess, 42nd Parl, 2016. MAiD also became available to federally incarcerated individuals: *CCRA, supra* note 22, s 19(1.1).

65   Canada, Office of the Correctional Investigator & Canadian Human Rights Commission, *Aging and Dying in Prison: An Investigation into the Experiences of Older Individuals in Federal Custody* (Ottawa, OCI, 2019), online: http://www.oci-bec.gc.ca/cnt/rpt/pdf/ oth-aut/oth-aut20190228-eng.pdf.

66   Correctional Service of Canada, "Response of the Correctional Service of Canada to the 38th Annual Report of the Correctional Investigator 2010–2011" (Ottawa: CSC, 2011), online: https://www.csc-scc.gc.ca/publications/ci10-11/index-eng.shtml.

67   CSC 1998, *supra* note 39; Correctional Service of Canada, "Older Offenders in the Custody of the Correctional Service of Canada," Research in Brief No. 14–21 (Ottawa: CSC, 2014), online: https://www.csc-scc.gc.ca/research/005008-rs14-21-eng .shtml [CSC 2014].

68   Leigh Greiner & Kim Allenby, *A Descriptive Profile of Older Women Offenders*, Research Report No. R-229 (Ottawa: Correctional Service of Canada, 2010), online: https:// www.csc-scc.gc.ca/research/092/005008-0229-01-eng.pdf; S. Michel, R. Gobeil, & A. McConnell, *Older Incarcerated Women Offenders: Social Support and Health Needs*, Research Report No. R-275 (Ottawa: Correctional Service of Canada, 2012); Renée Gobeil, "Older Women Offenders," Research Snippet No. 14–03 (Ottawa: Correctional Service of Canada, 2014), online: https://www.csc-scc.gc.ca/005/008/092/005008-rs14 -03-eng.pdf [Gobeil].

69   Gobeil, *supra* note 68 (includes quotation).

management and intervention strategies." Neither this study nor any other addresses the type of risk or needs these women raise, nor the kinds of strategies that may be required.[70] The most recent study with older people focuses on the number of people over fifty (24 per cent of the prison population in 2014); it is an attempt to minimize the growth and impact of this category of prisoner. The study asserts that the number of people over sixty-five is small, and few of them are in maximum security situations. It also justifies the increase in the overall number of elderly by noting that "the number of non-Aboriginal offenders has increased."[71] None of these studies are investigations into the shortcomings of the system in addressing the needs of the elderly, and none of them identify any need for immediate intervention. In its response to the 2019 OCI/ CHRC report and recommendations on this issue, the CSC stated that it had already created a new policy framework, "Promoting Wellness and Independence – Older Persons in Custody (2018)," which was consistent with the report's recommendations. The CSC addressed each recommendation by highlighting "various change initiatives completed and/ or underway," but noted that it recognized "considerable work remains" and that it "committed to ongoing quality improvement with the goal of maintaining optimal wellness and quality of life for older persons in custody."[72] How this commitment will play out remains to be seen.

Independent researchers have carried out very little investigation into the area of aging in Canadian prisons. In fact, only one exploratory study has been conducted specifically with older men, which signalled that they may have different types of problems than the general prison population.[73] More recently, other authors, while not working specifically with older prisoners, have highlighted health issues pertaining to the management of chronic diseases and dying in Ontario provincial prisons, which are common in old age.[74] In fairness, over the last few decades, both governmental and external research in federal correctional facilities has been limited. Ivan Zinger maintains that "[r]esearch remains the foundation for evidence-based and effective policies. The suppression of scientific and empirical research has been a unique feature of the

---

70   *Ibid.*
71   CSC 2014, *supra* note 67.
72   Correctional Service of Canada, "Response to the Office of the Correctional Investigator's Report – Aging and Dying in Prison: An Investigation into the Experiences of Older Individuals in Federal Custody – February 2019" (Ottawa: CSC, 2019), online: https://www.csc-scc.gc.ca/publications/005007-1509-en.shtml.
73   Gallagher, *supra* note 39.
74   Fiona Kouyoumdjian et al, "Health Status of Prisoners in Canada: Narrative Review" (2016) 62:3 Can Fam Physician 215–22.

Conservative government's tenure."[75] Significant barriers have also been created in relation to access to federal correctional institutions, and the CSC more often than not denies access to researchers and censors their work. The reasoning behind such administrative hurdles is often vague, and no realistic option exists for appealing decisions to deny access.[76] Such hurdles are serious barriers to knowledge advancement and, accordingly, to evidence-based policies.

Knowing the numbers and being familiar with the American work on older prisoners, I decided to look into the issue of aging in Canadian penitentiaries. I wanted to meet the older prisoners, talk to them, and give them a chance to express their worries, problems, and concerns. The ultimate goal of my work was to determine the general quality of life of incarcerated older prisoners in order to better understand the extent to which their rights were being upheld. My attempt to gain access to CSC institutions was met with the same resistance noted by other scholars and researchers.[77] Access to older prisoners came after one year of negotiation with the CSC, a significant amount of compromise on my side, many changes to the initial research protocol, and a denial of access to older female prisoners.

In 2012, when the study commenced, the population of male prisoners over fifty in federal institutions was roughly 2,000 according to data provided by the CSC (out of a total average number of 15,313 prisoners during the 2011–2012 fiscal year).[78] Based on these numbers, I initially decided to interview between 150 and 200 individuals, and I ended up interviewing 197 men. I conducted interviews in seven institutions in the Ontario region: two minimum, four medium, and one maximum

75 Ivan Zinger, "Human Rights and Federal Corrections: A Commentary on a Decade of Tough on Crime Policies" (2016) 58:4 Can J CCJ 609, https://doi.org/10.3138/cjccj.2016.E06.

76 Tara Marie Watson, "Research Access Barriers as Reputational Risk Management: A Case Study of Censorship in Corrections" (2015) 57:3 Can J Criminol Crim Justice 330 [Watson].

77 See *ibid*; Kelly Hannah-Moffat, "Criminological Cliques: Narrowing Dialogues, Institutional Protectionism, and the Next Generation" in Mary Bosnworth & Carolyn Hoyle, eds, *What Is Criminology?* (Oxford: Oxford University Press, 2011) at 440; Joanne Martel, "Policing Criminology Knowledge: The Hazards of Qualitative Research on Women in Prison" (2004) 8:2 Theor Criminol 157; Matthew G. Yeager, "Getting the Usual Treatment: Research Censorship and the Dangerous Offender" (2008) 11:4 Contemp Justice Rev 413.

78 Public Safety Canada, *Corrections and Conditional Release: Statistical Overview, 2014* (Ottawa: Public Safety Canada Portfolio Corrections Statistics Committee, 2015) at 36, online: https://www.publicsafety.gc.ca/cnt/rsrcs/pblctns/ccrso-2014/2014-ccrs-eng.pdf.

security, plus the assessment unit. Participation was purely voluntary, and, with the exception of maximum security where people were circumspect about talking to anybody, prisoners were generally eager to talk. I used fifty as the lower minimum age, based on CSC and OCI reports (which in turn relied on American literature) assessing that prisoners have the health problems equivalent to persons ten to fifteen years older than them in the general community,[79] and that prisoners also have a lower life expectancy than that of people in the community (the average age of natural death in prison is 60 compared to 78.3 in the community).[80]

Interviews with prisoners took between thirty and sixty minutes, and were based on a structured protocol of seventy-one questions. We talked about their health, the treatment they received in prison, the programming available, their adjustments to the prison environment, the maintenance of family relations, and the presence or absence of abuse. While I had initially planned to simply quantify their answers and have statistics as the product of this work, I soon realized that these prisoners had stories to tell. Some had spent decades in prisons. Like John, they had witnessed administrative, legal, and political changes. They had been through life experiences so disturbing that numbers alone could not do them justice. A number of the prisoners were so sick, so burned out, so alone, and so afraid that it was sometimes difficult for me to carry out the interview. Some were dying, and others were grieving or were struggling with disease and disability, all in the shadow of peer abuse and administrative neglect. As I was aware that I was one of the few fortunate external researchers who, over the last couple of decades, had received access to enter CSC institutions,[81] I decided to quantify the interviews but also to qualify some of the answers in order to give a voice to prisoners whose voices are so rarely heard by the public.

In this book, I employ the data gained from my research in two ways. First, the data are oriented towards offering the reader, in chapter two, an image of the health care available in prison older individuals. The image that the data depict shows a group whose quality of life is significantly altered, not just by incarceration but also by the inability of the correctional services to respond to their enhanced needs. Second, the data are used in chapters three, four, five, and six to illuminate a discussion about the difficulties this group of people face when attempting to ask

---

79 CSC 1998, *supra* note 39; OCI 2010–2011, *supra* note 8 at 20.
80 OCI 2013–2014, *supra* note 56 at 29.
81 For a description of the small number of research projects potentially approved by the CSC, see Watson, *supra* note 76 at 333.

for better health care in prison or for release to seek care in the community, either before administrative boards or in a court of law. In chapter
three, I argue that extensive prison reform and avenues for release for
the aging need to be developed. In chapter four, I provide an overview of
potential non-legal avenues for achieving prison reform, while I focus on
the need for more robust prison oversight. In chapter five, I discuss the
role of administrative boards and tribunals in addressing prisoner complaints, and in chapter six I engage in a discussion on the role of legal
action and the remedies available to prisoners through courts. Finally, in
most chapters, based on the experiences of the participants in my study,
I build a set of recommendations that would improve older people's conditions of confinement and ease their access to release, in particular, and
their access to justice, in general.

This book is thus a (non-fictional) tale about prisoners' access to justice in Canada in which the extreme situation of older prisoners who
need better health care is used as a case study. I approached the writing
of this book with a deep sense of responsibility to the people I interviewed and to the scholars whose work has been stalled by failed attempts
to obtain access to correctional institutions. The work contained in this
book is more than an attempt to shed light on the challenges that aging
presents to a system used to dealing with a younger population. It is an
attempt to give a voice to individuals who have been inside prisons for
decades and to those facing prison for the first time at an age when most
other people plan to retire. It is an attempt to shed much-needed light
on the forgotten.

Chapter Two

Age and Health Care Behind Bars

John and Eric are the faces of the aging experience presented in this book. Some details about them will keep reoccurring in the book as they connect to the different themes explored in each chapter. At the time I interviewed him in 2014, John was fifty-nine years old and serving a life sentence (he was what is colloquially referred to as a "lifer") in a medium security institution. In fact, John was very typical for the age group I worked with. Over half (55 per cent) of the people considered "old" by prison standards were between fifty and fifty-nine years of age, and 50 per cent of the whole sample were serving time in medium security institutions. Life sentences were the most common type of sentence among this age group (34 per cent). Thus, these individuals had essentially grown old in prison.

Eric, on the other hand, was part of a smaller group. He was seventy-four years old and serving a short sentence in a minimum security institution. People over seventy formed 12 per cent of the sample, leaving 33 per cent for individuals between sixty and sixty-nine years of age. People serving time in minimum security made up 34 per cent of the interviewees, while those in maximum security facilities comprised 9 per cent. Short determinate sentences (two to five years) were the second most common type of sentence (30 per cent), followed by medium sentences (six to ten years, 14 per cent), indeterminate sentences (similar in nature to life sentences, 12 per cent),[1] and long determinate sentences (over ten years, 11 per cent).

---

1 An individual who has committed three or more specific offences (*Criminal Code*, RSC, 1985, c C-46, s 753 [*CC*]) may receive a "dangerous offender" designation. This designation may attract an indeterminate sentence, which means the prisoner will serve time indeterminately (with possibility of applying for parole at regular intervals once he has served seven years). Once released, the individual may continue to be under supervision for the rest of his life [*CC*, s 761].

Neither John nor Eric had served time before their current sentences; hence, they fell within the non-recidivist group, which was roughly 50 per cent of the sample. In terms of time spent in prison, John and Eric were also representative. Individuals like John, who had spent a long time in prison (over ten years), formed half of the sample. Eric was part of the other half, with two years served. It is worth noting that 22 per cent of those interviewed had spent very long periods of time in prison when the interviews were conducted, with 11 per cent having served between twenty and twenty-nine years, and another 11 per cent over thirty years.

The data presented in this chapter are organized by the category of problems most participants in the study identified (chronic illnesses and physical disabilities, mental illnesses and associated problems, terminal illnesses, and emergencies) and by the ability of the institutions to respond to these problems. I have chosen this structure as the most efficient way to ensure a full overview of the challenges faced by older prisoners overwhelmed by health needs, as these challenges result from both the qualitative and quantitative data. Getting a complete picture of the complexity of the problems this population presents is essential to understanding the unique challenges of older prisoners. The overarching trends in health care in prison impact all prison age groups, but what makes the situation of older prisoners unique is the high number of conditions they face, the age-associated problems they present, and their increased weakness and vulnerability.

Similar to the foreign literature on this issue, many themes and trends emerged across the board in terms of the challenges faced by these individuals, regardless of the type of conditions presented. Some of the biggest issues encountered pertained to the lack of environmental accommodation for disabilities (both in terms of physical infrastructure and prison routine and demands); lack of availability of medical supplies, devices, and medication; lack of reasonable access to medical staff and long waiting times to see a doctor; lack of training for correctional personnel to deal with older individuals; disciplinary responses to health problems; and enhanced vulnerability of older prisoners to abuse by peers and staff. The desperation of aging in prison and the increased anxiety at the thought of dying or getting sick behind bars were overarching themes throughout the interviews. These themes were obvious across interviews and were particularly core concerns in my conversations with John and Eric.

Managing Chronic Illness and Physical Disabilities

Around here we don't call it health care. We call it death care. If you get sick between 4 p.m. and 6 a.m. you are as good as dead. (BB, 56, in prison 13 years)

John identified a number of challenges in taking care of his physical health, revolving mainly around access to appropriate services and to medical devices and supplies. First, the medical service was slow. He gave me a recent example. Three days prior, he felt dizzy at work and put in a request for a nurse. He was still waiting to hear back. John's problems, however, had been diagnosed, and the medical personnel were well aware of them. Specialized services were equally difficult to receive. John was now wearing hearing aids, but he complained that it had taken three years to have his hearing tested – the longest he had had to wait to see a specialist. Since turning fifty, he had seen a urologist, a neurosurgeon, an orthopaedic surgeon, an ear-nose-and-throat doctor, a chiropractor, and a speech therapist. He generally had to wait a few months for an appointment, for which he was sent to Kingston General Hospital (KGH). The trips to KGH were particularly unpleasant for John, so he tried to avoid asking for appointments. Regardless of health conditions, the protocol required that the prisoner be transported in a Correctional Service of Canada (CSC) van, with hands and feet shackled. The handcuffs and shackles stayed on for the duration of the medical consultation. John found it difficult to kneel down on the steel van stair for the shackles to be placed on him. Sitting upright on the plastic benches without being able to readjust his position was also challenging for his back.

Second, aside from medication, there was not much John could do to keep healthy in the institution. He received very little accommodation for his specific needs. John was aware that diabetes and circulation problems required an active lifestyle and regular movement. That is why, he said, he tried to do some stretches in his cell every evening before going to bed. He did not go to the gym or to the yard. He said the younger guys monopolized all the equipment and bullied the people who were not as strong:

> I have been through a lot. I have seen a lot. I am not putting up with that kind of attitude from those pricks. I don't care that they call me "old fart." But I don't want to be pushed. I can fall without them pushing me. I keep to myself and I avoid social interactions.

Third, medical devices and supplies were hard to come by. For any kind of supply, including things like an extra pillow to place under one's legs to improve circulation, a medical note was needed. The request attached to the medical note required further approval by the institution's warden. If approved, there were two possible outcomes: the prisoner received the item for free or they had to purchase it. John's institution was better than many others in that requests were not straight-out rejected; rather, individuals were allowed to purchase supplies if they had the money. Nothing except his eye glasses was given to John for free, but, as I soon found out, in many other places, purchasing items for medical needs was forbidden, even with a medical note. John purchased two orthopaedic pillows, orthopaedic shoes, hearing aids, a back brace, and a knee brace. He also needed to purchase any vitamins, dandruff shampoo, or creams for his skin and ulcer that he might require, as well as diapers in order to deal with his incontinence. These many expenses were part of the reason why John could not afford to lose his kitchen job. According to the prisoners interviewed, most of them earned $4 for a day of work. Moreover, in what is called the "current account," they are only allowed to have and use $500 in a year. While they are allowed to tap into their savings accounts for bigger medical purchases, they are limited to the current account for ongoing needs like vitamins, shampoo, and cream. A bottle of dandruff shampoo costs $10, meaning John had to save for over a month to purchase it.

Eric's institution was considerably more prepared to handle sick individuals, even compared to other lower security prisons. Eric had access to a physiotherapist every four weeks, he saw the nurse every month, and it took two weeks to see the dentist and two weeks to see the eye doctor. He received a number of medical devices to help with managing his disability: a medical mattress, a wheelchair, a cane, and a device to put socks on. Pittsburgh was one of the institutions where peer caregivers were available, and he had received one.

Eric found the infrastructure to be the most challenging aspect of his life in prison. The distances between his house and the medication distribution place or the administration buildings were long, and he found it difficult to wheel himself or walk those distances several times a day. The bathtub had a handicap rail, but he still struggled with bathing and was concerned about the lack of a panic button he could use in case he fell. Once in a while, he had to use stairs to get to the administration office because the elevators would break down. He said he fell many times on the stairs or on inappropriately cleaned paths, but he never really hurt himself because he was "really good at falling." Having to pick up his medication in person each morning made movement mandatory and took a toll on his health. Eric did not have to stand because he had the wheelchair, but getting there and waiting around for an hour was still challenging.

Pittsburgh was 70 per cent double bunked. The beds were side by side, which made it easier for people like Eric. He still found it very challenging, though, to share a one-person room. For example, his chair and his cane did not fit in the room, so he had to leave them at the door. In addition, because of his disability and pain, Eric was confined to his room for most of the day. His younger but also ill roommate was always very cold and kept a heater on, even in summer. Thus, Eric complained about the temperature of the room and was unhappy that he had virtually no control over the environment he lived in or the food he ate, even though minimum security was designed to give people higher levels of independence. On the one hand, his independence was virtually undercut by the younger, more vocal people he lived with. On the other, the overall independent living design worked against him when it came to moving around and caring for himself.

Chronic Disease and Access to Medical Services

CHRONIC DISEASES

John and Eric are not isolated cases, either in terms of physical struggles or concerns they identified regarding medical services and infrastructure. Almost every individual I interviewed reported having at least one chronic condition. With nine and twelve chronic illnesses respectively, John and Eric were part of the 28 per cent who were coping with between eight and sixteen illnesses. Of those I interviewed, 37 per cent were affected by at least four to seven different medical conditions. Like John and Eric, most prisoners interviewed (63 per cent), regardless of the time of incarceration, believed their health had declined considerably since they lost their freedom because of aging, conditions of confinement, and the stress of being incarcerated and away from family.

Unsurprisingly, many of the individuals interviewed reported a host of conditions often associated with aging:[2] arthritis and back issues, digestive problems, heart disease, diabetes, skin issues, cancer, physical disabilities, wounds due to falls, neurological conditions such as strokes, visual and hearing impairments, hypertension, oral problems, and incontinence (Table 2.1). It is difficult to compare these findings to those in the foreign literature because of the difference in methodologies used and sample sizes. However, overall, the types of problems, the reporting of at least three conditions per individual on average, as well as the percentages of most conditions tend to be consistent with those from studies of similar sizes with older prisoners.[3]

---

2 For general medical literature discussing age-associated diseases, see e.g. M. McKenna et al, "Assessing the Burden of Disease in the United States Using Disability-Adjusted Life Years" (2005) 28:5 AJPM 415 [McKenna et al]; Carol Jagger et al, "The Burden of Diseases on Disability-free Life Expectancy in Later Life" (2007) 62:4 J Gerontol A Biol Sci Med Sci 408 [Jagger et al].

3 Ronald H. Aday, *Aging Prisoners* (Westport, CT: Greenwood Publishing Group, 2003) at 20–1 [Aday, *Aging Prisoners*]; Seena Fazel et al, "Health of Elderly Male Prisoners: Worse than the General Population, Worse than the Younger Prisoners" (2001) 30:5 Age

Table 2.1. Distribution of physical illnesses

Disease	Frequency	Percentage
Asthma	24	12.2
Arthritis	100	50.8
Digestive problems	48	24.4
Skin problems	53	26.9
Severe heart problems	54	27.4
Cancer	14	7.1
Physical disability	37	18.8
Wounds	24	12.2
Diabetes	53	26.9
Hypertension	83	42.1
Severe oral problems	48	24.4
Cerebral–vascular problems/Epilepsy	19	9.6
Hepatitis	28	14.2
Circulation	39	19.8
Sleep apnoea	16	8.1
Severe hearing problems	52	26.4
Severe sight problems	162	82.2
Pinched nerve	6	3
Back problems	63	32
Hernia	13	6.6
Thyroid	10	5.1
Sciatic nerve	11	5.6
High cholesterol	48	24.4
Foot problems	33	16.8
Bladder	11	5.6
Constipation	9	4.6
Severe prostate problems	15	7.6
Other	94	47.7

Note: Percentages do not add to 100 per cent because of multiple illnesses.

A number of conditions that were likely symptoms from other diseases were also affecting this population, incontinence (14 per cent) being one of the most challenging to deal with in this environment. Likely under-reported (as the number is lower than that reported in the literature),[4]

Ageing 403 at 404–5 [Fazel et al]; Patricia L. Colsher et al, "Health Status of Older Male Prisoners: A Comprehensive Survey" (1992) 82:6 Am J Public Health 881 at 882–3 [Cosher et al]; Catherine M. Lemieux, Timothy B. Dyeson, & Brandi Castiglione, "Revisiting the Literature on Prisoners Who Are Older: Are We Wiser?" (2002) 82:4 Prison J 440 at 447–8 [Lemieux, Dyeson, & Castiglione]; Adrian Hayes, "Aging Inside: Older Adults in Prison" in Bernice Elger, Catherine Ritter, & Hein Stover, eds, *Emerging Issues in Prison Health* (Dodrecht: Springer, 2017) 1 at 4 [Hayes].

4   Brie Williams & Rita Abraldes, "Growing Older: Challenges of Prison and Reentry for Aging Population" in Robert Greifinger, ed, *Public Health Behind Bars* (New York: Springer, 2007) 56 at 63 [Williams & Abraldes].

incontinence was a loaded condition. The majority of the individuals who reported it felt the stigma of their situation and had to face jokes and petty comments from fellow prisoners or officers.

> I keep to myself because really ... if I fear something is that I will piss myself in front of them when I don't have a diaper on. And then there is no hiding that I am really weak. (PZ, 65, in prison 26 years)
>
>   The officers find it hilarious [him wetting himself]. Once, I was struggling to change my soiled clothes. This officer asked me if he should call an ambulance. (XX, 81, in prison 22 years)

A couple of people, including John, reported that one advantage of their incontinence was that they were housed in a single cell. I have, however, met individuals who still had to share double-bunked cells, who did not have access to diapers at all times, and who got into constant conflict with their cellmates over soiling the room.

> He yelled and screamed and hit the first couple times I pissed myself at night. He was sleeping in the bed underneath. The diapers help but it depends ... Then he gave me the lower bunk. He wasn't reasonable, but didn't like being pissed on either. I guess in the end, regardless of the reasons, he was more reasonable than the CSC who refused to assign me a different cell. (FF, 52, in prison 6 years)

ILLNESS AND DIET AVAILABILITY

A number of the conditions reported by the participants, most notably diabetes, required a medical diet in order to be appropriately managed. Including John, 35 per cent of the participants reported having been prescribed a medical diet. As a kitchen worker, however, John was privileged and among the few (11 per cent) who were able to respect that diet. The main reason for not following the diet was that "if I eat the medical diet they provide us with, I would starve to death." While the CSC Commissioner's Directive (CD) 880, "Food Services,"[5] requires that medical diets be available, the Standard Operating Practices (SOP) 800–01, "Food Services – Central Feeding,"[6] which implements CD 880,

---

5   Correctional Service of Canada, "Food Services," Commissioner's Directive No. 880 (Ottawa: CSC, 21 February 2000), online: https://www.csc-scc.gc.ca/acts-and-regulations/880-cd-eng.shtml.
6   Correctional Service of Canada, "Food Services – Central Feeding," Standard Operating Practices No. 880-01 (Ottawa: CSC, 21 February 2000), online: https://www.csc-scc.gc.ca/acts-and-regulations/880-1-sop-eng.shtml.

states that the general food served should be adapted to meet most therapeutic diets. By using a "one-size-fits-all" diet, all prisoners in need of a medical diet are deprived of nutrition at the highest level, regardless of their actual need.

Most of the 11 per cent who reported compliance with the medical diet were housed in independent living–type units. In such places, individuals living in the same house would order food, within a common budget, from the institution's catalogue and cook for themselves. In a number of situations, however, even this practice was problematic. As Eric explained, in houses where there were many younger, healthier people, they would be more vocal about their choice of foods when placing the monthly order. Thus, weaker people like Eric would not have the benefit of nutritional, dietary food because most of the house budget would be spent on junk food.

An additional nutrition-related issue was that 14 per cent of the participants had dentures, while 3 per cent had no teeth and no dentures, and another 2 per cent were waiting to receive dentures. For those without teeth or dentures, eating healthy and within the parameters of a medically prescribed diet was extremely difficult. Unless they were in an institution where they or their peer caregiver could cook their food, they did not benefit from a modified diet.

AVAILABILITY OF MEDICAL SERVICES

For people with chronic illnesses, the major challenge was access to appropriate medical services. Seeing a medical professional for any of these conditions or their symptoms was challenging. How challenging it was depended in large part on the institution where the individual was serving time. In general, CSC Health Services creates a list of medical positions to be filled in correctional institutions, and the number of people to be hired is decided at the regional health service level. Staffing decisions are then approved by each regional director of the CSC Health Services Department. For example, according to the current staffing protocol of the CSC for the region of Ontario, Warkworth Institution, a prison housing 600 prisoners of which close to 200 are over the age of fifty, has one physician and one psychologist, with the number of nurses undisclosed.[7] Other Ontario institutions have between three and five psychologists available, but none has more than one physician, and Bath Institution has no physician at all. The CSC regional hospitals also have

7   Correctional Service of Canada, Document A-2015–00641 [unpublished letter]. This document and explanations were obtained through an *Access to Information Act* request in May 2016.

only one physician and no psychologist;[8] no social workers or occupational therapists are available in any institution except Bath. A psychiatrist occasionally visits each regional institution based on respective clinic hours, but each institution is served by only one psychiatrist, with most institutions sharing the same psychiatrist.[9] For most other specialists, the prisoner would be escorted to a community hospital by a CSC officer.

The outcome of these hiring practices on older prisoners was clear from their reports. Overall, 54 per cent of the participants mentioned that no nurse was available 24/7 in their institution. The wait time to see a nurse was, in most institutions, between three days and a week, regardless of the problem. Access to specialized treatment differed from institution to institution. The dentist was by far the most sought after (45 per cent had requested to see one), and all institutions had a dentist come in at regular intervals. Many prisons had a reasonable wait time of a couple months, but in some institutions, like Millhaven Institution (maximum security), the wait time applied to emergencies as well. The optometrist and psychiatrist were also in high demand, with 31 per cent and 9 per cent of requests, respectively, and they would also come on-site. The optometrist was generally available within three months, but for some institutions the wait time to see a psychiatrist could be years if the individual was not suicidal. For other specialists such as oncologists, cardiologists, surgeons, and urologists, prisoners were seen at a community hospital, with wait times of generally over one year. In some of the most crowded institutions, people would sometimes be denied appointments: psychologist (14 per cent), optometrist (5 per cent), and cardiologist (14 per cent, while 43 per cent were still waiting to see a cardiologist). At Pittsburgh, Eric's institution, the biggest problem was the lack of escorts to the community. Only two officer escorts were available daily for a population of 270 people, 70 per cent of whom were old and sick. If, on the day of the community appointment, the prison did not have an escort available, the individual would simply lose the appointment and would have to be rescheduled on the next date available, perhaps months down the road.

Surgeries, common among people in this age group, would also take place in community hospitals and required available escorts. Approximate one-quarter (24 per cent) of the participants underwent surgery while in prison after the age of fifty. This number does not include the individuals who, like John, underwent surgery before the age of fifty, but still felt the consequences of the medical intervention in their older age (in John's case due to bladder removal). Protocol required that people be shackled during

---

8   *Ibid.*
9   *Ibid.*

surgery. However, the participants complained less about the shackles and more about the post-surgery recovery space. For example, 12 per cent were brought back to prison immediately after undergoing surgery, especially after hernia surgeries. Spending a night in hospital, even if highly recommended, was avoided as much as possible because security escorts would also have to spend the night, and that was an added cost. Most individuals spent about a day or two in hospital after surgery, and 8 per cent spent some time in a prison hospital after the more serious surgeries, such as heart or brain surgery. Most of the 25 per cent who underwent surgery reported being given little slack when it came to prison routines.

> Recovering from open heart surgery in a cell ... that was scary. They placed me by myself so that I am "protected." There was no person I could even ask to bring me water. They would check in on me twice a day. I was panicked and I constantly felt like I was going to have a heart attack. (ZZ, 61, in prison 7 years)

Numerous participants also complained about the improper post-surgery transportation conditions. One prisoner described being transferred back to prison immediately after a hernia surgery in a CSC steel van:

> I had just undergone surgery. They pumped me full of medication. Immediately after I woke up from surgery they had me sitting in the van for the forty minute drive back to the institution. I remember some pain, and just wanting to lie down. But what I clearly remember is being so nauseated and throwing up most of the trip. Throwing up ... that hurt. (CC, 57, in prison 15 years)

Disability, Access to Medical Supplies, and Infrastructure

PHYSICAL DISABILITIES

The difficulties in using CSC vans, as well as many of CSC's day-to-day pieces of equipment or infrastructure, increased when the individual had difficulty moving. Both John and Eric had mobility issues, with Eric being significantly disabled. Of the study participants, 24 per cent reported having mobility problems that interfered with their activities of daily living, mostly walking (37 per cent), getting in and out of bed (17 per cent), and climbing stairs (37 per cent). Of all individuals, 19 per cent were paraplegic and, hence, unable to move without a wheelchair. I was not able to speak to a number of individuals, despite their desire to be interviewed, because they were bedridden, and I was not allowed on their units. Thus, the most disabled individuals did not participate in this study.

Overall, slightly more than 6 per cent of the participants received regular help with their mobility issues, always from a peer assigned as a caregiver. In Collins Bay Medium Security Institution, where John was serving time, no peer caregivers were available. Such was also the case at Frontenac Minimum Security Institution (where more than 50 per cent were over fifty and had various disabilities), as well as at Joyceville Medium Security and Millhaven Maximum Security Institutions. Peer caregivers were available at Pittsburgh Minimum Security Institution, as well as at Warkworth and Bath, both medium security institutions. Where available, peer caregivers are supposed to help individuals transfer between places, assist them with cleaning their cells, and sometimes with eating, washing, and dressing. In addition to Eric, many other prisoners benefiting from this service complained about the lack of appropriate training for their peer caregivers.

He [the peer caregiver] means well really but he is clumsy. He has so much difficulty pushing my wheelchair. For example, last winter he stumbled down the ramp and I fell in the snow. (OO, 58, in prison 14 years)

I keep asking for new peer caregivers. They are useless. The one I have now is not bad. He fails to show up, like this morning I had to wheel myself here, and it's hard. But he is better than the last one. The last one I had was stealing my pills to sell them. I had him for a few months. It was hard time. I really need my pills. (QQ, 63, in prison 8 years)

ACCESS TO MEDICAL SUPPLIES

One of the biggest challenges for people living with physical disabilities was lack of access to medical supplies and devices. For instance, the more conditions an individual had, and the more disabled they were, the more demands for health care items they made. For example, over 30 per cent of those with over eight conditions had requested health items and were refused; approximately 27 per cent had asked for items and were granted; more than 18 per cent had asked for items and had been partially granted. Only about 23 per cent had never asked for anything other than what they were given by the institution. These statistics are in clear contrast with the people who had up to four conditions, of whom over 60 per cent had never asked for anything. However, as a rule, all individuals were more likely to be refused items they asked for than to be granted their requests. The items in most demand were extra pillows or blankets to deal with poor circulation or hypothermia, a better mattress for back problems, vitamins, and walking aids. Table 2.2 shows that, perhaps unsurprisingly, individuals with mobility problems requested more health

Table 2.2. Distribution of mobility problems per rate of health items requested and made available

	Were Health Items Requested and Made Available?				
Mobility Problems	None Needed % (n)	Needed, Not Granted % (n)	Needed and Granted % (n)	Needed, Partially Granted % (n)	Total % (n)
No	58.7 (54)	18.5 (17)	14.1 (13)	8.7 (8)	100 (92)
Yes	30.1 (31)	26.2 (27)	28.2 (29)	15.5 (16)	100 (103)

Chi-square = 16.691; df = 3; p = .001

items. However, the more items they requested, the less likely they were to receive them.

Like the availability and the wait time to see medical personnel, the availability of medical supplies and devices depended on the institution where the individual served their sentence. The *National Essential Healthcare Framework* is a document from the Health Care Department within the CSC signed by the Deputy Commissioner. Among other things, it lists the supplies that may be prescribed by a physician to sick prisoners.[10] Annex A lists a number of items that may be granted, such as walkers and canes, and forbids items such as medical mattresses, extra pillows or blankets, heated pads, and orthopaedic shoes. In addition, the document mentions that other items need "special authorization from the Warden or the regional director, based on the recommendation of the institutional physician or dentist along with the medical justification for the request."

Pittsburgh was by far the best institution that I visited in terms of granting medical supplies. Eric received, despite the CSC's general policy, an orthopaedic mattress and a device to help him put on socks. Many prisoners there had sleep apnoea machines. In other institutions, like Collins Bay where John was, the doctor would write a note for the devices needed, but, aside from eye glasses, the prisoner would have to purchase everything himself. In John's case, he had to purchase his orthopaedic shoes, hearing aids, orthopaedic pillows, and back and knee braces. Some people had difficulty even obtaining walking aids.

> I wasn't granted a cane. [The physician] said "There are no canes available for people like you who hurt themselves playing sports." I just move less and slower. (VV, 53, in prison 10 years)

---

10 Correctional Service of Canada, *National Essential Healthcare Framework* (Ottawa: CSC, 23 July 2015). This document was obtained in April 2016 through an *Access to Information Act* request. The quotation is found on page 6.

The difficulty in purchasing medical items, a problem often mentioned in my interviews (especially by those serving long sentences who had no outside sources of income), was, first, that prisoners were paid very little (at that time, $4 per day). Second, prisoners had two accounts: a savings account and a current account. The current account could hold an upward limit of $500 per year (now $750). With the exception of certain pieces of medical equipment, most other expenses, including medical, had to come out of the current account. When the $500 was used up, prisoners would have to wait until the next year to purchase something else. This policy was particularly challenging for people affected by several medical conditions at once, who regularly needed to supplement their food with items purchased from the canteen or from the regular vegetable and pastry drives (something similar to a monthly "market" in which prisoners could purchase specialized food items) or who wanted to purchase cards for their families and also needed creams, vitamins, Tylenol, on top of the medical equipment not provided by the institution. Third, the items prisoners were allowed to have in their possession could be valued at no more than $1,500, including clothing, electronics, books, and health care items. Thus, the more health care items an individual needed, the less entertainment or other types of personal items they could have. For certain individuals, like John and Eric, the total value of medical devices was well over $1,500. This rule meant that, when changing institutions, everything in excess of that amount would be confiscated. For people like Eric, who spent their entire sentence in one institution, the rule was not an issue. But Eric was the exception. Most people, like John, would eventually be transferred. In fact, John had been transferred every second year in the last decade. With each transfer, some items would always be confiscated. In the new institution, he would have to put in a new request for items to replace the ones taken, with a new wait time and a potential new expense if he had to pay for the items himself.

INFRASTRUCTURE

Infrastructure accessibility also depended on the institution. Aside from Millhaven Maximum Security Institution, all other penitentiaries were double bunked in different proportions. The general rule was that the newcomer took the top bunk. Nobody wanted the top bunk, so a younger roommate was unlikely to make a concession for an elderly cellmate. A prisoner at Joyceville described the experience:

> I am only fifty and I don't want to ask to be in segregation where I would be in a single cell. But I am a DO [dangerous offender], and I will spend a long time in here. Once you ask for segregation you have a target on your

back. You can never come out. I can't stay isolated for another ten years. So I put up with this shit. I have a top bunk. It has no rails and no stairs. I have to jump up and out of bed. It's not great. It's hard on my back, hard on my knees, hard on everything really. I hope my cellie [cellmate] will be transferred and then I can take his lower bunk. (UU, 50, in prison 8 years)

Of those interviewed, 35 per cent reported having fallen in prison within the prior year, and 19 per cent fell more than twice during the same period of time. This study confirmed that the likelihood of falling was directly related to the number of chronic conditions and mobility problems an individual presented. The majority of those who had fallen within the last twelve months fell in icy conditions, which should have been taken care of. Institutions like Warkworth, Pittsburgh, and Collins Bay are very large, and going outside is mandatory in order to get from one's cell to the pill distribution centre, the infirmary, the eating place, the canteen, or the program building. For many, every step taken outside in winter was a hazard. Other common falling spots were from the top bunk, on the stairs, and in the shower. For example, all the cells at Frontenac Minimum Security Institution were upstairs, while programs and food distribution took place downstairs. Showers and toilets had no accessibility handrails.

I fall mostly on the stairs because I can't avoid them. I need to eat and I need my pills. I also can't avoid the shower. I wet myself and I need to clean up. Otherwise I wouldn't ever wash. Not since I know I may bash my head every time I come out of the shower. (XX, 81, in prison 22 years)

A similar problem was reported at Warkworth Medium Security Institution.

The showers have no handicap rail, floors are glossy, and no ramps come out of the building. (OO, 58, in prison 14 years)

Interestingly, the number of physical disabilities reported in my study was higher than the numbers reported in the non-Canadian literature.[11]

---

11 Williams & Abraldes, *supra* note 4 at 61; Cynthia Massie Mara, "Chronic Illness, Disability, and Long Term Care in the Prison Setting" in Paul Katz, Mathy Mezey, & Marshall Kapp, eds, *Vulnerable Populations in the Long Term Care Continuum*, vol 5 (New York: Springer, 2004) 39 at 44 [Mara]; Melvin Delgado & Denise Humm-Delgado, *Health and Health Care in the Nation's Prisons: Issues, Challenges, and Policies* (Lanham, MD: Rowman & Littlefield, 2009) at 41–2 [Delgado & Humm-Delgado].

However, the concerns regarding availability of medical supplies and prison infrastructure were reported in nearly all studies dealing with older prisoners, and some of these papers have discussed at length, through qualitative or quantitative data, the impact of inadequate environment and lack of accessibility to resources for older individuals with disabilities.[12] The literature clearly shows that these kinds of institutional struggles caused by unaccommodating prison conditions accelerate deterioration and decline,[13] and cause "hidden injuries" to prisoners.[14]

Chronic Pain Management

Chronic pain was common among the participants, and this problem also tapped into the overarching issue of access to medication and medical supplies. John lived with pain caused by his advanced arthritis, his back, and his knee. Eric experienced chronic headaches that could have been caused by a number of his multiple medical conditions. Overall, 62 per cent of the participants reported having severe pain on a regular basis.

When asked what was the source of their pain, participants listed arthritis and other joint pain at the top of their list (49 per cent of the total sample), along with headaches and migraines (9 per cent). Other pain sources were cancer, foot pain, muscular pain, and nerve pain. In addition, those who experienced pain were more likely than those who did not to have a wide range of different ailments including arthritis, physical disabilities, long-term severe back problems, digestive issues, outstanding wounds, diabetes, hypertension, severe oral

---

12 Aday, *Aging Prisoners, supra* note 3 at 143–4; Elaine Crawley, "Imprisonment in Old Age" in Yvonne Jewkes, ed, *Handbook on Prisons* (Cornwall: Willan Publishing, 2007) 224 at 225 [Crawley]; Laura Addison, Delores Craig-Moreland, & Connie L. Neeley, "Addressing the Needs of Elderly Offenders" (1997) 59:5 Corrections Today 120 at 123; Anita Blowers, Jennifer M. Jolley, & John J. Kerbs, "The Age-Segregation Debate" in John Kerbs & Jennifer Jolley, eds, *Senior Citizens Behind Bars* (London: Lynne Rienner, 2014) 133 at 149–52 [Blowers, Jolley, & Kerbs]; Natalie Mann, *Doing Harder Time? The Experiences of an Ageing Male Prison Population in England and Wales* (Farnham, UK: Ashgate, 2012) at 41–2 [Mann, *Doing Harder Time*]; Chris Trotter & Susan Baidawi, "Older Prisoners: Challenges for Inmates and Prison Management" (2015) 48:2 Austl & NZ J Crim 200 at 209–10 [Trotter & Baidawi].

13 Natalie Mann, "Older Age, Harder Time: Ageing and Imprisonment" in Yvonne Jewkes, Ben Crewe, & Jamie Bennett, eds, *Handbook on Prisons* (London: Routledge, 2016) 514 at 516–18 [Mann, "Older Age"].

14 Elaine Crawley & Richard Sparks, "Hidden Injuries? Researching the Experiences of Older Men in English Prisons" (2005) 44:4 Howard J 345 at 350–3 [Crawley & Sparks, "Hidden Injuries?"].

problems, hernia, sciatic nerve, high cholesterol, and foot problems.[15] Furthermore, while not statistically relevant, the data showed a tendency for people reporting pain to also report in higher percentages conditions such as pulmonary disease, severe hearing problems, and severe vision problems.[16]

Tylenol was generally available at the canteen for prisoners to purchase and use at will. Nonetheless, all the individuals that I counted as reporting severe pain for the purpose of this study maintained that Tylenol did not ease their pain. Thus, my question regarding pain treatment, as well as their answers to it, referred to medication prescribed by the prison physician. The medication the prison physician generally prescribed in cases of chronic or acute pain was Tylenol 3, as the only compound available. The *CSC National Drug Formulary* is the official list of medication available.[17] This document confirms that the only prescription painkillers available in penitentiaries are Tylenol 3 and, in special cases, methadone or morphine.[18] It also mentions that all community prescriptions for painkillers will be changed to Tylenol 3, since it is the cheapest compound.[19]

The majority of people living with chronic pain reported receiving Tylenol 3. Those who did experience pain but were not treated explained that they were not prescribed anything by the prison doctor (7 per cent of the total sample) or that they did not want to take medication, generally because it would mean going to pick it up every day, which added stress on their bodies and made the pain worse (7 per cent). Of those who received pain treatment, 43 per cent reported it as ineffective in alleviating their pain. Some of them mentioned being on stronger medication in the community. Numerous people serving life sentences remembered

---

15 The percentages for medical conditions reported by people who also reported pain versus those reported by individuals who did not report pain are as follows: 64 per cent versus 28 per cent for arthritis, 26 per cent versus 7 per cent for physical disabilities, 44 per cent versus 12 per cent for long-term severe back problems, 34 per cent versus 8 per cent for digestive problems, 19 per cent versus 1 per cent for outstanding wounds, 32 per cent versus 19 per cent for diabetes, 50 per cent versus 30 per cent for hypertension, 33 per cent versus 11 per cent for severe oral problems, 10 per cent versus 1 per cent for hernia, 9 per cent versus 0 for sciatic nerve, 30 per cent versus 15 per cent for high cholesterol, and 22 per cent versus 8 per cent for foot problems.

16 The percentages for these reports are 15 per cent versus 7 per cent for pulmonary disease, 30 per cent versus 19 per cent for severe hearing problems, and 86 per cent versus 76 per cent for severe vision problems.

17 Correctional Service of Canada, *National Drug Formulary* (Ottawa: CSC, 2013). This document was obtained in April 2016 through an *Access to Information Act* request.

18 *Ibid* at 35–6.

19 *Ibid* at 57.

the time when stronger painkillers were available. Policy, they said, had changed because in the past people receiving painkillers were often robbed by younger prisoners. Participants also mentioned numerous situations of "fake pain" on the part of some prisoners, which made officials and physicians apprehensive about permitting access to medication.

I was provided with numerous examples of people who had inadequately addressed pain. An extreme example was given by a number of the people I interviewed at Pittsburgh, who described a cancer patient transferred to their institution in order to have access to chemotherapy. He waited a few months for his treatment, and in the first week he was not granted any pain medication. Apparently, he screamed in pain most of the day, to the point where the prisoners in his building collected money and bought him the regular Tylenol available at the canteen. When he finally received his chemotherapy, he was on it for six weeks. I was told the individual was now in a terminal stage and was receiving morphine. He was in his room at all times, very rarely lucid.

From the 50 per cent who were responsive to pain treatment, a small number were not on Tylenol 3. Some received methadone to manage drug addictions, which also functioned as a painkiller. In some institutions, like Pittsburgh or Millhaven, morphine was available. However, apart from Tylenol 3 and morphine, there was nothing else.

> When I came in after my accident they put me on morphine for my headaches [this individual suffered from a brain injury as a result of a car accident]. I was on it for a couple weeks and it was not working. After two weeks they went back to my chart and realized I was a heroin addict and that's why it didn't work. So now I am back on Tylenol 3. Doesn't do any good. (RR, 53, in prison 8 years)

Some of the individuals who mentioned that Tylenol 3 was ineffective acknowledged they had been offered morphine, but had turned it down. They felt it was a "last resort" medication and were afraid of becoming addicted or worried that at some point morphine would not work any longer and they would be left with nothing stronger to take.

> They pump me up with morphine, where do I go from there? I am not terminally ill. I just have really life-sucking arthritis. I was told I can live many more years with this pain. I will postpone morphine for as long as I can, but I am telling you, Tylenol 3 barely makes a difference. (KK, 55, in prison 24 years)

Ineffectively treated chronic pain was a risk factor for a number of other problems. One, as mentioned, was the risk of falls. Some of the others were sleep deprivation and substance abuse. Of those reporting regular pain, 63 per cent also reported having serious sleeping problems, as opposed to 37 per cent of those not in pain. This finding was of particular concern, since a different set of results from this study, discussed later, also identified sleep deprivation as having negative effects on other aspects of prisoners' well-being, especially mental health. In addition, it appeared that those in pain were more likely to self-identify as drug users, before and/or while in prison (46 per cent as opposed to 23 per cent).

> They prescribed me some Tylenol 3 but I have to pick it up every morning, rain or shine, and stand for an hour to pick it up. And it doesn't do anything for me. I'd rather drink in my cell. It doesn't make it all right, but at least I don't have to stand to get it. [His dealer] brings it to my cell. (CC, 57, in prison 15 years)

As interviewee CC noted, distribution of medication, including painkillers, was also problematic. Over 90 per cent of the people in this age group took at least one prescription medication, with people like John and Eric taking upwards of twenty-five pills a day. Some seniors with mobility issues mentioned having to choose between breakfast and medication because, with the waiting in line, they could not make both. They also spoke out about standing for long periods next to people with contagious diseases. Generally, those who took medication so strong that it required a daily pickup were in bad shape to begin with. Getting there and standing without being given priority in line was an ordeal for individuals with disabilities or for those in extreme pain. In addition, the medication lines in a couple of institutions formed outside. Hence, the sick prisoners had to line up, sometimes for over an hour, in rain, snow, freezing temperatures, or heat to pick up their medication.

> My gall bladder has been removed and I have diabetes and circulation problems. It's difficult to stand outdoors daily, for hours, with a diaper on, to pick up my pills. (FF, 52, in prison 6 years)

Consequences of Pain and Disease

Chronic pain and disease were connected to major themes that seemed to mark the lives of older prisoners: isolation, vulnerability, and abuse. The use of segregation was not very commonly reported by this age group. Being a well-behaved group, most of them, like Eric, had not spent time in solitary confinement since turning fifty. From this perspective, my study confirms the general view in the literature that older prisoners are a calm group, with few disciplinary incidents.[20]

Interestingly, however, the number of physical conditions seemed to influence or be influenced by the time individuals spent in segregation.[21] The more conditions individuals had, the more likely they were to have spent time in segregation for disciplinary or administrative reasons – almost half of those who spent time in segregation had over eight conditions (Table 2.3). John is a good example: with rapidly declining health, he had been in and out of solitary confinement regularly.

On the other hand, physical health was connected to increased vulnerability. The greater the number of conditions individuals reported, the more likely they were to also report spending time in segregation by their own request. They also reported higher percentages of abuse at the hands of both peers and staff members (Tables 2.4 and 2.5), as well

Table 2.3. Time spent in segregation per number of physical conditions

| Time Spent in Segregation for Disciplinary Reasons | Number of Conditions | | | Total |
	1–4 % (n)	5–7 % (n)	8–16 % (n)	% (n)
No	38.1 (61)	37.5 (60)	24.4 (39)	100 (160)
Yes	21.6 (8)	32.4 (12)	45.9 (17)	100 (37)

Chi-square = 7.467; df = 2; p = .024

Table 2.4. Number of physical conditions per rate of abuse by peers

| Physical Conditions n | Abuse by Peers | | Total |
	No % (n)	Yes % (n)	% (n)
1–4	66.7 (46)	33.3 (23)	100 (69)
5–7	43.1 (31)	56.9 (41)	100 (72)
8–16	32.1 (18)	67.9 (38)	100 (56)

Chi-square = 15.970; df = 2; p <.001

20 Aday, *Aging Prisoners, supra* note 3 at 116; John J. Kerbs, "The Older Prisoner: Social, Psychological and Medical Considerations" in Max Rothman, Burton D. Dunlop, & Pamela Entzel, eds, *Elders, Crime, and the Criminal Justice System: Myths, Percentions, and Reality in the 21st Century* (New York: Springer, 2000) 207 at 218.

21 The influence of solitary confinement on the physical health of older prisoners has also been documented in Brie Williams, "Older Prisoners and the Physical Health Effects of Solitary Confinement" (2016) 106:12 Am J Public Health 2126, https://doi.org/10.2105/AJPH.2016.303468.

Table 2.5. Number of physical conditions per rate of abuse by staff

Physical Conditions n	Abuse by Staff Members		Total % (n)
	No % (n)	Yes % (n)	
1–4	60.9 (44)	39.1 (29)	100 (69)
5–7	51.4 (37)	48.6 (35)	100 (72)
8–16	35.7 (20)	64.3 (36)	100 (56)

Chi-square = 7.883; df = 2; p = .019

as feelings of vulnerability and of being in danger in prison. Like John, who was now pacing his cell for a workout, many people with declining health felt weak and stopped using the gym or the yard. They sometimes avoided participating in programs as well.

> I don't go to the gym. That's where things go down. That's where fights start for no reason. And then they lock everyone in and throw tear gas. (NN, 52, in prison 7 years)
> It's the nature of the place. You get weak, you get picked on. They cut in line, they steal things from you, they call you names, they hit and push. Just don't show weakness, assert yourself. (GG, 61, in prison 32 years)

The non-Canadian literature,[22] as well as the numbers emanating from this study, support the allegations of increased vulnerability and peer abuse (Table 2.4).

---

22 Aday, *Aging Prisoners, supra* note 3 at 145–7; Joann Brown Morton, "Implications for Corrections of an Aging Prison Population" in Richard Tewksbury, ed, *Behind Bars: Readings on Prison Culture* (New Jersey: Pearson Prentice Hall, 2006) 61 at 65 [Morton]; John J. Kerbs & Jennifer M. Jolley, "A Commentary on Age Segregation for Older Prisoners: Philosophical and Pragmatic Considerations for Correctional Systems" (2009) 34 Crim J Rev 119 at 126 [Kerbs & Jolley, "Age Segregation"]; Jason S. Ornduff, "Releasing the Elderly Inmate: A Solution to Prison Overcrowding" (1996) 4 Elder LJ 173 at 175 [Ornduff]; Canadian Public Health Association, "A Health Care Needs Assessment of Federal Inmates in Canada" (2004) 95, suppl 1, Can J Public Health 1 [CPHA]; Andrew Tarbuck, "Health of Elderly Prisoners" (2001) 30:5 Age Ageing 369 at 369 [Tarbuck]; Australia, Corrections Victoria, *Growing Old in Prison: A Review of National and International Research on Ageing Offenders*, Corrections Research Paper Series 3, 2010 at 10 [Corrections Victoria]; Human Rights Watch, *Old Behind Bars: The Aging Prison Population in the United States* (New York: Human Rights Watch, 2012) at 57 [HRW]; Margaret E. Leigey, "Bio-Psycho-Social Needs of Older Inmates" in John Kerbs & Jennifer M. Jolley, *Seniors Behind Bars: Challenges for the Criminal Justice System* (London: Lynne Rienner, 2014) 43 at 57; John J. Kerbs & Jennifer

Abuse by members of the staff (Table 2.5) appeared to often be caused by the same individuals in each institution, who seemed to find entertainment in demeaning weaker prisoners and were not stopped by anyone. Pranks related to walking aids were reported at Warkworth Medium Security Institution, basically by everyone who used one.

> This one CO [correctional officer] ... he takes my wheelchair as a prank. I come out of the washroom or I wake up, the wheelchair is gone. He sneaks it in younger guys' cells and then they rip on me for finding it there. (SS, 52, in prison 10 years)

Pranks were also reported at Pittsburgh Minimum Security Institution.

> It's really just the two [women] COs. When they search the cells they take bags of chips, pop, whatever they can find. Not from everyone, from those who can't say anything about it. (FF, 52, in prison 6 years)

The incidents of staff abuse tended to be more frequently reported in my study than in the literature, where the incidents of indifference or improper training were deemed to be a greater problem than those of intentional abuse.[23] Nonetheless, I also received reports of staff members who tried to be helpful or encouraging, but their lack of appropriate training made them insensitive and rude.

> You know what [the nurse] told me when she delivered my cancer diagnosis? She said, "You are lucky you got cancer. We actually treat you for it in here." (II, 65, in prison 40 years)

John and Eric's stories are typical of the physical deterioration that occurs within the age group of this study. Their cases are illustrative of how access to treatment and to appropriate environmental conditions differs from one institution to another. They also serve as examples showing that, even in the best of circumstances, the current model of incarceration cannot deal with the wave and the diversity of age-related chronic conditions infiltrating the prison space.

J. Jolley, "Inmate-on-Inmate Victimization Among Older Male Prisoners" (2007) 53 Crime Delinq 187 [Kerbs & Jolley, "Victimization"]; Ken Howse, *Growing Old in Prison* (Prison Reform Trust, 2008) at 30, online: http://www.prisonreformtrust.org.uk/uploads/documents/Growing.Old.Book_-_small.pdf [Howse].

23 Trotter & Baidawi, *supra* note 12 at 351; Mann, *Doing Harder Time*, *supra* note 12 at 48–9.

Unfortunately, these challenges are not limited to the management of chronic diseases. Mental well-being is also shaped differently by aging. As well, acute conditions and medical emergencies increase in frequency as people get older. Ultimately, death and terminal illness is the outcome of aging. The CSC is not any more prepared to address these issues than it is to deal with chronic illnesses.

Mental Health Care

At the time I met John, two years had passed since his wife died. He was still aggrieved, partly because of her passing and partly because he felt that he did not get to say goodbye. When she was given an end-of-life diagnosis, John was not granted a pass to go into the community and see her. He received day parole when she passed, and he was able to go to her funeral. This sequence of events appeared to be a pattern, as at least ten men in medium or maximum security had lost their partners or parents within recent years and had been denied leave to see them before their passing. In some cases, they were also denied a pass into the community for the funeral.

Having served twenty-eight years of a life sentence, John was what is often referred to as "institutionalized." He was well adjusted to the environment and functioned well within the prison system. He was not burned out by incarceration either, and imprisonment did not cause him anxiety or depression. The loss of his wife, on the other hand, did cause him significant sorrow. After her passing, the institution offered him "psychological counselling if he felt suicidal." That was the extent of the support he received with the grieving process.

Eric was in a very different position. He was not institutionalized, and he was far from being well adjusted. As a first-time offender entering prison in old age, he was extremely anxious because of his health, security, and family. His recent trial was still fresh in his mind, and the embarrassment was acute. Eric was diagnosed with depression and was being treated for it. He had seen the psychiatrist the week before the interview and had no complaints about the mental health service. He was mostly keeping to himself and tried not to get involved in any group activities.

Mental Health Issues and Access to Medical Treatment

MENTAL HEALTH ISSUES

Fear and anxiety is to be expected in a prison setting. Even more so, it is to be expected among older and sick individuals. The greatest fear prisoners identified was that of dying in prison (29 per cent), followed by concern for their families on the outside. Fear, however, is particularly devastating when coupled with a multitude of mental health problems. To a certain extent, John and Eric were atypical for the group I interviewed. John was doing fairly well psychologically, aside from the normal grief related to the loss of his wife. Eric was chronically depressed, which was common among this group; again, it was not unexpected, given his poor physical health and his concerns for his elderly wife and for his safety in prison. However, considering the circumstances, Eric was in a better institution and had substantial access to mental health care. This kind of access proved atypical for the older federally incarcerated population.

Overall, 39 per cent of the individuals interviewed reported having, like Eric, at least one chronic mental health condition. Certain mental disorders frequently reported have been associated with aging by the general medical literature. These include depression, anxiety, dementia, memory loss, and suicidal ideation.[24] Because of the stigma associated with mental illness, as well as the lack of awareness sometimes present in cases of psychiatric illness, the rates of such diseases may possibly have been underreported by the participants in this study (Table 2.6).

The non-Canadian literature on the prevalence of mental illness among this group shows contradictory results, with some studies showing markedly higher rates than others.[25] A rough estimate of mental illnesses among this group offers a range between 29 and 78 per cent.[26] Thus, my findings fall within this range. However, for specific psychiatric disorders, the numbers are not always consistent. For instance, depression

Table 2.6. Distribution of mental health illnesses (not mutually exclusive in an individual)

Mental Health Conditions	Percentage/Frequency % (n)
Depression	24.4 (48)
Bipolar disorder	3.6 (7)
Schizophrenia	3 (6)
Anxiety disorder	17.3 (34)
Dementia	4.6 (9)
PTSD	4.1 (8)
Other	11.2 (22)

PTSD = post-traumatic stress disorder

24 McKenna et al, *supra* note 2; Jagger et al, *supra* note 2.
25 Leigey, *supra* note 22 at 51–3.
26 Harald Dressing, Christine Kief, & Hans-Joachim Salize, "Prisoners with Mental Disorders in Europe" (2009) 194:1 Br J Psychiatry 88.

and anxiety were the leading reported mental illnesses in my study. These numbers were similar to those in some studies,[27] but significantly lower[28] and significantly higher than in others.[29] However, consensus exists across the board that mental illness among this prison group is higher than among both younger and older people outside of prison.[30]

The 5 per cent rate of dementia in my study was particularly surprising, especially because those reporting it tended to be prisoners in maximum security and, more generally, people serving life sentences.

> I have been here [maximum security] for a while. Last year I was diagnosed with Stage 1 dementia. I don't think anything worse can happen. I am serving life and no one will release me directly from here. However, by the time I will be transferred to a lower level of security I will not even remember my name. That's scary. That's very scary. (LL, maximum security, in prison 7 years)

Some people did not have a dementia diagnosis but admitted to suffering from severe memory loss.

> I keep forgetting things. It's so frustrating. I am trying to hide it but it's getting hard at work. Staff yell at me all the time. (TT, 72, in prison 36 years)

The process of "cascading down the security levels" before being released is generally useful in that it helps prisoners readjust to life outside the institution. It is, however, highly problematic for individuals who get very sick at a high level of security early on in their sentence. While possible, early transfers due to illness to lower levels of security, hospices, or other centres require paperwork and often get caught up in bureaucracy. The rigidity of the process is even more problematic in

---

27 Massimiliano Piselli et al, "Psychiatric Needs of Male Prison Inmates in Italy" (2015) 41 Intl JL & Psychiatry 82; Howse, *supra* note 22 at 19–20; Judith J. Regan, Ann Alderson, & William M. Regan, "Psychiatric Disorders in Aging Prisoners" (2003) 26:1–2 Clin Gerontol 117 at 119, https://doi.org/10.1300/J018v26n01_10 [Regan, Alderson, & Regan]; Lisa C. Barry et al, "Disabilities in Prison Activities of Daily Living and Likelihood of Depression and Suicidal Ideation in Older Prisoners" (2017) 32:10 Int J Geriatr Psychiatry 1141 at 1147 [Barry et al].

28 Nicolas Combalbert et al, "Mental Disorders and Cognitive Impairment in Ageing Offenders" (2016) 27:6 J Forens Psychiatry Psychol 853 at 860–3, https://doi.org/10.1080/14789949.2016.1244277.

29 S. Fazel & J. Danesh, "Serious Mental Disorder in 23 000 Prisoners: A Systematic Review of 62 Surveys" (2002) 359 Lancet 545.

30 Leigey, *supra* note 22 at 52; Howse, *supra* note 22 at 19–20; Aday, *Aging Prisoners, supra* note 3 at 102; Barry et al, *supra* note 27 at 1147.

cases of prisoners with dementia, which challenge our understanding of punishment and the ability of incarceration to meet our desire for both rehabilitation and vindication. It is difficult to conceive how we can punish people who fail to understand where they are or why they are there, who cannot be rehabilitated, and who are already deterred from committing offences by their state of mind. However, people like LL can be considered for parole only after serving an amount of time in prison (in LL's case twenty-five years; he had barely served six years at the time of his dementia diagnosis). He is also not eligible to apply for the little-used compassionate release provision on medical grounds. Section 121.1 of the *CCRA* provides that individuals who are serving life cannot apply for compassionate release unless they are terminally ill (that is, within six months of dying). Nonetheless, dementia is not a terminal illness. This policy leaves a whole group of people in limbo. It also leaves prison workers and administrators grasping for solutions. A warden at a medium security institution explained:

> We have this one guy, I don't even know what to do with him. He suffers from some form of dementia. He was at Pittsburgh [minimum security]. They shipped him to us because he was a wanderer and got up and walked around at night. He bothered the other prisoners and the institution didn't know how to control him. They sent him to us. We can put him in segregation when he gets like that and then he can't move. We are not a nursing home, we can't care for him. He is very confused. (Warden, medium security institution)

Nonetheless, the rates and challenges presented by dementia and cognitive impairment were by no means unique to my study. Similar[31] or higher rates[32] have been identified in the literature,[33] and there is consensus that the prison environment is ill suited for individuals with these conditions.[34]

---

31 Regan, Alderson, & Regan, *supra* note 27 at 119.

32 Aday, *Aging Prisoners, supra* note 3 at 102–3; Brie Williams et al, "Addressing the Aging Crisis in US Criminal Justice Healthcare" (2012) 60:6 J Am Geriatr Soc 1150, https://doi.org/10.1111/j.1532-5415.2012.03962.x.

33 However, for dementia and cognitive impairment rates, there is also a large range across the literature, between 1 per cent and 30 per cent: Gabriele Cipriani et al, "Old and Dangerous: Prison and Dementia" (2017) 51 J Forensic Leg Med 40 at 42.

34 S. Fazel, J. McMillan, & I. O'Donnell, "Dementia in Prison: Ethical and Legal Implications" (2002) 28 J Med Ethics 156 at 156 [Fazel, McMillan, & O'Donnell]; Tina Maschi et al, "Forget Me Not: Dementia in Prison" (2012) 52:4 Gerontologist 441 [Maschi et al, "Forget Me Not"].

ACCESS TO MENTAL HEALTH CARE

As mentioned, access to medical services was an overarching theme regardless of what type of medical conditions participants reported. However, it appears that access to psychiatric services is even more limited than to other types of medical services, which is consistent with findings in the literature that mental health needs among older prisoners tend to be met at lower rates than physical ones.[35]

Institutions like Pittsburgh, where access to a psychiatrist and counselling is available, tended to be the exception. Only 14 per cent of the people with a mental health diagnosis reported seeing the psychiatrist after they turned fifty, and many of these men were already well into their sixties. Of the same group, 26 per cent said they were receiving some form of mental health counselling, either from a psychologist or a social worker. As mentioned, I obtained the list of medical hires for the Ontario region through an *Access to Information Act* request.[36] Earlier in this chapter, I referred to a shortage of psychiatrists and a lack of consistent access to mental health services, which explains the comments of the study participants that the psychiatrist is generally available for five minutes every second year or so, and their main role is to assess suicide risk.

> I am a lifer and the rule is I have to see the psychiatrist every two years. But it takes ... maybe five minutes? She just asks if I have suicidal thoughts, I say no, and that's that. (HH, 64, in prison 16 years)
>
> Last time I saw the psychiatrist was ten years ago when I arrived, because I came with a bipolar diagnosis. Since then the nurse has been renewing my prescription. Or someone, because it gets renewed. (SS, 52, in prison 10 years)

Warkworth Institution was particularly bad when it came to assisting those with mental illnesses. Because there was one psychologist to six hundred individuals, each individual was entitled to three counselling sessions for the duration of their stay in the institution.

> No, I don't see the psychologist. I have been in here for fifteen years and I have used them all up. We can only see the psychologist three times

---

35 Stephan Ardnt, Carolyn L. Turvey, & Micahel Flaum, "Older Offenders, Substance Abuse and Treatment" (2002) 10:6 Am J Geriatr Psychiatry 733 [Ardnt, Turvey, & Flaum]; Fazel, McMillan, & O'Donnell *supra* note 34; Lemieux, Dyeson, & Castiglione, *supra* note 3; Leigey, *supra* note 22 at 55.

36 Correctional Service of Canada, Document A-2015–00641 [unpublished letter]. This document and explanations were obtained in May 2016 through an *Access to Information Act* request.

because there is only one. And new people keep coming in. (WW, 50, in prison 25 years)

All thirty-six participants serving time in Warkworth Institution confirmed that getting access to a psychiatrist was close to impossible.

When you put in to see a psychiatrist, the nurse asks if you are suicidal. If you say no, well, there is no space. If you say yes, sure, you get to see one, but she might send you to suicide watch [which is essentially solitary confinement]. (WW, 50, in prison 25 years)

SUBSTANCE ABUSE

A distinct, but equally problematic, mental health issue was substance abuse, with 29 per cent of those interviewed self-identifying as addicts. Substance abuse was likely underreported, primarily because it is illegal in prison: 30 per cent of the participants reported drinking alcohol daily at least on the outside, but only 52 per cent of them also self-identified as alcoholics. Similarly, 38 per cent reported that they consumed drugs on a daily basis, while only 42 per cent of them self-identified as addicts. Because of these inconsistencies, and because these rates are much lower than those reported in the literature for older individuals,[37] substance abuse may have been underreported in my study.

Consistent with the overall lack of access to services, access to appropriate treatment for substance abuse is not always readily available. Alcoholics Anonymous and Narcotics Anonymous are available in all institutions and are typically well attended, either because individuals were required by their correctional plan to attend or because they volunteered to participate. Other types of programs, such as the National Substance Abuse Program (NSAP), are available. For example, John reported attending high-intensity NSAP when he was younger, though he did not self-identify as an addict. Of the participants, 9 per cent reported attending some form of NSAP.

However, medical treatment for addiction was much more rare, which was also reported as a problem in the literature.[38] Only 6 per cent reported receiving such treatment in my study, mostly because it is only available in community institutions and not in prisons. Because of

---

37 Ardnt, Turvey, & Flaum, *supra* note 35 at 735–7; Keith Morgen, "Substance Abuse and Older Adults in the Criminal Justice System" in Be the Evidence Project White Paper, *Aging Prisoners: A Crisis in Need of Intervention* (New York: Fordham University Press, 2012) 48 at 51–2 [Morgen].

38 Morgen, *supra* note 37 at 53–4.

security concerns, only some individuals qualify to be transferred to community institutions. A methadone program is available in most prisons, and some of the individuals who identified as addicts are part of these programs. Participation, however, raised other issues.

> I broke my conditions of parole. On purpose, because I wanted to return to prison. When I was released I couldn't get methadone from anywhere [but he was getting it in prison, before release]. So I started back on drugs. I knew my urine sample will come back dirty and that I would return to prison. Not much I can do, I can't go without [drugs]. (AC, 54, in prison 12 years)

SUICIDAL IDEATION

Likely underreported, suicidal ideation (21 per cent of the interview sample) is a controversial topic. A definite connection was seen between mental illness and suicidal thoughts (29 per cent of participants with a mental illness reported having suicidal thoughts, as opposed to 15 per cent of those not reporting a mental illness). The difference was even more apparent when participants were asked if they ever felt life was not worth living. Of those with various mental health conditions, 59 per cent answered yes, as opposed to 19 per cent of those who did not report any such illnesses. While individuals were more likely to report feeling that life was not worth living than that they experienced suicidal thoughts, as a rule, when the question came around, most were quick to deny anything that would resemble contemplating suicide.

> I think this is the question we get asked most frequently. It is the only thing they fear – that we will commit suicide. We get used to saying "no" when we hear the word suicide. So have I thought about it? In thirty-two years in this place? No. (GG, 62, in prison 32 years)

The majority of those who did speak openly about suicidal thoughts were well accustomed to the correctional system and did not appear to care about potential repercussions.

> If I think about suicide? Every single day. That day will come. I will never be released and I refuse to be sick in here. Not many other options. (AA, 63, in prison 43 years)
>
> Am I suicidal? No. Is life worth living in here? Absolutely not. (YY, 51, in prison 13 years)

The fact that only 5 per cent of those who reported having suicidal thoughts actually sought help says a lot about the manner in which prisoners perceive mental health services in prisons.

> Tell them what? What will they do? At best they will ignore, at worst they will send me to the hole [solitary confinement]. No, I just work things through my way. I try to keep hope alive. (CC, 57, in prison 15 years)

Many people did not give a reason for not seeking help, but 8 per cent said they feared the consequences of reaching out. Of the total number of participants, 5 per cent mentioned being punished or ignored when they sought help regarding their suicidal ideation.

> Two months in the hole. That's what I got for seeking help. Never doing that again. (AB, 53, in prison 9 years)

Some literature exists on the issue of suicidal ideation among older prisoners; it attests to the increased vulnerability of older prisoners to suicide, not only because of the high rates of mental illness but also because of their difficulty in coping with unmet health care needs in general.[39] Significant work also confirms the correlation between mental illness, imprisonment, and suicide. These studies underline the importance of appropriate programming, accommodation, treatment (such as substance abuse treatment and psychiatric care), and help with managing distress to enable prisoners to cope and thus reduce suicidal ideation.[40] This issue circles back to the fact that many of the challenges this population faces may stem from or be exacerbated by the lack of access to appropriate and timely services for their high physical and mental health needs. In addition, the lack of willingness of prisoners to report their suicidal ideation and seek help may be an illustration of how disciplinary responses to health problems expose prisoners to increased dangers.

---

39 Barry et al, *supra* note 27 at 1146; Kate O'Hara et al, "Links Between Depressive Symptoms and Unmet Health and Social Care Needs Among Older Prisoners" (2016) 45:1 Age Ageing 158 at 160–1, https://doi.org/10.1093/ageing/afv171.

40 Alison Liebling et al, "Revisiting Prison Suicide: The Role of Fairness and Distress" in Alison Liebling & Shadd Maruna, eds, *The Effects of Imprisonment* (London: Routledge, 2011) 209 [Liebling et al, "Revisiting Prison Suicide"]; Alison Liebling, "Vulnerability, Struggling, and Coping in Prison" in Ben Crewe & Jamie Bennett, eds, *The Prisoner* (London: Routledge, 2012) 53 [Liebling, "Vulnerability"]; Alison Liebling, "Prison Suicide and Its Prevention" in Jewkes, *supra* note 12 at 432 [Liebling, "Prison Suicide"].

Factors That Exacerbate Mental Health Problems in Prison

A number of factors present in prison appear to be statistically correlated to higher rates of mental illness. These factors may possibly be contributing to an exacerbation of mental decline in the older prison population. Statistically speaking, such factors appear to be the practice of segregating individuals presenting mental problems, the use of disciplinary charges for behaviour that may have a psychiatric explanation, an unsafe environment that leads to sleep deprivation and high levels of anxiety among this population, and the loss of family contact.

DISCIPLINARY ACTION

Instances of mental illness among prisoners seem to be commonly met with disciplinary charges and solitary confinement. As mentioned, the rate of disciplinary incidents was relatively low (about 31 per cent had been charged with disciplinary offences since turning fifty, mostly nonviolent ones, while 23 per cent had spent time in segregation). At the same time, those who reported they had been subject to disciplinary charges also tended to report mental illness in higher numbers than those without disciplinary charges (Table 2.7).

As well, it appeared that prisoners with mental illnesses were more often sent to segregation than their healthier counterparts (36 per cent as opposed to 15 per cent; Table 2.8). It is unclear from the study if

Table 2.7. Disciplinary charges per mental health rate

Disciplinary Charges since Turning Fifty	Does Prisoner Mention Mental Illness?		Total % (n)
	No % (n)	Yes (One or More) % (n)	
No	66.2 (90)	33.8 (46)	100 (136)
Yes	49.2 (30)	50.8 (31)	100 (61)

Chi-square = 5.109; df = 1; p = .024

Table 2.8. Mental Illnesses per segregation rate

Mental Illnesses Reported	Segregation since Turning 50		Total % (n)
	No % (n)	Yes % (n)	
No	85 (102)	15 (18)	100 (120)
Yes (one or more)	63.6 (49)	36.4 (28)	100 (77)

Chi-square = 11.961; df = 1; p = .001

segregation was used in response to mental illness or if segregation led to or exacerbated mental illness. It was likely both.

Those with a mental illness diagnosis were more likely to have been sent to segregation for disciplinary reasons than their healthier counterparts (60 per cent as opposed to 40 per cent). Similarly, of the people who requested segregation for their own safety, the majority reported having a psychiatric condition (73 per cent).

The disciplinary response of institutions to mental health conditions taps into the larger issue of institutional inability to respond to the needs of older prisoners and also underlines the need for better training for first responders in order for them to be able to differentiate between medical and behavioural issues. Significant work has been completed that confirms the correlation between mental illness and the use of segregation in general, and draws attention to the dangers of responding to mental illness with disciplinary action.[41] My findings add another dimension to that broader conversation.

ENVIRONMENT

As substantiated in the literature,[42] environmental conditions appeared to be an important factor contributing to mental decline. In my study, for example, many prisoners reported that they could not sleep at night, often because of safety concerns or because of their cellmates.

> I snore and when I snore [my cellmate] gets so angry and yells and hits me. I am trying really hard not to fall asleep before he does or to sleep during the day when he is working. (AD, 72, in prison 5 years)
>
> [The younger prisoners] play the music loud until late at night. There is no way I can sleep. (QQ, 63, in prison 8 years)
>
> God knows what will happen if I fall asleep. (DD, 52, in prison 5 years)
>
> [My cellmate] works out and gets heated and leaves the window open in the dead of winter. I only have one blanket. How do you think I can sleep? (OO, 58, in prison 14 years)

Mental health problems were significantly more prevalent among individuals who reported being sleep deprived. Of the participants,

---

41 See e.g. Kenneth Adams & Joseph Ferrandino, "Managing Mentally Ill Inmates in Prisons" (2008) 35:8 Crim Justice Behav 913 at 917; Angela Browne, Alissa Cambier, & Suzanne Agha, "Prisons within Prisons: The Use of Segregation in the United States" (2011) 24:1 Federal Sentencing Reporter 46; Ivan Zinger, "The Effects of 60 Days of Solitary Confinement" (2001) 43 Can J Criminol Crim Justice 109.

42 Mann, *Doing Harder Time, supra* note 12 at 42; Blowers, Jolley, & Kerbs, *supra* note 12 at 135–54.

47 per cent reported having sleeping problems on a regular basis, and 9 per cent stated that they had occasional issues falling asleep. People with mental health issues reported having more problems sleeping than those who reported no mental illnesses (70 per cent versus 46 per cent; Table 2.9). It is also equally true that the quality of sleep may be influenced by the mental illness itself. For example, 34 per cent of the people with sleeping disorders also reported having depression, and 26 per cent reported having anxiety. In contrast, only 16 per cent and 7 per cent of those without sleeping disorders reported experiencing depression and anxiety, respectively.

LACK OF FAMILY CONTACT

Considering the reports in the literature,[43] it was not surprising that lack of regular contact with family on the outside seemed to negatively impact the mental health of the study participants. A significant inverse relationship was observed between the frequency of family visits and suicidal thoughts. People who had never had suicidal ideation tended to report more frequent family contact (57 per cent reported weekly visits) than those who had experienced suicidal thoughts (37 per cent of whom reported weekly visits). Unfortunately, numerous participants in this study never received a visit during their time in prison (48 per cent), and most of the others received infrequent visits. These rates are consistent with the findings presented in the literature.[44]

A large number of older prisoners complained about the way their families were treated. I was told that generally if a prisoner was not well

Table 2.9. Distribution of mental health illnesses per sleep problems

Mental Health Illnesses Reported	Sleep Problems			
	No % (n)	Yes % (n)	Sometimes % (n)	Total % (n)
No	54.2 (65)	36.7 (44)	9.2 (11)	100 (120)
Yes	29.9 (23)	62.3 (48)	7.8 (6)	100 (77)

Chi-square = 12.920; df = 2; p = .002

43 Mann, *Doing Harder Time*, *supra* note 12 at 70–7; Alice Mills & Helen Codd, "Prisoners' Families" in Jewkes, *supra* note 12 at 678–9; Aday, *Aging Prisoners*, *supra* note 3 at 124; Judith Phillips, Anne Worrall, & Alison Brammer, "Elders and the Criminal Justice System in England" in Rothman, Dunlop, & Entzel, *supra* note 20 at 268–9; Rachel Condry, "Prisoners and Their Families," in Crewe & Bennett, *supra* note 40 at 67–78.

44 Aday, *Aging Prisoners*, *supra* note 3 at 125; Leigey, *supra* note 22 at 59–60; Hayes, *supra* note 3 at 7.

liked, his family was treated badly. Older prisoners took issue with that, especially if the family members were older relatives or small children. Participants pointed out that these behaviours acted as a deterrent for many family members to come and visit.

> My kids [eight and nine years old] don't want to come back. One is afraid of dogs. The guards always put the dogs on him. They let them jump up and down my boy. (UU, 50, in prison 8 years)

EXERCISE

The lack of exercise also appeared to lead to a decline in mental well-being. Thus, people who reported exercising on a regular basis also reported lower rates of mental illness (Table 2.10), confirming that exercise might in fact be the cheapest form of therapy.

Unfortunately, as John and other participants in the study explained, exercise was not always feasible for prisoners within this age group. The gym and the weight pit are sites associated with virility and strength. Numerous individuals claimed they were bullied or pushed aside from the gym for being too weak or too slow. A significant number of individuals stopped using the gym altogether in an attempt to hide their weakness and protect themselves. Most people tried to keep active on a daily basis (66 per cent). However, only 23 per cent used the gym. The rest walked the corridors (16 per cent), stretched in their cells (9 per cent), or walked in the yard when there was no ice on the ground (32 per cent). Because of improperly cleaned yards, the latter group were often left without any exercise space in winter. Eric was once again an exception. Being particularly sick and serving time in a better institution, he had access to a physiotherapist once a month. Nonetheless, aside from those sessions, he was unable to exercise in any manner.

The lack of an appropriate facility where seniors could work out was the second most common environment-related complaint, surpassed only by the lack of a seniors-only unit. When asked what program they would like to see introduced, 22 per cent of the participants (the most

Table 2.10. Distribution of rates of regular exercise per mental illnesses rates

| | Mental Illnesses Reported | | |
| | No | Yes | Total |
Regular Exercise	% (n)	% (n)	% (n)
No	51.5 (35)	48.5 (33)	100 (68)
Yes	65.9 (85)	34.1 (44)	100 (129)

Chi-square = 3.889; df = 1; p = .049

numerous) said it would be a seniors' fitness program. Others simply asked for either a seniors-only cardio room or a couple of hours set aside for seniors in the main gym. In general, 73 per cent believed that the institutions could offer more relevant programs and activities, physical and non-physical, in safer spaces for the elderly to attend and, thus, to maintain their mental alertness and avoid idleness.

> What's it to them? Over half of the population here are old people. Still only the young people use the gym, all the time. Why can't they set a time for us older people to be there without worrying about our safety? (TT, 72, in prison 36 years)

VICTIMIZATION

Fear for one's safety is a theme that occurred regularly in my conversations with older people, and I noticed a correlation between those who reported feeling fearful and those who were affected by mental illness. Of the 44 per cent of older prisoners who reported feeling unsafe and in danger, 56 per cent also reported having a mental illness. This study confirmed that their fears were justified, because people with mental illnesses were considerably more likely to be victims of different types of abuse than those not reporting a mental illness (70 per cent of those reporting a psychiatric condition; Table 2.11). The study does not show whether mental illness renders individuals vulnerable or if abuse enhances mental illness; it is likely both.

Overall, the most common types of abuse were insults (45 per cent) and ridicule (47 per cent); cutting in line, leading to some older prisoners having to stand in line longer (34 per cent); and physical violence and threats of physical violence (60 per cent).

> Old fart, kiddie diddler, pops, you hear that every time you get out of the cell. From inmates, from officers ... I learned to block them out. They won't go anywhere, and neither will I. (PP, 66, in prison 25 years)

Table 2.11. Distribution of mental illnesses reported per peer abuse rates

| Mental Illnesses Reported | Abused by Peers | | |
	No % (n)	Yes % (n)	Total % (n)
No	60 (72)	40 (48)	100 (120)
Yes (one or more)	29.9 (23)	70.1 (54)	100 (77)

Chi-square = 17.053; df = 1; p <.001

Property, particularly medication and food, was often stolen from people in this group (42 per cent). The frequent theft helps explain why 81 per cent of the participants felt that having a seniors-only sleeping and living unit would significantly increase the quality of their lives in prison.

> I must wheel myself down daily to pick up my pills. But I don't always get to take them. My peer caregiver snatches them when he can and sells them. (AE, 57, in prison 17 years)

Isolation and stigma due to age were also prominently reported (54 per cent). As encountered in John's case, there was a generally held view that older people are paedophiles. This belief attracted significant bullying from other prisoners and increased safety concerns, which, in turn, led to self-imposed isolation on one hand and peer-imposed isolation on the other.

There appeared to be no relevant statistical connection between mental illness and staff abuse, though incidents of bullying and lack of sensitivity in connection to mental illness were described by some participants.

> [The officer's] favourite phrase is "Hang yourself." The more depressed a guy is the more likely he is to hear it. He makes it clear we are all a waste of space. (AF, 58, in prison 25 years)

The literature does not address the correlation between mental illness, aging, and victimization. However, substantial work shows that both age and mental illness are factors rendering prisoners more vulnerable and hence at a higher risk of victimization. This finding may explain why the rates of victimization in my study are significantly higher than those reported against older prisoners in general in the literature.[45]

Mental health is often affected by one's environmental stability and security. Failure to provide adequate medical treatment to individuals with psychiatric conditions is worrisome. Much more can and should be done to prevent the enhancement of mental deterioration in general. Safety issues, unaddressed physical pain, sleep deprivation, lack of exercise and mental stimulation, lack of alcohol abuse interventions, and the use of punishment and solitary confinement are all interconnected, and are significant environmental factors that may accelerate mental

---

45 Morton, *supra* note 22 at 65; Aday, *Aging Prisoners, supra* note 3 at 113; Kerbs & Jolley, "Age Segregation," *supra* note 22 at 126; Ornduff, *supra* note 22 at 175; CPHA, *supra* note 22; Tarbuck, *supra* note 22 at 369; Corrections Victoria, *supra* note 22 at 15; HRW, *supra* note 22 at 58, Leigey, *supra* note 22 at 57–8; Kerbs & Jolley, "Victimization," *supra* note 22.

deterioration in a group already at risk. Ultimately, thoughts of death and/or anxieties about safety arose in most of the conversations I had with those interviewed. These matters slowly wear on the individual and can have significant, long-term effects.

Terminal Illness and End-of-Life Care

We have memorials every month now. You never know who will be next. (JJ, 56, in prison 30 years, about Pittsburgh Institution, aka "The Dead Men's Camp")

Terminal illness is commonly defined as an illness that causes an individual to be within six months of death.[46] Despite their many health problems, neither Eric nor John was terminally ill, though they knew of people who were and continued to be confined to a cell. Not all institutions house terminally ill prisoners. It appeared that once an individual became terminally ill they were sent to a minimum security institution. At the time of the interview, Pittsburgh was housing upwards of ten terminally or close to terminally ill individuals (hence the nickname "The Dead Men's Camp"). I was also informed that one such individual was housed at Millhaven Maximum Security Institution.

Terminally ill prisoners were out of my reach for the purpose of this study, either because they lacked motivation to talk to anybody or because they were bedridden. I was not allowed onto their units. Other prisoners, however, described the pain their peers suffered. A number of prisoners at Pittsburgh confirmed that ten terminally ill prisoners were housed at that institution. People like Eric were particularly distressed by seeing peers die in front of their eyes. The rate of individuals who identified dying as their number one fear was higher here than in any other institution (close to 80 per cent). Dying prisoners lived in the same houses as everyone else, and thus all prisoners could witness the end-of-life process unfolding. Horror stories spread fast and led to panic among individuals.

Two people died in here of cancer since I was transferred. They took them on the other side of the fence and declared them dead so [the prison administration] don't deal with the paperwork. And before they died? They just sat in their cells. (KK, 55, in prison 24 years)

As described in a previous section, many prisoners at Pittsburgh talked about a cancer patient, transferred there for chemotherapy, who waited

---

46   See e.g. Barry et al, *supra* note 27 at 445.

a few months for diagnosis and treatment and received no pain medication for the first week.

> He came here so sick. It took months before he got an esophagus cancer diagnosis. He was finally labelled as terminally ill. He was shaking and sweating in pain. We didn't know what to do. We bought him a bottle of Advil. (JJ, 56, in prison 30 years)

A different prisoner, talking about the same person, stated:

> My biggest fear is getting sick. I don't think I will ever be released so I might get sick. I just wish I will have a heart attack and die. If I get terminally ill like this guy, there will be a lot of suffering. (AG, 63, in prison 12 years)

The fear of getting sick and dying in prison was tightly linked to the high levels of anxiety expressed by all participants in the study. Witnessing end of life and disease in prison was a main trigger for those fears. This finding was not unique to this study, as fear of death and disease is a constant theme in older prisoner research,[47] while inappropriately addressed terminal conditions were deemed to trigger psychiatric conditions.[48]

None of the institutions I visited had a palliative care unit. In Peterborough, there was a hospice where dying prisoners from Ontario were sometimes sent. Indeed, a number of the participants from Pittsburgh mentioned that prisoners were sometimes sent there to die, though the space was limited and transfers required a significant amount of paperwork.

> We had a guy who died last month of cancer of something. They were planning to send him to Peterborough but the paperwork was not done in time. (AC, 54, in prison 12 years)

---

47 Elaine Crawley & Richard Sparks, "Older Men in Prison: Survival, Coping, and Identity" in Liebling & Maruna, *supra* note 40, 343 at 353–4; Ronald H. Aday, "Aging Prisoners' Concerns Towards Dying in Prison" (2005–2006) 52:3 OMEGA – J Death Dying 199 at 202; Aday, *Aging Prisoners, supra* note 3 at 127–8; John F. Linder & Frederick J. Meyers, "Palliative Care for Inmates" (2007) 298:8 JAMA 894 at 896; Susan J. Loeb et al, "Who Wants to Die in Here? Perspectives of Prisoners with Chronic Conditions" (2014) 16:3 J Hosp Palliat Nurs 173 at 178, https://doi.org/10.1097/NJH.0000000000000044 [Leob et al]; Mary Turner & Marian Peacock, "Palliative Care in UK Prisons: Practical and Emotional Challenges for Staff and Fellow Prisoners" (2017) 23:1 J Corr Health Care 56 at 64–5 [Turner & Peacock]; Yvonne Jewkes, "Loss, Liminality and the Life Sentence: Managing Identity through a Disrupted Life Course" in Liebling & Maruna, *supra* note 40, 366 at 370–8.
48 Annette Hanson, "Psychiatry and the Dying Prisoner" (2017) 29:1 Intl Rev Psychiatry 45 at 47.

While there may have been attempts to provide palliative care in prison on an individual basis, this venture was seriously restricted by the prisons' security policies. Without a palliative care unit, it was difficult to administer the strong medication available in the outside community to people in similar situations. The lack of a proper palliative care unit also meant that medical staff were not available at all times (only 20 per cent thought a nurse was available around the clock). There was no special housing for people who were terminally ill or in severe pain, and no adjusted infrastructure. Through an *Access to Information Act* request, I obtained a CSC guideline called *Hospice Palliative Care Guidelines for Correctional Service of Canada.* This document offers instructions to different staff members regarding how to interact with dying prisoners and emphasizes the need for a team of individuals to help with end-of-life care. The material makes it clear that palliative care is not systematic and that dying prisoners are housed in the same facilities as everyone else and, thus, subjected to the same security rules and medical regulations. For prisoners at Pittsburgh, that meant lack of appropriate painkillers, approvals needed for any kind of therapeutic intervention, trips in the community (in the CSC steel van) to the hospital for chemotherapy, and limited time with their family. They would generally be visited at their bedside by spiritual counsellors, but their family would not be allowed on the units. Hence, a prisoner's limited mobility made family reunions very difficult.

For Millhaven Maximum Security Institution, palliative care meant day after day spent in a cell in protective custody. One might wonder why a dying prisoner would be subjected to the highest security rules possible. When a prisoner is incarcerated, their risk is assessed based on personal traits and the offence committed. Regardless of anything else, murder scores so high on the risk assessment scale that the individual convicted of murder would generally have to spend a number of years in maximum security.[49] Such was the case with the terminally ill individual

---

49   The scoring system used to assess the risk level of any individual sentenced to imprisonment and, thus, the security level where they would begin their sentence was changed in the early 2000s to require spending time initially in maximum security. To determine an individual's risk level, a number of personal circumstances are scored (type of offence and sentence, results of the psychological assessment, presence of a previous criminal record, and so on); if an individual scores above the minimum points threshold, they are sent to the corresponding higher security level. On the new system, extra points are given to murder and life sentence so that individuals in such situations automatically score above the minimum points for maximum security. See Correctional Service of Canada, "Yes, SIR! A Stable Risk Prediction Tool" (1997) 9:1 Forum on Corrections Research, online: https://www.csc-scc.gc.ca/research/forum/e091/e091a-eng.shtml.

at Millhaven. While a transfer to a lower level due to illness was in sight, such a transfer required paperwork that was not expeditiously completed. In the meantime, the prisoner was confined to a protective custody cell without any kind of end-of-life care.

The *Corrections and Conditional Release Act* (*CCRA*) provides in section 121 that an individual who is terminally ill may be released based on what is called "parole by exception." Individuals such as those dying at Pittsburgh or Millhaven fell squarely under such provision. However, none of the individuals I interviewed had ever heard of this provision or of anyone being released for compassionate or medical reasons outside the regular parole process. Not being able to interview people who were terminally ill, I could not confirm if they had been presented with this option.

The concerns expressed by participants regarding dying in prison are consonant with the ones expressed by the Office of the Correctional Investigator (OCI). The OCI found that "natural" death is on the rise in prisons because of the aging process and longer sentences. The OCI criticized the approach taken by the CSC in dealing with such deaths, the small number of compassionate releases based on *CCRA* section 121, and the far-from-dignified "dying conditions" prisoners experienced. The OCI also confirmed and criticized the fact that no systematic approach to palliative and end-of-life care exists for individuals who perhaps should not continue to be incarcerated at all.[50] In a separate report on death in prison, the OCI found that for half of the dead prisoners whose files it reviewed, the procedure used to deal with their illnesses was affected by tardiness or was incomplete, or their medical files simply did not elaborate on that procedure. While this report dealt with death in general, not just that of older individuals, this category of prisoners is the most affected by the CSC's inability or unwillingness to deal with the terminally ill.[51]

The concerns expressed regarding end of life in prison revolve around the same challenges identified by participants regarding their other needs. Challenging infrastructure, lack of access to appropriate services, and lack of access to pain management medication and medical supplies, as well as the overwhelming anxiety caused to individuals anticipating they will die behind bars, make the prison environment a very inappropriate place for someone to spend the end of their life. While other

---

50 Canada, Office of the Correctional Investigator, *Annual Report, 2013–2014* (Ottawa: OCI, 2014) at 20, online: http://www.oci-bec.gc.ca/cnt/rpt/pdf/annrpt/annrpt20132014-eng.pdf.

51 Canada, Office of the Correctional Investigator, *An Investigation of the Correctional Service's Mortality Review Process* (Ottawa: OCI, 2014) at 18–23, online: http://www.oci-bec.gc.ca/cnt/rpt/pdf/oth-aut/oth-aut20131218-eng.pdf.

jurisdictions have noted some improvements in terms of providing palliative care for prisoners (addressed in the next chapter), the inability of correctional systems to provide quality end-of-life care at a level comparable to the community for similar reasons as those identified in this study has been well documented.[52] In 2016, Canada decriminalized assisted dying,[53] an option that is now also available to incarcerated individuals.[54] While at the time of writing there have not yet been any cases, significant concerns have been expressed that many terminally ill prisoners may not have a meaningful choice in terms of end-of-life care. Unless palliative services and compassionate release are significantly improved, we may face situations where prisoners would choose assisted dying for lack of a realistic palliative care option.[55]

Emergency Care

I was having a heart attack. They made me walk to the front gate because the ambulance is not allowed on the alley. (KK, 55, in prison 24 years)

Once a guy in here had a heart attack. He had to wait one hour for the ambulance after they made him walk to the front gate. So my biggest fear? Getting sick in here. (JJ, 56, in prison 30 years)

Terminal illness is not the only cause of death in the community or in prison. Sudden, acute conditions, especially when inappropriately

---

52 Mara, *supra* note 11 at 50; Crawley, *supra* note 12 at 234; Turner & Peacock, *supra* note 47 at 61–4; Marina Richter & Ueli Hostettler, "End of Life in Prison: Talking Across Disciplines and Across Countries" (2017) 23:1 J Corr Health Care 11 at 17; Irene Marti, Ueli Hostettler, & Marina Richter, "End of Life in High-Security Prisons in Switzerland: Overlapping and Blurring of 'Care' and 'Custody' as Institutional Logics" (2017) 23:1 J Corr Health Care 32 at 36–9; Janice Penriod, Susan J. Loeb, & Carol A. Smith, "Administrators' Perspectives on Changing Practices in End-of-Life Care in a State Prison System" (2014) 31:2 Public Health Nurs 99 at 7–9, https://doi. org/10.1111/phn.12069; Rachel K. Wion & Susan J. Loeb, "End-of-Life Care Behind Bars: A Systemic Review" (2016) 116:3 AJN 24 at 32; Loeb et al, *supra* note 47 at 177–82; Meridith C. Burles, Cindy A. Peternelj-Taylor, & Lorraine Holtslander, "A 'Good Death' for All? Examining Issues for Palliative Care in Correctional Settings" (2016) 21:2 Mortality 93 at 98–101; John F. Linder, "Health Issues and End of Life Care" in Kerbs and Jolley, *Senior Citizens, supra* note 12, 177.

53 *An Act to amend the Criminal Code and to make related amendments to other Acts (medical assistance in dying)*, SC 2016, c 3.

54 *Corrections and Conditional Release Act*, SC 1992, c 20, s 19 [*CCRA*]; Correctional Service of Canada, "Medical Assistance in Dying," Guideline 800-9 (Ottawa: CSC, 29 November 2017), online: https://www.csc-scc.gc.ca/politiques-et-lois/800-9-gl-en.shtml.

55 On this issue, see also Canada, Office of the Correctional Investigator, *Annual Report, 2016–2017* (Ottawa: OCI, 2017) at 8–10, online: http://www.oci-bec.gc.ca/cnt/rpt/pdf/annrpt/annrpt20162017-eng.pdf.

addressed, may lead to death. Even in the best of institutions, such as Pittsburgh, the issue of emergency medical intervention is significant, and people were eager to share stories that they had lived, seen, or heard about. As with any word of mouth story, its telling amplifies and creates an environment of fear and unease. Unfortunately, when it comes to medical care, such panic is not always unjustified.

Designed for health emergencies, the panic button is made to ensure that prisoners do not die in their cells. John, as a veteran prisoner, knew better than to push the panic button. He explained to me that he had never used it himself, though he had seen or heard of numerous people across institutions who had pushed it. When they did, hell broke loose.

> You don't push the panic button, and especially you don't push the panic button at night. The only thing that panic button will do is create enemies for life out of the officers who have to respond to your call.

Some prisoners who were less experienced in the prison environment had made the mistake of pushing the panic button.

> I was in terrible pain. I was rather new in prison but had already heard of people dying in here. When I couldn't take it anymore I pushed the button. They came running but they were yelling, "You'd better be dying." I was not dying. They did not take that lightly. They gave me shit and told me to put in a request in the morning to see the nurse. I saw the nurse three days later. The pain was gone by then. (AI, 56, in prison 2 years)
>
> I touched it [the panic button] by mistake during my first week. It's such a small cell, you barely have space to move. I must have touched it when I was changing or something. They yelled and shouted and told me I should hope I'll never have a real emergency because they won't respond to one coming from me. (AH, 51, in prison 1.5 years)

Eric presented me with the other face of the panic button issue: the minimum security house where he lived had only one button by the entrance. In the bathroom or bedrooms, the most likely places accidents would happen, such a button did not exist. With his disability, Eric was terrified of slipping and falling in the shower. "It will be a while before they'd find me," he said.

The issue of the panic button is rather illustrative of a bigger, systemic problem: the attitude and ability of front-line workers to intervene in crisis situations. Few of the stories I heard were as horrific as those told by prisoners who at some point found themselves in immediate need of medical intervention. Many of them believed that such poor response was due to the lack of a nurse available 24/7 and the fact that officers were very poorly trained in performing cardiopulmonary resuscitation (CPR). In addition, the bureaucracy involved in even calling for an ambulance, as well as the time it took for one to arrive on remote locations, did not help.

> I had a stroke a couple of years back. What saved my life was this nurse who is very humane. She leaves at 4 p.m. but the stroke was in the morning. Normally they won't see you immediately. You put in a request, even if it is an emergency, and they see you when they see you. But this lady knew me. And I knew it was a stroke because I had one before. Someone called for her and she saw me immediately and helped me and sent me to the hospital. She saved my life. Had it been someone else, or after 4 p.m., I'd likely be dead now. (HH, 64, in prison 16 years)

As an example of what happened when an emergency occurred outside the nurses' working hours, a prisoner described having a heart attack while at Pittsburgh. The ambulance was called, but for security reasons it was not permitted to enter the premises. The correctional officers made the inmate walk through the yard to the ambulance. An even worse heart attack story was told by a prisoner at Bath Medium Security Institution:

> I had a heart attack at 6 p.m. There is no personnel at that hour. I was just out in the yard walking and I felt this terrible pain. I fell down. Another guy alerted the officer on duty. The officer didn't know what to do. He is not allowed to call the ambulance. The keeper must give permission for the ambulance to be called. He ran back inside while I was on the ground and tried to get a hold of the keeper. Finally he did, and the keeper called the ambulance. It took about an hour or more the whole thing. I was sure I was going to die then and there. (AJ, 58, in prison 6 years)

In the same institution, another prisoner described his experience:

> Last year an aneurysm exploded in my leg. It was so painful, I can't even describe. But they didn't call the ambulance. It takes a while to get here. They put me in the CSC van to take me. At the gate the officers jumped off because it was change of shift. I had to wait for fifteen to twenty minutes on the bench in the van for the two other officers to come before we took off to KGH. (EE, 54, in prison 10 years)

The prison medical services appeared to be unable to provide prompt help, not only for emergencies but for acute problems in general.

In Millhaven Maximum Security Institution, one prisoner mentioned that it took over two weeks to see a dentist when he developed tooth abscesses:

> It was terrible. The infection was so bad, my cheek went huge. I was placed on a waiting list for two weeks and bought Advil from the canteen. Didn't help greatly. (MM, 50, in prison 32 years)

Another prisoner, talking about the same person, commented:

> Ask MM about the time he suffered a tooth abscess and what they did to him. He looked like a hamster for two full weeks. He was in so much pain. (AL, 50, in prison 6 years)

As people age and their bodies and minds are invaded by chronic conditions, their vulnerability exposes them to an increased number of acute conditions and medical emergencies. It is to be expected that in places where 70 per cent of the individuals are over fifty, and where 99 per cent of such individuals have at least one serious chronic condition, emergencies will occur with regularity. General challenges reported in the study, which pertain to limitations of the health services, understaffing, and lack of proper training, are painfully present in older prisoners' encounters with emergency situations.

Conclusion: Are Prisons High Security Nursing Homes?

> I entered vertically. I will leave here horizontally. (AA, 63, in prison 43 years)

John and Eric are good examples of the range of conditions that older individuals experience in prison, regardless of whether they have lived their lives inside an institution or were imprisoned at an older age. The difference between the two groups is that those who did grow old in prison (half of the sample) presented many old age–associated diseases at an earlier age. John was fifty-nine at the time of the interview, but he looked and felt a decade older. Eric, who entered prison in his seventies, was significantly ill, but he was also fifteen years older than John. They were both typical of the group I interviewed, not only in terms of chronic conditions but also in terms of the diversity of medical and non-medical therapy needed, their loss, grief, anxiety and depression, need to come to terms with mortality and the possibility of dying in prison, mobility issues that rendered them unfit in a prison environment, and, ultimately, their significant weakness due to age and illness in a space marked by the need to assert virility and to dominate.

The significant increase in the number of people like John and Eric means an increased demand in the quantity, quality, and diversity of medical services. Because of their confinement, John and Eric were left without the option of seeking treatment of their choice, were away from their families, and were deprived of activities that could contribute to their well-being. In such circumstances, their incarcerators have a duty to provide them with the necessities of living, as defined by this group's current and enhanced needs. These necessities may mean access to painkillers, surgery, medical devices, accessibility accommodation, medical specialists, end-of-life care, first-aid, age-informed mental health intervention, a safer environment, grief counselling, and, ultimately, the possibility of release for extenuating circumstances. Without these things, people like John and Eric are essentially sentenced to serving time on death row.

Currently, older prisoners are not recognized as a group with special or heightened needs, and the correctional services apply blanket treatment – in terms of both medical and non-medical services – to all individuals, regardless of age or health status. Whether affected by chronic, mental, acute, or terminal illnesses, the experiences of older individuals follow the same thread. First, lack of access to medical services, medication, and devices is highly problematic. The blanket prohibition of medication and medical products through documents like the *National Essential Healthcare Framework*, the *CSC Drug Formulary*, and institutional wardens' decisions create undue hardship on older prisoners who need special medical and non-medical interventions to manage their chronic conditions. The significant restriction on mental health care in certain institutions leaves older prisoners at higher risk of self-harm and defies the rehabilitation purpose of incarceration. The lack of systematic palliative care for the increasing number of people dying in prison after a long disease and the failure to promptly respond to medical emergencies for a group whose health status by definition exposes them to such emergencies are outright inhumane. Second, the unaccommodating infrastructure, the placement of older people with younger individuals in double-bunked cells, and the lack of priority for elderly, sick prisoners to medication pickup and medical services are placing significant stress on a group of individuals who are at higher risk of victimization and present disproportionate rates of physical disability. Third, directives like administrative segregation, which allow punitive responses for the management of prisoners, lead to mentally and physically ill older prisoners being placed in solitary confinement at higher rates, with potential devastating effects on their health. Fourth, inappropriate treatment of older people adds a significant amount of stress to a group already burned out by incarceration and terrified of dying in prison.

For the remainder of this book, I will explore potential reform avenues for policies that stand out as problematic. Filtered through the experiences of John, Eric, and other participants to the study, I will further engage with the legal and non-legal options for release and for obtaining the needed medical services if policy reform is not willingly undertaken by the CSC. The legal options all prisoners currently have to request the fulfilment of their needs in a court of law lack substance and are hampered by bureaucracy. By looking specifically at elderly individuals, it becomes clear that these legal avenues are unable to protect the well-being of prisoners who are older, sick, and disabled. The fact that older people are overlooked as a prison group is sad. But the fact that prisoners in general, and older, higher-needs prisoners in particular, are overlooked by our legal system, which fails to take their rights seriously, is unacceptable.

Chapter Three

Reform for Older Prisoners: Release and Institutional Accommodation

Legal Obligations for a Senior-Respectful Correctional System

Age brings about a host of new problems. Older people have considerably more chronic and acute health problems than younger individuals. They are more exposed to age-associated diseases like diabetes, cancer, digestive problems, arthritis, and mental illnesses, some of which may prove terminal. Chronic pain becomes a part of life. Diseases are less likely to be cured and increasingly require management. Disability is common. In such circumstances, maintaining quality of life at age seventy looks very different for people than it did when they were in their thirties.

Many practices surrounding the Correctional Service of Canada's (CSC's) treatment of older prisoners could be seen by some as inhumane: a drug restriction prevents older people from using anything but Tylenol 3;[1] people have to pick up medication in person each day by lining up outdoors in some location, regardless of the weather conditions; individuals go through terminal illnesses while incarcerated without any systematic pain management and other palliative care; older people are housed in institutions that lack hand rails, elevators, clean pathways, and disability-accessible washrooms; mentally ill prisoners, including those with dementia, are placed in solitary confinement at higher rates; access to medical diets and medical items that could help manage illness and disability is severely restricted, either by policy documents (such as the *National Essential Healthcare Framework*) or wardens' discretionary decisions; staff members are poorly trained in emergency care and many institutions do not have a 24/7 nurse on-site; in some

---

1 See Correctional Service of Canada, *National Drug Formulary* (Ottawa: CSC, 2013). This document was obtained through an *Access to Information Act* request in April 2016.

institutions, people have restricted access to psychiatric care unless they are suicidal; post-surgery, prisoners often recover in their cells without round-the-clock medical supervision; some officers regularly play pranks on older prisoners and call them degrading names; older, disabled, and incontinent prisoners are still sleeping on top bunks with no significant exemption from the "first-come, first serve" basis; prisoners who are wheelchair users must crawl to their beds because there is no room to take a wheelchair into the cell; people have to choose between breakfast and pill pickup because they do not move fast enough to make it to both; and younger prisoners systematically victimize older prisoners without the CSC providing safer accommodation.

The following chapters deal in greater detail with the potential statutory and constitutional violations raised by the practices examined in this study, as well as the legal challenges that prisoners may utilize in their quest for accommodation of their needs. For now, take note that the practices described in the previous chapter may not just be immoral or repugnant – they may also be against the law. In such a context, the pressure on the CSC to reform its policies, both in terms of release and the conditions of confinement, is greater.

For example, the *Corrections and Conditional Release Act* (*CCRA*) states in section 4(h)[2] that correctional policies, programs, and practices must respect gender, ethnic, cultural, and linguistic differences and be responsive to the special needs of women and Aboriginal peoples, as well as to the needs of other offender groups with special requirements. Moreover, section 70[3] of that act states that the CSC must take reasonable steps to ensure that the prison environment, including living and working conditions, are safe, healthy, and free of practices that undermine a person's reintegration into the community. Section 76[4] directs the CSC to provide a range of programs designed to address the needs of offenders and contribute to their successful reintegration into the community. According to section 86,[5] the CSC is under an obligation to provide every prisoner with essential health care and reasonable access to non-essential mental health care. As well, the provision of health care must conform to professionally accepted standards. Mental health care is seen as paramount and regulated by section 85.[6] In addition, section 87 requires that the health status of an individual be taken into account for all decisions

---

2 *Corrections and Conditional Release Act*, SC 1992, c 20, s 4(h) [*CCRA*].
3 *Ibid*, s 70.
4 *Ibid*, s 76.
5 *Ibid*, s 86.
6 *Ibid*, s 85.

related to transfers, placements, administrative segregation, disciplinary matters, release, and supervision.[7]

Some of the practices identified by prisoners are blatantly against the law. Clearly, the issues inherent in the lack of infrastructure, the use of top bunks, and slippery pathways can be quite problematic under section 70 of the *CCRA*. Other issues are more subtle. For example, one may ask the question, "What is essential health care as guaranteed by the *CCRA*?" Psychiatric care, which many prisoners are deprived of, squarely falls under essential health care. What about pain management? One could argue that when chronic pain is so distressing that a prisoner cannot sleep or move or function, failing to address it signifies a failure to provide essential health care. In addition, medical items such as orthopaedic mattresses and pillows may not be essential health care in general, but for older people these items may significantly reduce their distress. Should they not be considered essential health care? When access to such items is qualified as non-essential health care, how is a blanket prohibition of these items, per a warden's direction, within the boundaries of section 86 of the *CCRA* (that prisoners be given reasonable access to non-essential health care)? Also, when faced with terminally ill prisoners, is palliative care not essential health care? Are the acceptable levels of the profession, required according to section 86(2) for the provision of health care, met when palliative care is not systematically available and terminally ill prisoners are housed together with everyone else, deprived of pain medication? Moreover, the data collected in this study indicate that mentally and physically ill individuals are disciplined and placed in solitary confinement more than healthier individuals. The data thus suggest that the CSC uses punitive measures as responses to medical problems, and that, in fact, it does not always take into account prisoners' health status before they are segregated as required by section 87 of the *CCRA*.

The *Canadian Human Rights Act* (*CHRA*) prohibits discrimination against individuals based on age or disability when providing services.[8] Thus, blanket treatments – such as a general obligation to pick up medication outside after standing for an hour, limited access to painkillers for everyone, lack of disability-friendly infrastructure, and so on – without accommodation for older people and those with disabilities may in fact be discriminatory practices under this statute.[9]

---

7   *Ibid*, s 87.

8   *Canadian Human Rights Act*, RSC 1985, c H-6, s 5.

9   See e.g. *Kavanagh v Canada (AG)* (2001), 41 CHRR 119 (CHRT), where the lack of medical and housing accommodation for transgender people was found to breach this provision.

The provisions of this statute are constitutionally supported by section 15 of the *Canadian Charter of Rights and Freedoms* (*Charter*), which also prohibits discrimination based on grounds such as age or disability.[10] When reflecting on the potential physical and physiological harm that the lack of appropriate medical treatment may bring to older prisoners, other constitutional guarantees also come to mind. For instance, section 12 of the *Charter* ensures that everyone is free from cruel and unusual treatment or punishment.[11] In addition, section 7 guarantees that everyone has the right to life, liberty, and security of the person in accordance with the principles of fundamental justice.[12] While courts apply complicated analyses to individual cases to decide the instances where such constitutionally protected rights have been breached, it is not a stretch to imagine that some of the practices described in the previous chapter could be the subject of future *Charter* challenges.

Canada has also signed, ratified, or adheres to international conventions and other instruments that stipulate rights for prisoners. Canada is a dualist state, which means the breach of international instruments that it has ratified cannot be challenged directly in a national court. Rather, the provisions of those international instruments must become national law, and only the breach of national law (like the provisions described above) can be directly challenged. However, the Supreme Court of Canada (SCC) has recognized that the national legislation must be interpreted in accordance with Canada's international obligations.[13] As early as 1987, for instance, the SCC stated that the *Charter* is built as a response to Canada's international human rights obligations and that international documents, binding and non-binding,[14] are essential in the interpretation of the *Charter*.[15] Thus, even if international provisions cannot be the only basis for a court challenge, they are important in determining the rights of Canadian prisoners. In terms of conventions

---

10 *Canadian Charter of Rights and Freedoms*, Part I of the *Constitution Act, 1982*, being Schedule B to the *Canada Act, 1982* (UK), 1982, c 11, s 15 [*Charter*].

11 *Ibid*, s 12.

12 *Ibid*, s 7.

13 See e.g *Baker v Canada (Minister of Citizenship and Immigration)*, [1999] 2 SCR 817 at paras 69–71; *R v Hape*, [2007] 2 SCR 292 at para 53.

14 Binding international documents, like conventions and treaties, create an obligation on the states that ratified them to either apply them directly (for monist states) or incorporate them in national law (for dualist states). Non-binding documents, such as declarations, principles, rules, and codes, are standards that states recognizing them aim to achieve.

15 *Reference Re Public Service Employee Relations Act (Alberta)*, [1987] 1 SCR 313 at 348.

that Canada has ratified,[16] a host of them require that incarcerated people be treated with dignity,[17] that all prison systems should have as a goal reformation and rehabilitation,[18] that states must ensure everyone's protection against cruel and unusual treatment and punishment,[19] that all individuals have the right to the highest attainable standard of mental and physical health,[20] and that people with disabilities need appropriate access to justice, while prison officers must be trained to work with people with disabilities.[21] People with disabilities must enjoy the same range, quality, and standard of programs and health care as everyone else.[22]

Canada has also recognized a number of non-binding documents, highly relevant for prisoners. For instance, the *United Nations Standard Minimum Rules for the Protection of Prisoners (the Nelson Mandela Rules)* requires that all prisons provide adequate sanitary installations and showers,[23] expeditious medical treatment, and sufficient medical personnel;[24] that health problems that may hamper rehabilitation are identified and addressed;[25] that everyone who complains of illness is immediately seen;[26] that people who receive disciplinary punishment are mentally and physically fit for it;[27] and that mentally ill or physically disabled prisoners are not placed in solitary confinement.[28] Other instruments address the obligation of prison officers to protect the life and health of

---

16 The list of conventions, as well as Canada's level of commitment to them, can be found on the United Nations Human Rights Office of the High Commissioner website, online: http://indicators.ohchr.org.

17 *International Covenant on Civil and Political Rights*, 19 December 1966, 999 UNTS 171 (entered into force 23 March 1976, accession by Canada 19 May 1976), art 10 [*ICCPR*].

18 *Ibid*, art 10(3).

19 *Ibid*, art 7; *Convention Against Torture and Other Cruel, Inhuman or Degrading Treatment or Punishment*, 10 December 1984, 1465 UNTS (entered into force 26 June 1987, ratification by Canada 24 July 1987), art 2(1).

20 *International Covenant on Economic, Social and Cultural Rights*, 16 December 1966, 993 UNTS (entered into force 1 March 1976, accession by Canada 19 August 1976), art 11.

21 *Convention on the Rights of Persons with Disabilities*, 13 December 2006, 2515 UNTS (entered into force 3 May 2008, ratification by Canada 10 April 2010), art 13.

22 *Ibid*, art 25.

23 United Nations, General Assembly, *United Nations Standard Minimum Rules for the Treatment of Prisoners (the Nelson Mandela Rules)*, A/Res70/175, 17 December 2015, rules 15–16, online: https://undocs.org/A/RES/70/175.

24 *Ibid*, rules 24–31.

25 *Ibid*, rule 25.

26 *Ibid*, rule 31.

27 *Ibid*, rule 36–45.

28 *Ibid*, rule 45.

prisoners[29] and the ethical obligations prison medical personnel have to adequately treat prisoners.[30] The *United Nations Principles for Older People* require that incarcerated older people receive an appropriate level of health care, rehabilitation opportunities, social and mental stimulation, and a humane and secure environment.[31] All older people have the right to be treated fairly[32] and to live in dignity, free from physical and mental abuse.[33] The United Nations (UN) also sets principles for the treatment of people with mental illnesses and calls for these principles to be applied in prisons to the fullest extent possible.[34]

All of these international provisions should inform the services and treatment available to older prisoners. Moreover, the international provisions provide context and a new level of detail to the national norms and to prison systems' obligations towards their charges. They also bolster the case that failure to appropriately address the heightened needs of older people is not just an unfortunate event. It is a denial of statutory and constitutional rights, which, in certain circumstances, exposes the CSC to legal liability.[35]

---

29 *Code of Conduct for Law Enforcement Officials,* GA Res 34/169, 1979.

30 *Principles of Medical Ethics Relevant to the Role of Health Personnel, Particularly Physicians in the Protection of Prisoners and Detainees Against Torture and Other Cruel, Inhuman or Degrading Treatment or Punishment,* GA Res 37/194, 1982.

31 *United Nations Principles for Older People,* GA Res 46/91, 1991, s 13.

32 *Ibid,* s 18.

33 *Ibid,* s 17.

34 *Principles for the Protection of Persons with Mental Illness and Improvement of Mental Health Care,* GA Res 46/119, 1991, s 20. Other relevant instruments include *Body of Principles for the Protection of All Persons under Any Form of Detention or Imprisonment,* GA Res 43/173, 1988; *Basic Principles for the Treatment of Prisoners,* GA Res 45/111, 1990.

35 Many conventions have been followed by optional protocols, which create international boards or oversight mechanisms to directly hold countries accountable for breaches of the corresponding convention rights. Canada has not signed most of these protocols (e.g. *Optional Protocol to the International Covenant on Economic, Social and Cultural Rights,* UN General Assembly, GA Res 63/117, 2008; *Optional Protocol to the Convention Against Torture and Other Cruel, Inhuman or Degrading Treatment or Punishment,* GA Res 57/199, 2002; *Optional Protocol to the Convention on the Rights of Persons with Disabilities,* GA Res 61/106, 2006). The one notable exception is the *Optional Protocol to the International Covenant on Civil and Political Rights,* GA Res 2200A (XXI), 1966, ratified by Canada in 1976. This protocol mandated the creation of the Human Rights Committee, an international human rights tribunal that can receive complaints directly from individuals (including prisoners) who believe Canada has breached their ICCPR-protected rights. Complaints against Canada have, however, been very few compared to those against other countries. On the importance for prisoners of Canada signing the optional protocols and recognizing international oversight mechanisms, see e.g. H. Archibald Kaiser, "Canadian Prisoners with Mental Health Problems: The Promise (and Limits) of the *Convention on the Rights of*

Because of the potential moral and legal issues with the continuing incarceration of older prisoners under present conditions, in this chapter I will explore two avenues that could help the CSC improve its treatment of this prisoner group. The first avenue is release. This option should be considered first when the correctional system is faced with old, sick, and terminally ill individuals. The second avenue is the improvement of institutional conditions. Faced with an increase in older individuals who appear to have different needs and whose rights may be infringed when treated the same as younger prisoners, the CSC needs to consider creating a framework that clearly acknowledges the particularities of older prisoners and procedures to incorporate practices that accommodate these particularities. With the current demographic shift in prisons, the CSC will need to rethink its infrastructure and services in order to provide humane accommodation for all of its charges and to avoid future litigation.

Early Release Reform

Since I completed the study, I have often discussed it with colleagues and at community events. Strikingly, what outraged most people was not the lack of services for older individuals. Rather, the first question tended to be, "Why are these people still in prison?" Release would, indeed, solve many of the potential legal issues that may be raised by insufficient medical services in prison. It would also be, by far, the most efficient option. Arguably, regardless of the improvements that the CSC may undergo, the nature and security concerns surrounding its locations, medical services, social services, and family support mean that it would likely never be of the same nature and quality as found in the community. For this reason, I believe investigating solutions to the problems older prisoners face needs to start with exploring the possibility of their decarceration and the current limitations for them to access release.

Parole in Older Age

Life stops and starts back when you get out. (QQ, 63, in prison 8 years)

Regardless of who they are, how much time they have spent in prison, what kind of sentence they received, whether they were incarcerated

---

Persons with Disabilities" (2011) 32:1 Health L Can 1; Ivan Zinger, "Human Rights Compliance and the Role of External Prison Oversight" (2006) 48:2 CJCCJ 127 at 136; Howard Sapers & Ivan Zinger, "The Ombudsman as a Monitor of Human Rights in Canadian Federal Corrections" (2010) 30:5 Pace L Rev 1512 at 1527–8.

for the first time in old age or grew old in prison, most prisoners have one common source of anxiety: parole. When paroled, individuals are allowed to continue serving their sentence in the community under supervision. Most times, parole is something prisoners look forward to; it motivates them to behave well, and they are anxious about failing to obtain it. For most people, parole equals freedom. They do not care that they have to spend time in halfway houses under curfews before they are allowed to move back with their families. They do not care that they have to report to an officer every so often or that they are under restrictions that most of us are not. For most of them, these conditions are nothing compared to the experience of confinement.

Parole is what keeps prisoners of all ages going. It makes them work harder, keep in touch with their families, and participate in programs. In short, it helps them keep their hopes up. With a handful of exceptions, every single one of the prisoners I talked to, regardless of how many times they had been denied parole before, still held on to the hope that they would be released someday and that they would be able to live and die in the community. Some of them were anxious about returning to society. They were afraid because they did not have any relatives left, because they might not find jobs. They worried that they had become too institutionalized to live on their own in the community, or that they might inadvertently do something to breach their parole conditions. However, their fears were mostly rooted in the fact that failure in the community would mean returning to prison. Examples of such failures and their consequences were common, particularly among people who have served very long periods of time.

John spent twenty-two years in prison before he was eligible to apply for day parole. He needed to complete three years of day parole before he would be eligible to apply for full parole. Unlike many other people, John received his day parole on his first application. He was fifty-four at the time and highly motivated: he had a large family on the outside, including a wife who had been battling cancer for many years. However, after twenty-two years, the community environment proved overwhelming to him. He continued to make small procedural mistakes upon going to or returning from the community, which often led to him being admonished by officers and threats to end his day parole. One such incident ended in John pushing an officer. Thus, his day parole was immediately revoked, and he was transferred to solitary confinement in a medium security institution. Back to square one, John had to make his way back down to minimum security. In 2012, he was granted day parole again, in time for his wife's funeral. When he returned from the funeral, John was overwhelmed with grief. What had kept him going for twenty-five years in prison was the hope of returning to his dying wife. Hence, following her funeral, John was, perhaps not surprisingly, not doing well. Returning to prison that night, John forgot to declare a $20 bill that he had in his coat. A person who has been incarcerated for twenty-five years is not used to having any money on them, so declaring cash is far from being a habit. Moreover, given the events of the day, one could understand that he had other things on his mind. Nonetheless, this misstep, arguably much less serious than intentionally pushing an officer, led to a contraband disciplinary charge, a transfer to medium security, sixty days in solitary confinement, and a revocation of his day parole, which eliminated any real chance for full parole in the foreseeable future.

Eric also had a parole story. His story did not involve parole revocation, but rather failure to receive parole in the first place. As someone who was assessed as low risk, who had served all of his sentence in minimum security with absolutely no disciplinary incident, who was a first-time offender, sentenced for a historic crime (a crime committed thirty or more years prior), and who was significantly ill and used a wheelchair, Eric had all the factors for receiving his full parole on his first application attempt. However, his application was rejected because he did not complete the programs required by his correctional plan. The completion of a correctional plan is so high on the priority list, regardless of any other considerations (for example, health status, extenuating life circumstances), that parole is virtually impossible without it. Eric's health status was so deteriorated – and continued to deteriorate in prison – that he simply could not stay alert for the duration of any required class. As a result, he had to serve two-thirds of his sentence, which is when he would likely be able to return home on statutory release. The CSC could also technically ask the parole board to detain Eric and have him serve his complete sentence in prison. Such a CSC request is discretionary, and one would hope that, in such particular circumstances, it would be highly unlikely.

John and Eric's stories are typical of the problems the population I interviewed encountered. Even though parole is eventually available to all prisoners in Canada, it is very difficult to obtain and to retain. Application of parole rules is rigid, and the experience of parole boards with elderly and sick individuals is limited. The CSC is also doing a poor job of preparing such "institutionalized" individuals to return to the community. This combination of problems obstructs the possibility of systemic decarceration for an increasingly old and sick prison population.

REGULATION OF PAROLE

The Canadian federal parole system is regulated by the *Corrections and Conditional Release Act* (*CCRA*)[36] and its *Regulations* (*CCRR*).[37] This legislation provides for a number of types of early release options for incarcerated people, with the purpose of contributing "to the maintenance of a just, peaceful and safe society by means of decisions on the timing and conditions of release that will best facilitate the rehabilitation of offenders and their reintegration into the community as law-abiding citizens."[38] The most common types of early release are day parole and full parole. In Canada, all prisoners are eligible to apply for release before their warrants expire. Early release, or conditional release, is also regulated at the federal level by the *CCRA*[39] and the *CCRR*,[40] which prescribe both the criteria and the process for the different forms of releases. In addition, individuals who serve determinate sentences, save in exceptional situations, are generally released once they have served two-thirds of their sentence.[41]

Criminological studies have shown that early release is successful in "ensuring the long-term protection of the public."[42] Early release allows individuals to be part of the community and to begin building a life on the outside, while they are still under supervision for the remainder of their sentence. Thus, at the heart of the provisions regulating this type of release are two key concepts: reintegrating individuals into and reducing the risk to the community. These concepts are present in the mission statement of the Parole Board of Canada (PBC), which is the administrative body charged by the *CCRA*[43] with hearing parole requests and making early release decisions.[44]

Day parole is a form of early, or conditional, release in which an individual is allowed to be released into the community for limited periods of time before being fully released. While on day parole, the individual is

---

36 *CCRA, supra* note 2.

37 *Corrections and Conditional Release Regulations*, SOR/92–620 [*CCRR*].

38 *CCRA, supra* note 2, s 100.

39 *Ibid*, ss 99–156.

40 *CCRR, supra* note 37, ss 145–68.

41 *Ibid*, s 127.

42 Anthony N. Doob, Cheryl Marie Webster, & Allan Manson, "Zombie Parole: The Withering of Conditional Release in Canada" (2014) 61 Crim LQ 301 at 304 [Doob, Webster, & Manson].

43 *CCRA, supra* note 2, ss 103–11.

44 Parole Board of Canada, "The Parole Board of Canada's Vision and Mission," online: https://www.canada.ca/en/parole-board/corporate/the-parole-board-of-canada-s-vision-and-mission.html [PBC].

generally housed in a halfway house or, in limited circumstances, in a minimum security facility. The eligibility criteria in regards to the time served for different types of offenders are regulated by section 119 of the *CCRA*.[45]

Full parole, another form of early release, allows for the release of incarcerated offenders before they complete their sentence. Except when they commit an offence that triggers a life sentence, prisoners are generally eligible to be released after serving one-third of their sentence. However, individuals serving life as a maximum sentence are eligible to apply for early release after seven years.[46] The *Criminal Code* also provides different criteria for those sentenced for murder. People imprisoned for first degree murder are eligible to apply for parole after twenty-five years served, while second degree murder carries a period of parole ineligibility of between ten and twenty-five years.[47] In addition to these limits, the *Criminal Code* permits the judge to increase the parole ineligibility to half of the sentence or to ten years, whichever comes first.[48] The *Protecting Canadians by Ending Sentence Discounts for Multiple Murders Act*[49] also allows for people convicted of multiple murders to be sentenced to life with a parole ineligibility of considerably more than twenty-five years. Parole ineligibility periods can now be made consecutive to one another. For example, since the act's introduction, people have been given parole ineligibility periods of up to seventy-five years.[50] Arguably, this ruling is akin to a life sentence without possibility of parole.

Individuals who do not get paroled (for various reasons) have the semi-automatic right to be released on the day when they have served two-thirds of their sentence. This provision is called "statutory release." Such individuals serve the rest of their sentence in the community under supervision, similar to parolees.[51] Statutory release is usually automatic as no application is required, but the parole board may deny it, upon recommendation of the CSC, and detain an individual convicted of certain offences that are deemed particularly high risk.[52] If that occurs, the

---

45   *CCRA, supra* note 2, s 119.

46   *Ibid*, s 120.

47   *Criminal Code*, RSC 1985, c C-46, ss 745, 745.1, 745.3, 745.4 [*CC*].

48   *Ibid*, s 743.6.

49   *Protecting Canadians by Ending Sentence Discounts for Multiple Murders Act*, SC 2011, c 5.

50   See the cases of Travis Baumgartner (*R v Baumgartner*, 2013 ABQB 761), Justin Bourque (*R v Bourque*, 2014 NBQB 237), Christopher Husbands (*R v Husbands*, 2014 ONCJ 89), and John Pail Ostamas (*R v Ostamas*, 2016 MBQB 136).

51   *CCRA, supra* note 2, s 127.

52   Correctional Service of Canada, "Detention," Commissioner's Directive No. 712-2 (Ottawa: CSC, 2015), online: https://www.csc-scc.gc.ca/acts-and-regulations/712-2-cd-eng.shtml [CD 712-2]; *CCRA, supra* note 2, s 129.

prisoner will serve the whole sentence in prison.[53] In any case, the sentence is deemed completed only when the warrant expires.[54]

APPLICATION OF PAROLE

Despite the somewhat robust regulation of different forms of release, the parole processes have been regularly described as bureaucratic and inefficient, and they fail time and again to meet the goals for which parole exists. In their seminal study, Doob, Webster, and Manson analysed the use of conditional release in the federal and provincial systems. They concluded that conditional release is so little used that it would make little numeric difference if it were altogether abolished (for example, the federally incarcerated population would increase by only 4.5 per cent).[55] Its use appears to be unnecessarily low, especially since the rate of reoffending for parolees is very low.[56] As Doob and colleagues pointed out, "if the purpose of parole is to facilitate the safe and peaceful reintegration of prisoners into society, it is failing."[57]

The low rate of use is not the only problem presented by conditional release. The parole process is poorly regulated, so decisions are quite unpredictable. Aside from the eligibility dates for different types of sentences, the *CCRA* and the *CCRR* do not provide other operational criteria that should be considered by parole board members in their conditional release decision-making. Clearly, however, the criteria used need to be centred on risk and on helping the individual reintegrate into the community.[58] More criteria are provided by the PBC's *Decision-Making Policy Manual for Board Members*. The manual elaborates on the main factors, which include criminal history, family relationships, employment, substance abuse, the gravity of current offences, breaches of previous conditional releases, history of reoffending, history of violent behaviour, attempts to escape, recommendations of the sentencing judge, and victim impact statements. Other factors relate to the offender's involvement in correctional programs, diagnosis of

---

53 For the release procedure upon warrant expiry, see Correctional Service of Canada, "Release Process," Commissioner's Directive No. 712-4 (Ottawa: CSC, 2018), ss 30–8, online: https://www.csc-scc.gc.ca/acts-and-regulations/712-4-cd-eng.shtml.

54 *CCRA, supra* note 2, s 128(3).

55 Doob, Webster, & Manson, *supra* note 42 at 315.

56 In fiscal year 2012–2013, only three people on parole for violent offences had their parole revoked, compared to 1,190 who successfully completed their full parole: *ibid* at 322. See also Ivan Zinger, "Conditional Release and Human Rights in Canada: A Commentary" (2012) 54:1 CJCCJ 117 at 119–20, https://doi.org/10.3138/cjccj.2011.E.19.

57 Doob, Webster, & Manson, *supra* note 42 at 317.

58 *CCRA, supra* note 2, s 100.

a mental disorder, behaviour during incarceration, and whether they have a release plan. Signs of change in behaviour, as revealed by the manner in which the prisoner completed their correctional plan and by professional report assessments[59] (that is, a psychological report), are also important.[60] A Commissioner's Directive (CD) mentions institutional behaviour and the completion of correctional plans (as well as attitude during completion) as information to be collected and presented to the parole board by the parole officer in each case.[61] Consideration of these factors is explained through the objective of not creating an undue risk to society.[62] However, factors like health status, disability, the physical capacity of committing further crime, and age are not listed at all, even though they might have at least as much influence on the very capacity of an individual to reoffend. More bluntly, it appears that the parole board is required to consider whether someone once convicted of a violent offence has received and responded appropriately to correctional programs, but is not encouraged to consider the impact of whether they are totally paralyzed.

Studies conducted in Canada point out two main problems with parole decisions: they rely on sometimes subjective and unpredictable criteria, and also on factors that are at least partially outside the prisoner's control (such as completion of correctional programs or having a release plan). Gobeil and Serin argued that the only factors that appear to consistently influence parole decisions are gender (women are released more often), type of crime (sex offenders are released more often, while those charged with domestic violence less often), ethnicity (Aboriginal status negatively impacts release decisions), and risk assessment reports. Other demographic factors, the victim impact statement, or mental health appear to be completely irrelevant to such decisions.[63]

---

59 The content of the case managers' report is regulated by CD 710-1: Correctional Service of Canada, "Progress Against the Correctional Plan," Commissioner's Directive No. 710-1 (Ottawa: CSC, 2018), online: https://www.csc-scc.gc.ca/acts-and-regulations/710-1-cd-en.shtml [CD 710-1]. It stipulates that the report will document the institutional adjustment and attitude of the prisoner, the programs they participated in, and their institutional employment history, as well as the professional counselling they received.

60 Parole Board of Canada, *Decision-Making Policy Manual for Board Members*, 2nd ed (Ottawa: PBC, 2018), ss 8–13, online: https://www.canada.ca/content/dam/pbc-clcc/documents/manual-manuel/Decision-Making_Policy_Manual_2nd_Ed_No_13.pdf [PBC Manual].

61 CD 710-1, *supra* note 59, Annex E.

62 PBC Manual, *supra* note 60, s 6.

63 Renée Gobeil & Ralph C. Serin, "Preliminary Evidence of Adaptive Decision Making Techniques Used by Parole Board Members" (2009) 8:2 Int J Forensic Ment Health 97 at 100–2.

More recently, Hannah-Moffatt and Yule conducted a similar study with a focus on incarcerated women. Their study revealed that the main factors considered were length of the total sentence (the shorter the sentence, the likelier the release), lack of psychological assessments, evidence of change (mainly through program participation), and attitude during incarceration. Other personal characteristics, type of offence, demographic factors, mental illness, or substance abuse did not play into the decision-making.[64]

In 2009, Jackson and Stewart published a report on the state of correctional affairs.[65] They were critical of the release criteria, which are mostly geared towards rewarding "good behaviour" (which is not a stated purpose of early release) and are sometimes out of the prisoner's control: "motivation," fulfilment of the correctional plan, attitude and statements made by the prisoner, early engagement in the parole process, and securing employment upon release.[66]

In 2010, Howard Sapers, the former federal correctional investigator, identified four major barriers to release: lack of efficiency in moving prisoners down the security level, program access and availability, case management and preparation, and restricted access to discretionary and conditional release.[67] Supporting the comments of scholars reporting on this matter, Sapers stated that, in 2009, one in four prisoners had to waive, postpone, or withdraw their parole application because they were "waitlisted" and had not yet completed their programs.[68] In addition, every day, only one in four individuals participated in a required program, generally because most prisoners are waitlisted. Priority for programs is given to people serving less than four years or to individuals late in their sentence. People who serve long periods of time (like half of older prisoners) do not have access to these programs until well into their sentences and often past their parole dates.[69] As well, 6 per cent of prisoners had to withdraw or waive their applications because their case

64 Kelly Hannah-Moffat & Caroline Yule, "Gaining Insight, Changing Attitudes and Managing 'Risk': Parole Release Decisions for Women Convicted of Violent Crimes" (2011) 13:2 Punishment & Society 149 at 157–9.

65 Michael Jackson & Graham Stewart, *A Flawed Compass: A Human Rights Analysis of the Roadmap to Strengthening Public Safety* (2009) at 109–115, online: http://www. justicebehindthewalls.net/resources/news/flawed_Compass.pdf [Jackson & Stewart].

66 *Ibid* at 109–15.

67 Howard Sapers, "Barriers to Conditional Release" in Patrick Healey & Patrick A. Molinari, eds, *Sentencing and Corrections: Sentencing Theory Meets Practice* (Montreal: Canadian Institute for the Administration of Justice, 2012) 167.

68 *Ibid* at 171.

69 *Ibid* at 171–2.

preparations were incomplete.[70] This situation explains why six in ten prisoners are past their initial parole eligibility date and 50 per cent of prisoners are past their full parole eligibility date.[71]

These trends have been confirmed by my study. Half of the study's participants were sentenced to life in prison; about 10 per cent had an indeterminate sentence, and the rest were serving determinate sentences. The majority of people serving life, indeterminate, or long sentences were convicted prior to turning fifty. Almost half of the participants had already served over ten years of their current sentence at the time I talked to them, with over 11 per cent having served between twenty and twenty-nine years and another 11 per cent having spent over thirty years in prison. Slightly over 33 per cent had not reached their parole date at the time of the interview. Half of this latter group, however, had a hearing scheduled within the following year. Only 3 per cent had to wait another ten years for their first parole eligibility date.

Thus, most of the participants were either eligible for parole at the time of the interview or had already passed their first parole eligibility date. In addition, 19 per cent had had their first parole eligibility date over ten years ago. Regardless, 18 per cent of the whole sample reported that they did not apply for parole at all. Of this number, 33 per cent did not apply because they were appealing their conviction or their sentence. This small group of people maintained that, for them, being cleared of the charges and having justice prevail was more important than serving their time in the community. Both people serving life and people with determinate sentences were in this group. A few individuals also reported dropping their appeals because they wanted to be paroled.

One individual had served twenty-five years in prison but continued to maintain his innocence. He was working with the Innocence Project to have his conviction for first degree murder thrown out. He had an excellent record, was housed in minimum security, and was serving as the head of the Inmate Committee. He was, however, not able to apply for parole, even if his first eligibility date had passed.

> You don't get paroled if you don't acknowledge and feel remorse for what you have done. They don't let you continue your appeal while serving your sentence in the community. You don't get to the community if you appeal. (AF, 58, in prison 25 years)

---

70 *Ibid* at 171.
71 *Ibid* at 172.

The majority of those who did not apply for parole (61 per cent) said it was "useless." The same reasons occurred with regularity.

> When you serve a short sentence like I do, it is common knowledge that they don't release people on their first eligibility date. At least that's what they say around here. (AI, 56, in prison 2 years)
>
> When you serve a life sentence they don't release people on the first try. Sometimes you have to try many times before they parole you. I haven't seen anyone serving life being paroled on their first try. (HH, 64, in prison 16 years)

In addition, 2 per cent also reported not applying because they had no interest in being released.

> I applied in the beginning. Like twenty years ago. Now I have been in prison for over forty-three years. What's there left for me out there? (AA, 63, in prison 43 years)
>
> I don't know how to use a cell, a computer, the bank, I have no skills, and I am sick. Good luck surviving. (TT, 72, in prison 36 years)

Of the participants, 24 per cent had applied for parole in the past (sometimes repeatedly), but were denied. The reasons they reported for denial were very similar to the reasons people gave for not applying. For example, the ability to fulfil the requirements of their correctional plan was a very big problem. More than half of the people serving life (who were 50 per cent of the sample) mentioned that they had not completed their correctional plan by their first parole eligibility date, generally because there were no spots available in the programs. In addition, there were a couple of special situations, such as Eric's, where prisoners were not able to complete their programs due to health issues.

> I haven't completed my correctional plan yet. I have to do a sex offender program but when you are serving a short sentence you are not a priority. It's kind of like, they don't plan on releasing you on your first eligibility date anyway, so they don't rush to give you a spot in the programs you need. And there is no point in applying before I complete my correctional program. (BB, 56, in prison 3 years)
>
> Well I still have one program to complete. I finished all the others over ten years ago, but this one program they never had spots. They give all spots to people who serve short sentences, who go out on stat [statutory release] or whatever. Us, lifers, are not a priority. We have a lifetime to do them, they say. (YY, 51, in prison 13 years)

As well, the lack of post-release plans was a major reason that participants reported, both for not applying for parole and for being rejected for parole.

> I feel I did everything right, but I couldn't secure a job. No one really wants to hire a seventy-five-year-old. What would I do? (AD, 74, in prison 5 years)
>
> My PO [parole officer] said she couldn't find a halfway house. I made inquiries, I talked to John Howard [the John Howard Society is a nongovernmental agency that helps prisoners reintegrate in the community]. It's really hard to secure housing when you are a lifer. I'll keep trying. Something will come up I guess. (KK, 55, in prison 24 years)

Almost 45 per cent of the participants in the sample were over sixty, and some mentioned being already retired when they entered prisons. Others just grew old in prison. While most of them were working in prison (about 80 per cent), they mentioned that at their age and level of disability, finding work on the outside was highly problematic. This factor was negatively impacting their reports; they were not seen as good candidates for parole because they were old, unemployable, and difficult to house.

Despite their odds and previous experiences, most participants were keeping their hopes up. Over half of the participants were planning to apply at their next parole date, and over 37 per cent of the entire sample believed they had a good chance of being released. Some of these people had been in prison for over thirty years; they had had their first parole date twenty years before, and they had applied and were denied parole every time.

> I'll keep applying. It will happen some day. (AC, 54, in prison 12 years)
>
> Why wouldn't they parole me? I've done really well. (TT, 72, in prison 36 years)
>
> I have found a halfway house and I have family on the outside. I know they don't release lifers on their first parole date but maybe they will release me. (EE, 54, in prison 10 years)
>
> My former boss said he'd take me back. So I have a job lined up. I am hoping this will matter to the [parole] board. (ZZ, 61, in prison 7 years)

Finally, 18 per cent were close to their statutory release date, and they were sure they would get out then.

> They never gave me parole. All the same now, my stat [statutory release] is coming up this year. (DD, 62, in prison 5 years)

I never applied for any parole. I keep seeing people returning for silly breaches of conditions. You can't do this, you can't do that. You can't do anything on parole. And it has fuck all to do with my crime. What's the point? I'll go out on my stat release date. If not, my warrant expires in two years anyway. What's the point in being on the outside without being free and having to worry that I make one wrong step and they'll ship me back here? (AH, 51, in prison 2 years)

The success of parole applications seems to be random and unpredictable, and this uncertainty affects all prison groups. However, circumstances that actually make individuals low risk (disease, age, and so on) do not appear to be systematically taken into account, a fact that disproportionately affects older people. In addition, older people are less likely to find jobs or, considering that half of them have served very long sentences, to still have support in the community. The reasons for parole application rejections highlight key institutional shortcomings, as release plans (for example, supporting individuals in finding housing and employment in the community), as well as availability of required programs, are the responsibility of the CSC. These matters do not reflect the individual's risk or rehabilitation potential, but the failures of the system instead. Among other things, such failures lead to low-risk senior prisoners potentially spending longer periods in prison than their younger counterparts.

WHERE TO?

As mentioned, many of the individuals I interviewed had very short lists of disciplinary offences or of time spent in segregation. Also, literature clearly shows that older individuals are good candidates for release due to what is sometimes referred to as "aging out of crime." Because of age and health alone, older individuals are a significant lower risk to reoffend.[72]

Still, many of the participants in the study spent decades in prisons, considerably past their first parole eligibility date and well into their golden years. They are vulnerable and sick, and while they present a high

---

72 Andrew C. Sparkes & Jo Day, "Aging Bodies and Desistance from Crime: Insights from the Lives and Stories of Offenders" (2016) 36 J Aging Stud 47; Kristie R. Blevins & Anita N. Blowers, "Community Reentry and Aging Inmates" in John Kerbs & Jennifer M. Jolley, eds, *Seniors Behind Bars: Challenges for the Criminal Justice System* (London: Lynne Rienner, 2014) 201 at 205–6 [Kerbs & Jolley, *Seniors Behind Bars*]; John Kerbs & Jennifer Jolley, "The Implications of Age-Graded Desistance" in Kerbs & Jolley, *supra*, 157 at 160.

burden on prisons, they are a low risk for communities. The Canadian parole system relies heavily on criteria that are perhaps appropriate for younger prisoners but not for many aging prisoners. For example, prisoner risk is assessed based on the crime they committed twenty years ago, on victims' statements that may not reflect who the individual offender is today, and on fulfilling correctional and release plans, which are often outside the prisoner's control. In turn, their age and health, the very factors that render them low risk, are ignored.

Recasting the parole system is outside the scope of this book. However, it bears repeating that the criticisms and suggestions of Jackson and Stewart regarding the reform of the parole process are as valid today as they were when first produced.[73]

I will instead turn my attention to two release-related issues that are more specific for older individuals and are currently completely non-existent in Canada: preparation for release for aging prisoners and compassionate release. It is worth noting, first, that an effective parole system is long overdue. Part of the reason why we see the current increase in the number of older inmates today is the malfunctioning of this system. When parole reform is finally undertaken, it will need to be done with the needs of the changing prison demographic in mind. Thus, the criteria for release will need to reflect realistic expectations for people who are sixty or seventy years of age. Such criteria will need to include age and health (both physical and mental), as well as an evaluation of the prisoner's behaviour in prison (for example, program participation and socializing) based on their age and physical and mental abilities. An evaluation of the prisoner's behaviour will also need to reflect the findings of these and other studies that suggest prisoner misbehaviour may be caused by improperly attended mental or physical problems. Aside from better guidelines to assist in their decision-making process, parole board members need appropriate training on the needs and characteristics of vulnerable groups of prisoners who appear before them. Like all other aspects of the correctional system, a one-size-fits-all approach for parole adjudication is unfair and harmful to older prisoners.

Preparation for Release in Old Age

> I have been in here since the 80s. I don't even have a piece of ID on the outside. I don't have a bank account and I have never used a cell phone. That's why people come back in here. How can I succeed outside if you don't help me? I don't recognize the world anymore. (II, 65, in prison 40 years)

---

73 Jackson & Stewart, *supra* note 65.

STATUS QUO

The parole process is slow and keeps older prisoners away from their families often longer than necessary. Sometimes, as in John's case, people receive parole only once their family members have passed away and their community support is considerably diminished. Other times, as in Eric's case, people are released in such bad health that there is very little hope for them to recover on the outside.

Most incarcerated individuals are released back into the community at some point, which is why preparing prisoners for community reintegration and ensuring they have the tools needed to succeed in society should be of paramount importance. Ultimately, all other aspects of the correctional system are justified by the goal of reintegrating released offenders: this objective is why prisoners cascade down security levels; why they are gradually given more independence; why they are released under supervision before their warrant expires; and why they are placed in halfway houses (institutions where a mild form of security is in place and curfews are enforced) before they can live on their own. Nonetheless, this study's participants often felt that the institutions set them up for failure because, after decades of incarceration, they were sent back into communities they did not recognize with no skills or support to help them adapt.

Some research has been conducted in England and the United States pertaining to the challenges and unique needs of older prisoners as they re-enter the community. A number of themes are prevalent in the literature on the matter. The fact that appropriate preparation for release is often inexistent and completely inappropriate for aging individuals was a serious concern,[74] especially since research shows that appropriate reintegration programs are affecting people's non-criminal survival curve.[75] The lack of proper communication and creation of a concrete, tailored plan for release negatively affected all individuals assessed in non-Canadian studies and significantly increased their anxiety level.[76]

Old men lack basic life skills due to spending long periods of time in prison. Hence, upon release everything is challenging: getting a bank

---

74 Katrina Forsyth et al, "'They Just Throw You Out': Release Planning for Older Prisoners" (2015) 35:9 Ageing Soc 2011 at 2016 [Forsyth et al]; Blevins & Blowers, *supra* note 72 at 212.

75 K. Kamigaki & K. Yokotani, "A Reintegration Program for Elderly Prisoners Reduces Reoffending" (2014) 2:4 JFSC 401 at 404 [Kamigaki & Yokotani].

76 Elaine Crawley & Richard Sparks, "Is There Life after Imprisonment? How Elderly Men Talk about Imprisonment and Release" (2006) 6:1 Criminol Crim Justice 63 at 73 [Crawley & Sparks]; Elaine Crawley, "Release and Resettlement: The Perspectives of Older Prisoners" (2004) 56:1 CJM 32 at 32 [Crawley].

account, cooking meals, and so on.[77] These individuals also have great difficulty securing employment, and the prison services are all too often not supportive enough of their efforts, which impacts their financial independence as well as their ability to function as prosocial individuals.[78] Another major concern for older prisoners is accommodation upon release. Most prison services do not offer enhanced support for individuals looking for housing, and accommodation catering to old and sick individuals is lacking. These factors explain why homelessness among older released individuals is particularly high.[79] Another major issue for older prisoners is the discontinuation of medical services upon release, and they often lack the skills to seek medical care by themselves in the community.[80] Finally, anxiety related to release was fuelled by prisoners' concern that they would be paroled only to have parole revoked for minor breaches committed inadvertently.[81]

Some of the same themes were apparent in my research as well. Half of the participants were incarcerated when they were young. They did not recognize the world they had left behind, and their life skills were not sufficiently developed to navigate technological changes, for instance. Also, over half of the people in this group experienced a high level of institutionalization and would probably experience difficulty readjusting even if the world were the same place they had left behind. The kind of community support and intervention needed to help these people is very different than what a twenty-year-old, who has spent two years behind bars, needs. Once again, CSC services consistently fall short in addressing this former group's needs.

Of those interviewed for this study, 15 per cent had been released on parole at some point after turning fifty, but then had their parole revoked for various reasons. However, only a few of the 15 per cent returned to prison with new charges. Almost all of them had had their parole revoked, sometimes more than once, for administrative reasons only (such as breach of curfew, for example). While administrative

77 Blevins & Blowers, *supra* note 72 at 211; Tina Maschi, Mary Beth Morrisey, & Margaret Leigey, "The Case for Human Agency, Well-Being, and Community Reintegration for People Aging in Prison: A Statewide Case Analysis" (2013) 19:3 JCHC 194 at 206 [Maschi, Morrisey, & Leigey]; Forsyth et al, *supra* note 74 at 2019.

78 Blevins & Blowers, *supra* note 72 at 209.

79 *Ibid* at 211; Crawley & Sparks, *supra* note 76 at 73; Kamigaki & Yokotani, *supra* note 75 at 403.

80 Blevins & Blowers, *supra* note 72 at 207–8; Crawley & Sparks, *supra* note 76 at 74; Crawley, *supra* note 76 at 33; Kamigaki & Yokotani, *supra* note 75 at 403; Forsyth et al, *supra* note 74, at 2019.

81 Forsyth et al, *supra* note 74 at 2021.

rules for parole are strict, they are sometimes not properly explained to prisoners, who fail to understand which actions violate their release conditions. Other times, some of the individuals have modest cognitive skills and are unable to understand rules that are too elaborately formulated. For example, an individual in minimum security had been sent back to prison three times for breaching the rules. He said he had tried really hard to understand what he was expected to do but kept failing. He had been in prison for over twenty years and showed me his psychiatric evaluation that qualified him as "institutionalized" and having "cognitive impairment." He described his latest parole revocation experience:

> I have been in the halfway house for eight months. A work colleague introduced me to this woman. We liked each other and we had coffee a couple of times. She invited me over for Christmas evening. Her eight-year-old son and her brother were there. It was very nice, very festive. I returned home before 10 p.m., which was my curfew. The innkeeper had me sign in and asked where I'd been. I told him, quite proud, that I spent Christmas Eve with this woman I started seeing and her family. He asked me why I didn't report dating her because I was supposed to report people I was dating. Like nothing happened. We didn't have sex or anything. Her son was there for God's sake! Like she wasn't my girlfriend yet. I didn't think I had to report every person I saw. At least not yet, it wasn't a relationship yet. He called my PO and they revoked my parole. Here I am, for the third time. The time before this, I arrived fifteen minutes after my curfew. So now I am not sure what will happen. Some say if you get your parole revoked three times you won't get paroled again. I don't know. I have a young kid. (AM, 50, in prison 15 years)

Another person I interviewed, this one in a medium security prison, described his experience as an individual who had been released after spending sixteen years in prison:

> I left Canada when I was five. I lived all my life in [the] States, but I am not an American citizen. When I was arrested, they deported me back to Canada. I don't know anybody here. I don't know the system. I don't know where to go to get a health card or a social security number. When I found myself on the streets, I didn't feel I had much choice. Who was going to hire a sixty-year-old with no social insurance number? I called my associate in Detroit, and he hooked me up with someone here and I started selling [drugs] again. I got caught ... to be expected. (AN, 60, in prison 16 years)

Failure to continue to provide medical treatment to people upon release was also mentioned as an issue.

> I really needed that methadone. That's [why] I went back on crack. I knew my piss sample will come back dirty and they'll send me back. Now I get methadone. (SS, 52, in prison 10 years)

Even though 15 per cent of the individuals had been previously paroled and 18 per cent were less than a year away from their statutory release, only three people of the whole sample attended a preparation for release program. When such a program was offered, space was limited, and younger people, who were more likely to become productive members of society, were prioritized. Many people also did not think the programs offered would be of any use. A number of prisoners thought they should be taught how to use computers. They felt that upon release they should have already been set up with a bank account, a social insurance number, a health card, and an identification card.

> They need to build us an identity on the outside. Otherwise, we can't survive. (AN, 60, in prison 16 years)

One of the few other studies looking at release program availability for older men noted that one in nine older prisoners had been enrolled in a release program, and, even then, the program tended not to be age appropriate.[82] In my study, overall 13 per cent of the participants believed there should be more space for them in the programs available; 7 per cent said there should be a release program for older people; 7 per cent asked for computer skills programs; 4 per cent requested basic banking courses; 7 per cent wanted to learn general life skills to help them survive (for example, cooking, cleaning, and other basic skills); 6 per cent wanted a course on health care maintenance (in order to know how to prevent disease when released); and 30 per cent asked for very specific things that they believed would help with their transition.

There was consensus among participants in my study that virtually no substantial preparation for release was offered; that the support they were given was insubstantial, especially after spending decades in prison; and that their success depended largely on how much family support they had on the outside. Hence, improving formal access to release for these people is not enough; parole reform also means improved preparation and support for release.

---

82 Forsyth et al, *supra* note 74, at 2017.

WHERE TO?

Half of those interviewed for this study consisted of people who had spent or would spend over twenty to thirty years in prison before being released. A quarter of the sample comprised individuals who had been in and out of prison for most of their lives. Many of the older prisoners were highly institutionalized and significantly lagged behind societal developments. Someone re-entering society after twenty years away will have considerable difficulty readjusting to independent and responsible living as a free person and navigating in a world that has changed in fundamental ways. A number of steps should be taken in order to ensure that federally incarcerated older individuals are given a real chance at reintegration.

First, diverse community reintegration programs must be made available to all individuals before their release. Such programs need to be adapted to the age of the individual and the duration of time spent in prison. A seventy-year-old who has spent forty years in prison will have very different reintegration needs from a twenty-five-year-old who has spent two years in prison. The former does not need to learn about job opportunities and job hunting, about raising children, or enrolling in a college program. By the same token, the twenty-five-year-old is less likely to need a computer crash course or to learn how to use an ATM or access old-age benefits and make end-of-life preparations. Older people, especially long-term prisoners, need to be given hands-on opportunities to learn how to use a computer, how to use a cell phone, how to do online and in-person bank transactions, and how to use public transit. They need to understand the utilities they need to pay and how to pay them, and become aware of the services for seniors that communities offer. Such programs have started to emerge in other jurisdictions. While these programs are still few in number, the preferred model is one in which older individuals are placed in a living unit where most programs are targeted towards specific age-related needs. The aim of this model is to support individuals seeking to develop life skills and help them connect with community organizations that can offer them support outside the institution.[83]

Second, in addition to training, prisoners should be helped, prior to release, to create an identity: social insurance number, health card, and bank account. Their case manager should be tasked with ensuring that each individual who does not have a job lined up or who cannot work, for whatever reason, has financial support and is signed up for programs

---

83 Programs such as Recoop and Restore 50+ are described in Maschi, Morrisey, & Leigey, *supra* note 77 at 207.

like old-age pension, disability, and other available programs. A couple of US programs have been created to do just that, either through community organizations established to have volunteers act as mentors for recently released older individuals, guide them, and provide emotional support, or through law schools that work with older individuals to prepare a plan for their release.[84]

Third, as they transition to the community, older individuals should be referred to a family doctor who is provided with the former prisoner's medical file. Ensuring continuation of care is very important, and it should be the CSC's responsibility to ensure that its prisoners do not suffer gaps in their health care when they leave CSC institutions.

Some services in the community and agencies (such as the John Howard Society and the Elizabeth Fry Society) do significant work in providing released individuals with support. However, their programs should be add-ons beyond the CSC's work to ensure a successful transition. With support from their families and from non-governmental agencies, some individuals do fairly well once released. An old, disabled, poor, and institutionalized individual, though, is considerably less likely to know who to ask for help or even the kind of help to ask for. The CSC should teach these individuals before release what they will need in the community, and then take substantive steps to ensure that they receive what they need. Without such support and preparation, individuals are set up for failure. While such a release plan requires resources, it has the potential to save substantial prison costs in the long run by ensuring that individuals are successful on the outside and do not return to prison.

Compassionate Release

STATUS QUO

The general parole system is ill equipped to account for situations where individuals are old, sick, disabled, or on their death beds. Conditional release is part of the offender rehabilitation and reintegration program, based on risk-predicting criteria. However, neither health nor physical capacity to reoffend is part of such criteria.

Canadian law provides for two types of release that target extenuating situations outside the mainstream parole system: the royal prerogative of mercy and parole by exception. The royal prerogative is not granted by the parole board; it is instead an executive power technically exercised by the Governor General of Canada in the name of the Queen. It is not

---

84 A description of the Senior Ex-Offender Program (SEOP) and the Project for Older Prisoners (POPS) is provided in Blevins & Blowers, *supra* note 72 at 217–19.

governed by the *CCRA*.[85] While the royal prerogative is largely discretionary, and technically anybody is eligible to apply, parole by exception is, in contrast, regulated by section 121 of the *CCRA*. By all accounts, parole by exception appears to be Canada's current version of compassionate release.[86] The provision states that parole may be granted at any time to an offender if they are terminally ill; their mental or physical health is likely to suffer damage if incarceration continues; continued incarceration for that person would constitute excessive hardship not reasonably foreseen at the time of sentencing; or they are subject to an order of surrender under the *Extradition Act*. Individuals sentenced to life in prison or to an indeterminate sentence[87] are not eligible to apply for this type of parole,[88] which means that those serving the longest sentences are outside its reach.

The purpose of parole by exception under the *CCRA* is to ensure the release of people (a) who are terminally ill, (b) whose health is incompatible with incarceration, (c) whose health is threatened by continued incarceration, or (d) who are under an extradition order.[89]

On average, thirty-five people die annually in federal custody as a result of different illnesses; the number of people succumbing to medical conditions and those whose death was expected is growing significantly.[90] Even though many of my study's prisoners were very sick, none of the participants had ever heard of parole by exception, let alone been encouraged to apply for it by their case manager or other counsellors. On one hand, 60 per cent of the sample (those serving life or indeterminate sentences)[91] would not be eligible to apply for parole by exception at all.

---

85 It is, however, mentioned in the *CCRA*, *supra* note 2, s 110.

86 Canada, Office of the Correctional Investigator, *Annual Report, 2012–2013* (Ottawa: OCI, 201) at 20, online: http://www.oci-bec.gc.ca/cnt/rpt/pdf/annrpt/ann-rpt20122013-eng.pdf [OCI 2012–2013].

87 In Canada, an offender may be incarcerated for an indeterminate period of time if they are labelled a "dangerous offender" (DO). This label can be applied by a judge, upon sentencing, to an individual found guilty of three or more violent offences in their lifetime. Dangerous offenders are generally treated as "lifers" (those sentenced to life in prison). Under the current regime, DOs, unlike lifers, are eligible for parole after serving seven years, after which they are entitled to a parole hearing every second year. However, most DOs spend extended periods of time in prison and, even when released, they, like lifers, are under lifetime supervision. Essentially, their warrant never expires, and neither category is entitled to statutory release. See *CC, supra* note 47, ss 752 to 761(1).

88 *CCRA*, *supra* note 2, s 121.

89 *Ibid*, s 121.

90 Public Safety Canada, *Corrections and Conditional Release Statistical Overview, 2016* (Ottawa: Public Safety Canada Portfolio Corrections Statistics Committee, 2017) at 45.

91 *CCRA*, *supra* note 2, s 121(2).

On the other hand, even the 40 per cent of elderly prisoners who could theoretically apply for parole by exception would appear to have extreme difficulty in succeeding on a section 121 application. For example, the *Annual Report, 2010–2011* of the Office of the Correctional Investigator (OCI) addressed the issue of compassionate release in a chapter related to death and dying in prison.[92] The report noted that twenty-two requests for parole under section 121 were made between 2005 and 2010, and that twelve were granted. In addition, there were twenty-one applications for release by royal prerogative, and none was granted.[93] The *Annual Report, 2012–2013* again examined compassionate release and criticized the fact that "few inmates [are allowed] to die in some semblance of dignity in the community."[94] In 2018, as a result of an *Access to Information Act* request, I received data from the Parole Board of Canada (PBC) showing that twenty-eight parole by exception requests made it before the board over ten years, and twenty-one were granted.[95] Additional testimony to the scarcity of parole by exception comes from records showing that the Federal Court has only heard two judicial reviews of related negative decisions by parole boards. Neither of them was based on a request for release due to medical issues. They were instead grounded in section 121(1)(d), which covers release while awaiting deportation.[96]

First, the current parole by exception provision has a number of problems. It is poorly regulated, does not provide for a coherent and expeditious process, and is unduly restrictive. Section 121 is regulated by CD 712-1, "Pre-Release Decision Making."[97] Unfortunately, the CD does not bring further clarity and only reiterates the text of section 121, stating that the "PBC will determine if the s. 121 criteria are met." No direction is given about how such determinations will be made. The main shortcoming of section 121 is therefore reinforced by the CD. Those

---

92 Canada, Office of the Correctional Investigator, *Annual Report, 2010–2011* (Ottawa: OCI, 2011) at 34–5, online: http://www.oci-bec.gc.ca/cnt/rpt/pdf/annrpt/annrpt20102011-eng.pdf [OCI 2010–2011].

93 *Ibid* at 34.

94 OCI 2012–2013, *supra* note 86 at 20.

95 Parole Board of Canada, "Parole by Exception 2007–2017" (Ottawa: Parole Board of Canada, 2018) [Parole by Exception 2007—2017]. This document (A-2017–000021) was obtained through an *Access to Information Act* request in February 2018.

96 *Hutchins v Canada (National Parole Board)*, [1993] 3 FC 505; *Daoud v Canada (AG)*, [1997] FCJ No. 57. The issue was also mentioned prior to the enactment of the *CCRA*, *supra* note 2, in *R v McDonald* (1980), 56 CCC (2d) 1.

97 Correctional Service of Canada, "Pre-Release Decision Making," Commissioner's Directive No. 712-1 (Ottawa: CSC, 2018), online: https://www.csc-scc.gc.ca/acts-and-regulations/712-1-cd-eng.shtml [CD 712-1].

sentenced to life in prison are not eligible to apply "unless they are terminally ill." Thus, the offence committed – perhaps decades earlier – determines eligibility, not a prisoner's actual health and low-risk status. The CD mentions that people in this group can apply for a royal prerogative of mercy. However, as mentioned earlier, such a release has not been granted to anyone in over ten years.[98]

Second, an individual cannot apply for exceptional forms of parole without the CSC's support. The parole officer must initiate the pre-release.[99] The OCI has been critical about how the CSC discharges its responsibility to seek alternatives for incarceration; it has noted that many potential meritorious requests are not brought before parole boards at all because caseworkers are unwilling or unable to go through the necessary administrative steps.[100] Often, even when the caseworker supports the application, the process is lengthy and bureaucratic, and the applicant dies before their case is heard. These circumstances explain why over ten years only twenty-eight parole by exception applications have been brought before PBC.[101]

Third, the conditions stated in the provision are extremely difficult to meet because of the procedure followed for such applications. An application for parole by exception requires "substantive evidence" given by a prison doctor that the prisoner has a disease incompatible with incarceration.[102] Rarely are prison health professionals willing to give evidence of that type in writing, especially considering the perceived risks associated with releasing a prisoner.[103] By making such a judgement, the health professional could be seen as chancing potential professional liability issues, and this action is unlikely to be a good professional move. In contrast, refusing to grant "substantive evidence," even where the individual is severely ill, carries no risk to the health practitioner.

---

98 OCI 2010–2011, *supra* note 92 at 34.

99 CD 712-1, *supra* note 97 at ss 55–60. This procedure means that the parole officer will have to assess, based on the medical information indicating that the individual is eligible for parole by exception, what are the best alternatives to incarceration. It is the parole officer who has to collect the paperwork, including the risk and psychological assessments and the medical documentation; write their own assessment of the individual; put together recommendations for community options if the individual is released; contact potential family members and victim(s); and so on.

100 Canada, Office of the Correctional Investigator, *Annual Report, 2014–2015* (Ottawa: OCI, 2015) at 8, online: http://www.oci-bec.gc.ca/cnt/rpt/pdf/annrpt/ann-rpt20142015-eng.pdf [OCI 2014–2015].

101 Parole by Exception 2007–2017, *supra* note 95.

102 OCI 2010–2011, *supra* note 92 at 35.

103 OCI 2012–2013, *supra* note 86 at 20.

Fourth, despite the humanitarian grounds enumerated for compassionate release in *CCRA* section 121, the key criteria are disconnected from these grounds, partly because parole by exception is seen and treated as if it were part of the general parole system. The legislation governing parole by exception is situated under the general parole section, both in the legislation and in the CD. This placement suggests that compassionate release is considered to serve the same purpose as other early release provisions (that is, safe reintegration and rehabilitation), as opposed to humanitarian purposes. CD 712-1 states that the information to be forwarded to the parole board by parole officers is the same as for regular parole, with a focus on the way the offender completed their correctional plan, their criminal history, and their institutional behaviour. By overlapping the information required for a section 121–based decision with that needed for general parole, CD 712-1 effectively abolishes any hope that a section 121 decision is actually grounded in humanitarian goals. As noted earlier, older people have difficulty fulfilling the regular parole criteria, and such criteria are not always relevant for truly proving rehabilitation and risk. For compassionate release, where only health and risk status should matter, not only is the relevance of such other factors even more questionable but the chances of very sick individuals meeting these additional requirements is less likely. Understandably, completing correctional programs and working to build a release plan might not be a dying person's priority.

WHERE TO?

In Canada, compassionate release is essentially an extinguished subgroup in a dying breed of early release mechanisms. The failures of the general parole system are also partly to blame for the failure of compassionate release. Accordingly, improving the parole system should include consolidating the role that the CSC has in helping individuals fulfil their correctional plans, providing them with post-release support, and using more predictable release criteria that account for age and illness. Such changes will allow for old, low-risk individuals with rehabilitative potential (provided age-appropriate support is given) to serve the remainder of their sentence in the community.

Rehabilitation, however, means more than just being low risk, so these concepts are instead treated as separate conditions in the legislation. Being rehabilitated does imply low risk: the offender has learned from their mistakes and is committed to reintegrate into society and be a productive citizen (for example, work, go to school, and stay away from the "wrong crowd"). A terminally ill individual, however – or one with a permanent disability – may not be rehabilitated. They may have a history of bad behaviour in prison up to the moment they became ill; they may not care about the consequences of what they have done; they may not care about their outside family; or they may not have any remorse. Regardless, they are still low risk because they are physically incapacitated. In discussing those near death, Jalila Jefferson-Bullock, an American scholar, suggests that "[i]n such situations, the granting of compassionate release relies on a determination that impending death extinguishes any threat that an otherwise dangerous offender might levy upon release, and on a basic, fundamental belief that, due to the inmate's altered circumstances, humanity and decency demand early release."[104] In addition, if this individual were serving life, even with a great rehabilitation potential, they would not be considered for parole for up to twenty-five years (and, in special circumstances, up to seventy-five). It is for this small – but growing – group of individuals in exceptional life circumstances that a good compassionate release system is needed.

At the moment, section 121 of the *CCRA* is a useless provision. It adds nothing to the parole system and does not create true compassionate release opportunities. Section 121 needs to be repealed and replaced by a humanitarian-based provision. The compassionate release provision must also be appropriately regulated by the *CCRR* and Commissioner's Directives, separately from other forms of parole. The following are some guidelines as to how this reform could be achieved.

A New Provision in the CCRA. A new provision will need to be separate from the general parole provisions in order to illustrate the different basis for its use. The humanitarian rationale needs to be clearly stated in the provision to prevent any future misinterpretations.

Criteria for Compassionate Release. Health status (for example, terminal illness and health incompatible with incarceration) should be the only criteria used for compassionate release. In order to properly reflect its humanitarian grounds, compassionate release will need to be available to all prisoners regardless of the length or type of their sentence, or the duration of time they have served before applying for it. Other factors may be considered collaterally to prove diminished risk: psychological assessments, disciplinary record, report of the parole officer, and other such items. These factors, however, should not be determinative where

---

104 Jalila Jefferson-Bullock, "Are You (Still) My Great and Worthy Opponent? Compassionate Release of Terminally Ill Offenders" (2015) 83:3 UMKC L Rev 521 at 523 [Jefferson-Bullock].

medical evidence can establish that the prisoner is so sick that they could not reasonably be believed to pose a risk.

CSC's Concomitant Obligation for Post-Release Support. Post-release plans and support should never be factors for release. That is not to say they should not exist or that a prisoner should be released without ensuring they have some place to go. But these plans and support should be the CSC's obligation and should never be used as an argument against a prisoner's release. A variety of avenues exist through which such obligations could be met, some of which are illustrated by the American experience. For example, internal case management that helps prisoners find nursing homes or retirement homes should be available. As well, cost-sharing between the CSC and the appropriate province would offer the support needed on the outside and increase the chances of inmates finding appropriate medical facilities that would take them in. As already mentioned with respect to the cost issue, it is implausible to think that providing decent living quarters outside of a prison could rival the cost of imprisonment in a secure facility.

Who Should Provide the Evidence of Disease. A list of diseases and symptoms incompatible with incarceration should be put together by a committee of experts appointed by the government. This committee should include different types of physicians, including prison doctors. This list should not be exhaustive. The evidence of disease should be provided, and recommendations made, by a physician. Few prison physicians are willing to sign off and affirm that a prisoner's health is incompatible with incarceration. To ensure the objectivity of the process, the link between the condition and the capacity of the individual to endanger society should be established by a fully independent physician.

Who Should File a Compassionate Release Request. Currently, only prisoners and their parole officers can apply. Some prisoners have health conditions that do not allow them to prepare such applications, while some parole officers are not willing or do not have the expertise to recognize the need for making such recommendations. The family of the prisoner, as well as the prison doctor, must be allowed to make requests for compassionate release when such prisoners are incapable of doing so.

Adjudication of Compassionate Release Requests. A specialized body is needed to adjudicate compassionate release requests. The number of old and sick people will increase and, if properly regulated, so will – and should – the number of compassionate release requests. As illustrated by the experiences in California, New Jersey,[105] and France,[106] a court seems to be the best functioning mechanism for granting such release. In Canada, judges have taken into account the health status of the accused in order to minimize the sentence in numerous sentencing cases. It would make sense to allow judges to release the individual upon a radical change of circumstances, as well as to decide when and if continuing supervision upon release is needed. Judges are also highly familiar with balancing different factors, and they are not directly involved in the correctional process, which offers them enhanced objectivity. Other scholars have also agreed that placing the duty of hearing such requests upon a judge would best ensure fairness and competency.[107] The judges assigned for such cases could be either a judge specializing in such particular matters or someone who deals with sentencing on a regular basis. For the group of judges deciding such cases, specialized training on matters related to the conditions of compassionate release (for example, medical issues) should be expected and provided.

If judges are not invested with such responsibilities, at the very least a special panel within the PBC should be created to hear such compassionate release requests. Creating a special body for this purpose would allow for the appropriate training on medical issues likely to arise in such cases. Also, through developed experience, a special panel would more likely be capable of quicker and fairer assessment of all the relevant factors, especially since compassionate release cases are time sensitive. As the OCI *Annual Report, 2012–2013* mentioned,[108] such a case currently takes months under section 121, months an ill and dying prisoner may not have. A special adjudicative body would allow for such requests to be heard with priority and for decisions to be made expeditiously without compromising quality.

Knowledge Mobilization. Once an appropriate provision exists and is regulated, it needs to be acknowledged and publicized so that prisoners and their families know that compassionate release is an option. Presently, neither the CSC's nor the PBC's websites mention section 121.[109] Lawyers do not inform their clients about compassionate release, likely

---

105 Marjorie P. Russell, "Too Little, Too Late, Too Slow: Compassionate Release of Terminally Ill Prisoners – Is the Cure Worse than the Disease?" (1994) 3:2 Widener J Pub L 799 at 820–1.

106 Eva Steiner, "Early Release for Seriously Ill Elderly Prisoners: Should French Practice Be Followed?" (2003) 50:3 Probation J 267.

107 Jefferson-Bullock, *supra* note 104 at 563.

108 OCI 2012–2013, *supra* note 86 at 20.

109 See PBC, *supra* note 44, and Correctional Service of Canada, www.csc-scc.gc.ca.

because many of them are not aware of it either. Parole officers and case managers also need to include compassionate release information in a package available to prisoners.[110] If the criteria are well regulated, the risk of abuse of such a provision would be minimal. Proper regulation, while more difficult, is a better way to avoid abuse of the system than keeping prisoners uninformed.

Oversight. Currently, it is very difficult to obtain up-to-date information on the number of times a section 121 release was applied for and how many times it was successful. It would be useful if a tracking system could be put in place to monitor the implementation of a new compassionate release provision. Having a special adjudicative body for these requests would facilitate the creation of such a system.

Institutional Reform

At the end of their respective interviews, I asked John and Eric what they would like to see changed in prison, if there was anything that would make life better for people like themselves. For both of them, release was the number one answer. Eric did not care about anything else, and he did not share any specific opinions regarding confinement conditions. "You can draw your own conclusions from what I told you about life in here," he said. He was simply disheartened that he could not access parole in a meaningful manner that would have allowed him to be with his wife.

On the other hand, John was a prison veteran. He knew that, as much as one may dream of being released, it is not the reality for many elderly people. Their reality is behind bars. The cell is their home, and it must be "survivable." Based on his experience and that of people he saw coming and going in different correctional facilities, he shared some suggestions with me. He believed that the current accommodation was unacceptable – older people should never have to use a top bunk, and they should rarely have to share a cell, especially if they were very sick or incontinent. They should have more opportunity to keep mobile, such as a safer place to exercise and cleaner, less cluttered yards in winter. John also believed that seniors-only units should be available. He thought that being together with people his own age would reduce the bullying he experienced and increase people's willingness to socialize.

---

110 The current policy does not require such information to be made available to prisoners: Correctional Service of Canada, "Sentence Management," Commissioner's
Directive No. 703 (Ottawa: CSC, 2017), s 20, online: https://www.csc-scc.gc.ca/acts-
and-regulations/703-cd-eng.shtml.

In addition, opportunities to keep in touch with families should be a priority. He suggested that there be better speakers in the phones because many people his age were hard of hearing and talking to their families through the regular prison phones was difficult. John also believed that having some monitored Skype conversations with family members would be an easy way to ensure that, regardless of distance, prisoners kept in touch with their loved ones. Internet connections are not available in any federal facilities, but a monitored "visit" room, where prisoners sit at computers that they can use only to Skype with approved "visitors" would not be very difficult to implement.

John had some words to say about health care as well. He was disheartened by the neglect and the bureaucratic hurdles he had to navigate in order to access any service at all. He was afraid he would die in prison, not from sickness but rather killed by indifference. John believed older prisoners should have access to speedier medical assistance, to better pain medication, and to key medical supplies such as adult diapers.

Living in prison is different from dying in prison. Even individuals who were so institutionalized that they did not feel they would succeed in the community did not want to die in prison. Thus, release was by far the number one answer to the question, "What would make your life better?"

Measures taken to improve conditions of confinement in prison may mean an investment in resources that could be better spent by improving release mechanisms and creating supports in the community for aging individuals coming out of prisons. No matter how improved conditions of confinement are, there may still be little justification for the continued incarceration of the old and the sick.

Unfortunately, it is unlikely that any type of parole reform, including compassionate release reform, would be applicable to all old and sick individuals. As the population ages, a significant number of prisoners will continue to grow old behind bars and thus rely on what correctional services makes available to them. The suggestions I provide in the following section for improving these services are not exhaustive – much more will need to be done. They are simply starting points to enable the creation of a general policy framework inclusive of older people's needs.

Improvement of Commissioner's Directives

> We don't exist. Since we don't exist, why would anyone bother with us?
> (PP, 66, in prison 25 years)

Commissioner's Directives are administrative documents meant to set a framework for uniformly regulating issues in CSC institutions. A CD regulating the treatment of older prisoners behind bars would go a long way towards protecting this group's needs. CDs have been issued that recognize the differences of women and Indigenous prisoners compared to the mainstream population.[111] Hence, each correctional institution has the duty to adapt to those needs in accordance with the directives' guidelines.

A similar directive is needed for older prisoners. The OCI has already noted that aging people, people with a mental illness, and those in need of palliative care are some of the most vulnerable prison populations.[112] The indiscriminate application of the same medical practices across all age groups fails to account for seniors' particular problems and potentially enhanced medical needs. It would not be surprising if future medical research proves that such a uniform application is medically inadequate and may not respond to the needs of older people. A correctional framework that accounts for enhanced medical and programming needs, created in accordance with gerontology studies, would eliminate treatment differences that currently exist among institutions and ensure a minimum degree of protection in accordance with human rights. A directive on managing the problems of senior prisoners would also reflect the CSC's understanding of such problems, as well as its commitment to act in accordance with these people's needs. It would also serve as guidance for CSC staff members who deal with such people and their issues on a daily basis.

In addition to a CD addressing seniors' needs, the already existing directives require improvement and revision. The health care directives are extremely important, but they are currently vague and very difficult to apply. Little guidance is given regarding the practical definition of primary or essential health care. It is also not clear what is meant by "acceptable standards of the profession." This lack of clarity is why, for example, chronic diseases are being managed by granting prisoners medical equipment in some institutions, while in other institutions the doctor is completely forbidden to prescribe them. The directives and Standard Operating Practices should not be a mere reiteration of the

---

111 Correctional Service of Canada, "Staff Protocol in Women Offender Institutions," Commissioner's Direction No. 577 (Ottawa: CSC, 2013), online: https://www.csc-scc.gc.ca/lois-et-reglements/577-cd-eng.shtml; Correctional Service of Canada, "Intensive Intervention Strategy in Women's Institutions," Commissioner's Directive No. 578 (Ottawa: CSC, 2017), online: https://www.csc-scc.gc.ca/lois-et-reglements/578-cd-eng.shtml.

112 Canada, Office of the Correctional Investigator *Annual Report, 2013–2014* (Ottawa: OCI, 2014) at 15, online: http://www.oci-bec.gc.ca/cnt/rpt/pdf/annrpt/ann-rpt20132014-eng.pdf [OCI 2013–2014].

existing legislation. They should instead clarify the laws and provide for a relevant practical and useful framework that helps meet prisoners' needs.

Reconfiguration of the Health Care System

> It's really not that terrible. Until you get sick. If you get sick, you are screwed. (YY, 51, in prison 13 years)

The Office of the Correctional Investigator noted in its last few reports that prison health care needs to be reformed with an aging population in mind.[113] The insufficient treatment options for chronic pain due to "ill-defined security, administrative, or institutional concerns" have been noted by the OCI based on an extensive qualitative review of the CSC's *National Drug Formulary*. Based on this review, the OCI recommended that the CSC amend its formulary in areas such as chronic pain management (where treatment options appear to be lacking).[114] Previously, the OCI also mentioned that neither pain management nor assistive medical devices for the aging exist in satisfactory quantities and quality.[115] OCI also noted the need for staff members and specialists in this environment to be trained in gerontology and palliative care.[116]

The findings of this study confirm and add to these concerns raised by the OCI. They re-enforce the need for a restructuring of prison health care. Considering the growing number of older prisoners and the CSC's lack of experience with them, restructuring should be done in consultation with gerontology specialists. Before this reform can happen, a few things should be considered and used as starting points.

First, the medication available for pain management is insufficient and of limited diversity. The little medication available appears to lead to pain going untreated, which in turn seems to alter the quality of life of older prisoners, who cannot rest properly and are turning in higher numbers to drug and alcohol abuse.

---

113 OCI 2010–2011, *supra* note 92 at 25; OCI 2013–2014, *supra* note 112 at 16; OCI 2014–2015, *supra* note 100 at 11, online: http://www.oci-bec.gc.ca/cnt/rpt/index-eng.aspx.

114 OCI 2014–2015, *supra* note 100 at 10; Canada, Office of the Correctional Investigator, *National Drug Formulary Investigation* (Ottawa: OCI, 2015), online (summary and recommendations): http://www.oci-bec.gc.ca/cnt/rpt/oth-aut/oth-aut20150127-eng. aspx [OCI, *Drug Formulary Investigation*].

115 OCI 2010–2011, *supra* note 92 at 22.

116 *Ibid* at 25.

Second, the consequences of ineffective treatment of pain and chronic diseases, as well as lack of medication, may have unique impacts on the well-being of older people. Hence, the prison doctor should be able to consult with a gerontology specialist on a regular basis. The CSC should contract with gerontology specialists who would be on-site regularly in institutions with a higher number of older prisoners. This provision would be similar to the CSC contracts with other specialists such as dentists and psychiatrists. Where gerontologists cannot be brought on-site, they should be available via teleconferencing. Consultation by electronic means is also not an unusual practice, as the CSC already uses telepsychiatry in some of its more remote locations. In addition, in locations with high numbers of seniors, a nurse trained in gerontology should be available at least during the day. Consulting with gerontology specialists can prove crucial in determining whether behaviours need to be responded to with treatment or with discipline. For example, it appears that mental or physical problems commonly cause disruptive behaviour in older prisoners. Solitary confinement and other forms of punishment are not appropriate responses in such cases.

Third, in light of the increased number of chronic and acute diseases leading to pain and other complications that seniors face, all prison facilities should have a nurse on-site at all times. Fewer than half of the prisons I visited had a nurse available 24/7, and the same goes for institutions in remote locations, where even ambulances take a long time to arrive.

Fourth, chronic disease management is more than an adequate range of effective painkillers. The current list of assistive devices available is restrictive. Supplies such as extra pillows, medical mattresses, heating pads, and orthopaedic shoes are currently never prescribed. Others, such as braces, can be prescribed, but the interviews with older prisoners show that such prescriptions vary from institution to institution. Clearly, these rules have not been made with the problems of aging prisoners in mind. They need to be reconsidered, perhaps with the help of gerontology specialists.

Fifth, distribution of medication for the elderly needs to be redesigned. It is counter-intuitive to ask someone who is in pain to stand in line for an hour, outside, rain or shine, to pick up their pain medication. Of the seniors I interviewed, 90 per cent reported taking prescription medication. Clearly, they are the most likely population to pick up medication daily, while also being affected by pain associated with aging. If, for security reasons, they cannot be given a month's worth of medication at a time, a nurse should be tasked with bringing medication to their cells on a daily basis. This process should be an integrated part of pain and disease management. While such a reform is in progress, seniors should be given priority in picking up their medication, and pill distribution should begin for them half an hour or so earlier than for everyone else.

Creation of Seniors-Only Units

A senior-centred health care system would be more achievable in prison if at least some of the institutions offered seniors-only units. Such arrangements would also address other age-related concerns, such as lack of appropriate programming and care, vulnerability, victimization, and infrastructure.

An overwhelming number of the participants in this study (93 per cent) indicated that they believed their quality of life would increase if they were housed in seniors-only units. None of the institutions I visited provided such units, or even a seniors' lounge for daytime activities. Some institutions had a quieter unit where vulnerable individuals were generally housed. Even in those institutions, though, the study participants indicated that only so many seniors would fit in those units, and many were left on the outside. There was also a tendency to house younger, vulnerable prisoners there as well, as a mild form of protective custody. In addition, in maximum security, a notoriously dangerous place, seniors tended to be placed in protective custody or on a mental health range. However, protective custody meant that the prisoner was locked up for twenty-three hours a day. Also, stigma was associated with this type of accommodation. Once an individual was placed in protective custody, they could not be released into the general population without serious repercussions to their well-being.

A seniors-only (living) unit could be created in a manner that offers appropriate stimulation and socialization. It would also provide managerial benefits. Older prisoners reported relatively low disciplinary incidents (31 per cent with only 6.1 per cent for violent behaviour) and relatively low rates of time spent in segregation (23.4 per cent with only 20 per cent for violent behaviour). They also reported good relationships with staff (89.3 per cent). The OCI also reported that older prisoners are, as a general rule, a low-risk population.[117] Both my study and the OCI report confirmed that disruptive behaviour in this population tends to be associated with illness.[118] Consequently, the security cost in seniors-only units could be lower in favour of higher investments in related health and programming services. It would allow for specialized medical care without the same concern about drug abuse or dealing. Medication could be distributed in a more age-sensitive manner, and the infrastructure could be adapted to be more accessible to people with disabilities. Such accommodations would not have to be available in all institutions, but

---

117 OCI 2010–2011, *supra* note 92 at 23.
118 *Ibid.*

prisons that cannot offer them should not house seniors. As an interim measure, study participants indicated that even a seniors' lounge where they could spend their daytime without fear of being bullied would be an improvement over the current state.

Some US models of senior prisoner care units (for example, True Grit at Nevada Correctional Centre; Ohio Hocking Correctional Facility; Angola Prison, Pine Bluff, Arkansas; Hartwick Georgia; The Minnesota Correctional Facility Stillwater Seniors' Dormitory; Mississippi State Penitentiary; and Old Men's Colony West Virginia) could be used as examples for enhancing correctional practices, especially in the areas of programming, pain management, mental health, and end-of-life care.[119] The creation of these units (often living units) is not just about the space; rather, it concerns the quality of programming in support that exists in such places, with reduced segregation and activities tailored for geriatric prisoners.[120] Studies showed that such programs successfully enhance the physical health of older people (through recreational programs and physical therapy), their mental health (through group and individual therapy), and their emotional well-being (through spiritual counselling and targeted peer and staff support). For instance, in Nevada, True Grit is based on a system in which individuals are required to maintain good personal hygiene to stay in the program, and they are assigned work and programming tasks based on their capabilities. This accommodation keeps their motivation high, increases their quality of life, and makes their community reintegration more likely.[121] The literature is ambivalent regarding the cost-benefit of special housing only for older people. However, strong evidence shows the benefit of having safe living units with specialized programs and services for seniors.[122] The success of

119 Ronald H. Aday, *Aging Prisoners* (Westport, CT: Greenwood Publishing Group, 2003) [Aday, *Aging Prisoners*]; R.V. Rikard & Ed Rosenberg, "Aging Inmates: A Convergence of Trends in the US Criminal Justice System" (2007) 13:3 J Correct Health Care 150 at 151 [Rikard & Rosenberg].

120 Martha H. Hurley, *Aging in Prison: The Integration of Research and Practice* (Durham, NC: Carolina Academic Press, 2014) at 164; Chris Trotter & Susan Baidawi, "Older Prisoners: Challenges for Inmates and Prison Management" (2015) 48:2 Austl & NZ J Crim 200 at 215.

121 Ronald Aday & Jennifer Krabill, "Social Programming and Activities" in Kerbs & Jolley, *Seniors Behind Bars, supra* note 72, 69 at 87–90 [Aday & Krabill]; Aday, *Aging Prisoners, supra* note 119 at 85–6.

122 Anita Blowers, Jennifer Jolley, & John Kerbs, "The Age-Segregation Debate" in Kerbs and Jolley, *Seniors Behind Bars, supra* note 72, 133 at 154–5.

such programs has been attributed to their having at least one of the following characteristics: age and cognitive appropriate environmental modifications, interdisciplinary staff and volunteers trained in geriatric issues, complementary medicine, specialized case coordination, the use of family and volunteers, mentoring, and self-help advocacy groups.[123]

However, should such units be created, the hope is that they would be tiny: the number one priority in dealing with older prisoners should still be to ensure that adequate release mechanisms and preparation for release are in place.

Mandatory Staff Training on Geriatric Matters

Yes, officers call us names. I wouldn't even call that abuse; that's what they all do. (AB, 53, in prison 9 years)

Findings from my study, to which I referred in the previous chapter, suggest that some seniors are being stigmatized and their vulnerability due to age and disability is exploited inside prisons. It is unacceptable to have correctional staff members making fun of incontinent individuals. It is equally unacceptable to steal prisoners' walking aids in order to play tricks on them. Name-calling by staff members was reported by the participants as part of their day-to-day living. While calling prisoners "old fart" and "pops" may not be regarded as a big deal in a correctional setting, it still has negative psychological consequences. Name-calling reminds older people that they are more vulnerable and suggests that they are less worthy of respect.

In Ohio, geriatric correctional training called "Try Another Way" was introduced, with positive results reported.[124] Correctional officers are not just security guards; they should be role models, and a prison environment is only as good as its front-line workers. It might be hard for officers to understand that care needs to be combined with security even more than before with an aging prison population, which is why proper training is very important. While the Ohio program is one of the most successful training programs, it is by no means the only one; many

---

123 Tina Maschi, Deborah Viola, & Fei Sun, "The High Cost of the International Aging Prisoner Crisis: Well-Being as the Common Denominator for Action" (2012) 53:4 Gerontologist 543 at 550 [Maschi, Viola, & Sun].

124 Rikard & Rosenberg, *supra* note 119.

jurisdictions that run geriatric programs or living units are increasing training for staff members in geriatric matters.[125]

Palliative Care Units

> It's really difficult to live with someone who is dying. When you hear them scream, you can't not think that that's what awaits you. (JJ, 56, in prison 30 years)

Currently, no hospice beds are available in Canadian prisons, and palliative care is not systematically available.[126] Palliative care is sometimes given to prisoners, but that happens because of the efforts of different agencies and volunteers, not because of the CSC.[127] Coupled with the fact that compassionate release options are highly restrictive, the situation of terminally ill prisoners is not very good. Compassionate release is not available to people serving life sentences, and it is rarely used even for other groups.[128]

Palliative care units have been described as places where the focus is placed on interdisciplinary health care teams meant to ameliorate suffering.[129] They are "guardians of the patient's comfort while helping the patient and their family grapple realistically with which goals and treatments best suit a particular patient."[130] Prison hospices and palliative care units have flourished throughout the United States in response to the increased number of people who die in prison (for example, Angola, Maryland, Hospice Program; Federal Medical Center at Carswell, Ft. Worth; Broward Correctional Institution, Florida; Oregon State Penitentiary; US Medical Center for Federal Prisoners, Missouri; Vacaville State Prison, California; Michael Unit, Tennessee Colony; and the Dixon Correctional Center, Illinois). These places are more health care–oriented than other type of units. They focus on pain relief, are safer, and have better trained teams

---

125 Aday & Krabill, *supra* note 121 at 75; Maschi, Viola, & Sun, *supra* note 123, at 550; Rikard & Rosenberg, *supra* note 119 at 155.

126 OCI 2013–2014, *supra* note 112.

127 OCI 2010–2011, *supra* note 92 at 24.

128 *CCRA*, *supra* note 2, s 121; OCI 2012–2013, *supra* note 86 at 20.

129 Meridith C. Burles, Cindy A. Peternelj-Taylor, & Lorraine Holtslander, "A 'Good Death' for All? Examining Issues for Palliative Care in Correctional Setting" (2016) 21:2 Mortality 93 at 95–8 [Burles, Peternelj-Taylor, & Holtslander].

130 John F. Linder, "Health Issues and End-of-Life Care" in Kerbs & Jolley, *Seniors Behind Bars*, *supra* note 72, 177 at 185–6 [Linder].

and reduced security.[131] Thus, as a matter of harm reduction, having such units is better than not having them.[132]

However, while these units are better than regular units for terminally ill individuals, and they are necessary as long as terminally ill prisoners continue to be incarcerated, the quality of care has been deemed to be either lower than that in the community due to the unique prison environment,[133] or, at the very best, unclear, due to lack of systematic research and because such units may be marginalizing spaces.[134]

All prisoners approaching death should be able to choose the course of their treatment, in particular now that medical assistance in dying is available.[135] Resources should be overwhelmingly invested in ensuring that individuals are released before they opt for medical assistance in dying in order to ensure a fully voluntary consent to treatment. The palliative units are expensive, and not enough evidence supports their effectiveness. That said, for those who do spend their end of life in prison, there ought to be some space where security is relaxed, medical care is enhanced, palliative care specialists are available 24/7, and family visits are strongly encouraged and facilitated. These prisoners should also have access to legal advice for the writing of wills and advance directives.

Conclusion

Creating a correctional system that accounts for the differences of vulnerable groups – such as aging prisoners – requires a reform of confinement conditions and especially of release mechanisms. Such extensive

---

131   Melvin Delgado & Denise Humm-Delgado, *Health and Health Care in the Nation's Prisons: Issues, Challenges, and Policies* (Lanham, MD: Rowman & Littlefield, 2009); Annette Hanson, "Psychiatry and the Dying Prisoner" (2017) 29:1 Intl Rev Psychiatry 45 at 46; Mary Turner & Marian Peacock, "Palliative Care in UK Prisons: Practical and Emotional Challenges for Staff and Fellow Prisoners" (2017) 23:1 J Corr Health Care 56 at 64.

132   Ami Harbin, "Prisons and Palliative Politics" in Geoffrey Adelsberg, Lisa Guenther, & Scott Zeman, *Death and Other Penalties: Philosophy in a Time of Mass Incarceration* (New York: Fordham University Press, 2015) 158 at 166–7 [Harbin].

133   Linder, *supra* note 130 at 194–7.

134   Harbin, *supra* note 132 at 167; Burles, Peternelj-Taylor, & Holtslander, *supra* note 129 at 100, 103; Susan J. Loeb et al, "Who Wants to Die in Here? Perspectives of Prisoners with Chronic Conditions" (2014) 16:3 J Hosp Palliat Nurs 173 at 182–3; Rachel K. Wion & Susan J. Loeb, "End-of-Life Care Behind Bars: A Systematic Review" (2016) 116:3 AJN 24 at 31–2.

135   Correctional Service of Canada, "Medical Assistance in Dying," Guideline 800–9 (Ottawa: CSC, 29 November 2017), online: https://www.csc-scc.gc.ca/acts-and-regulations/800-9-gl-en.shtml.

reform will be needed in order to align the CSC's practices to its moral duties and legal obligations.

The suggestions made in this chapter are based on the experiences of the study's participants. However, valid suggestions for improvement in these two correctional areas – even if not always age-centred – are being made on a rolling basis, both by scholars and the OCI. The major issue, as I argue in the next chapters, is that evidence-based policy reform does not come naturally within the CSC. Getting such an intransigent institution to change its practices often turns out to be a very difficult endeavour.

In the next chapter, I trace the history of CSC's undertakings to reform and its previous reception of various recommendations made by different external prison oversight mechanisms. I look at a number of particularly problematic CSC prison practices that underwent significant external investigation and pinpoint the resulting reform recommendations. In addition to showing the CSC's historical resistance to reform, these examples also show a culture of disrespect towards the law, the recommendations of oversight institutions, and individual rights.

Chapter Four

Democracy in Action: Implementation of Policy Reform and Prison Oversight

Every time I sat across a desk, I lost. I don't ask staff for anything. I don't talk to anybody anymore. There's nothing to say. (CC, 57, in prison 15 years)

Eric was in prison for a brief period of time compared to other individuals, and he mostly kept to himself. Incarcerated for the first time in old age and faced with the shame of spending his "golden years" in prison, all he wanted to do was serve his time and get home to his wife.

John, on the other hand, was a prison veteran. Having spent many years in prison and in declining health, he faced the inadequacy of prison policies numerous times. When his health conditions became aggravated, he began putting in more frequent requests to see the nurse or to receive treatment or items to help him with his conditions. In 90 per cent of the situations, his requests were denied or took a long time to be addressed. When a federally incarcerated individual believes their rights are being abused, they have access to the Office of the Correctional Investigator (OCI), the prison ombudsman, through a toll-free number. John said he called about five times in ten years to complain about inadequate health care, about being kept in solitary confinement for too long, and about being denied an escort to see his dying wife. However, he said that nothing ever happened. When he called to follow-up, he was told that "they are investigating" or that "they investigated and ... the correctional authorities were informed about the situation and recommended to rectify it." John has never seen any changes as a result of his complaints or those of his peers. In the last few years before his interview, he no longer complained to anyone when he felt his rights were being infringed. "Waste of time and only adds to my frustration," he said.

I asked John if the Correctional Service of Canada (CSC) or another agency came to talk to him about his needs or how his rights were being upheld. He said that the CSC occasionally had them fill out surveys for "research" or "policy" purposes. He never really expected much of them. He also thought that a couple of people who were not CSC talked to him over time, but he could not remember who they were. He said perhaps the OCI came once. He was never presented with any reports or other outcomes of that talk. For his part, Eric said that I was the first person to have a discussion with him on the matter.

Task Forces and Non-Governmental Reports

As a governmental agency and the administrator of the federal correctional system, the CSC has wide discretion, coming from its delegated power, to create and implement prison policies.[1] In so doing, it is bound by the *Constitution*,[2] the *Canadian Charter of Rights and Freedoms* (*Charter*),[3] and the relevant legislation.

Because the correctional environment significantly restricts individual rights and liberties by its nature, and thus an ongoing risk of abuse exists, prison affairs cannot be hidden from the public eye in a democratic state. The separation of powers and a respect for the delegated power of the CSC to create its own policies is crucial, but so are prisoners' rights and respect for the law. On more than one occasion, CSC policies have raised ethical and legal issues by going either against the letter or the spirit of the law. For example, correctional administrators often took advantage of legislative gaps to justify morally problematic policies or offered their own interpretation of the law. In the words of Parkes and Pate, "too often, the power of the Commissioner to make policy and the implementation of that policy are understood as freedom to any measures not specifically prohibited by the *CCRA* and regulations," without further assessing their legality against provisions of the *Charter* or the *Canadian Human Rights Act*.[4]

In an ideal world, the CSC should be able to reform its own policies when they are deemed to be problematic, or when they become obsolete, without major outside interventions (such as parliamentary or judicial). However, to ensure compliance with the law, the creation and implementation of such policies need to be transparent and subject to

---

1   *Corrections and Conditional Release Act*, SC 1992, c 20, s 5–6 [*CCRA*].
2   *Constitution Act, 1982*, being Schedule B to the *Canada Act 1982* (UK), 1982, c 11.
3   *Canadian Charter of Rights and Freedoms*, Part I of the *Constitution Act, 1982*, being Schedule B to the *Canada Act 1982* (UK), 1982, c 11 [*Charter*].
4   Debra Parkes & Kim Pate, "Time for Accountability: Effective Oversight of Women's Prisons" (2006) 48:2 CJCCJ 251 at 254–5.

external oversight. When a major issue with a CSC policy arises, the government (or sometimes the CSC itself) often creates a committee or a task force to review the issues surrounding that policy and make recommendations. The CSC should then reform its policy based on those recommendations. Other times, non-governmental agencies with expertise in imprisonment take it upon themselves to research, report, and make recommendations (often quite regularly) about such policy flaws (for example, the Elizabeth Fry Society, the John Howard Society, and the HIV/AIDS Canadian Legal Network).

Nonetheless, the recommendations made by these committees are not binding on the CSC. While their work is essential in uncovering key legal violations and bringing together experts who are in a position to make viable reform suggestions, only the CSC itself decides how and if it will implement the recommendations. In an evocative piece on the CSC's policymaking, Lisa Kerr traces the birth, development, and abolition of a highly problematic CSC document.[5] The Management Protocol (Protocol) was the final section within a larger document, the *Secure Unit Operational Plan*, created in 2003. The Protocol enabled the CSC to use an enhanced form of security on certain women, a disproportionate number of whom were Aboriginal. The technique, Kerr argues, was in full contradiction with the *CCRA*, the *Charter*, and the Supreme Court of Canada's case law. Before it was created, numerous stakeholders, including the OCI and the Canadian Association of Elizabeth Fry Societies (CAEFS), brought targeted objections to the Protocol during a consultation process. All of the objections were brushed aside, and the Protocol survived almost in its original form for nearly ten years. It was abolished only after a decade of criticism and after the BC Civil Liberties Association brought a *Charter* challenge in court to its use. Kerr argues that the history of the Management Protocol is emblematic of the challenge Canada faces to entrench a culture of legality in its correctional system and to ensure access to an external review of its policies.[6]

As is apparent from Kerr's case study, the CSC has a history of responding defensively to external recommendations and ignoring or distorting recommendations it does not like. This flaw within the prison policymaking process may create problems for seniors behind bars. The acceleration of aging in Canadian prisons is a relatively novel problem

---

5 Lisa Kerr, "The Origins of Unlawful Prison Policies" (2015) 4:1 Can J Hum Rts 89. [Kerr, "Prison Policies"]; Office of the Deputy Commissioner for Woman, *Secure Unit Operational Plan* (Ottawa: Correctional Service of Canada, September 2003) at Part 8, "Management Protocol." Note that Part 8 has been removed from the CSC website.

6 Kerr, "Prison Policies," *supra* note 5 at 119.

that requires extensive institutional and policy reform related to medical interventions, infrastructure, availability of drug and non-drug services, and so on. These types of reforms presuppose a potential diversion of resources from security to other kinds of interventions. One can only hope that this book's recommendations will result in some sort of reform or will perhaps lead to the appointment of a governmental committee, with more authority than in the past, to further research the matter and issue a set of guidelines on how to create an age-sensitive prison environment. This process would be the most common way to produce change within this administrative branch. Sadly, the chances of that happening are illustrated by the words of one of the study's participants:

> I will talk to you because I have nothing better to do. I talked to many people over the last forty years – CSC people, government people, Office of the Correctional Investigator people. They do their reports, they check the activity, and then the resulting paper collects dust somewhere. No one cares and nothing will change. You may be hopeful now, but I am telling you, from experience, all this research does not lead to anything. Not for us in here. Never has, never will. It will make a good story for you to tell when you are old, though. (DD, 62, in prison 5 years with repeat previous incarcerations)

Another individual stated:

One time a woman – I don't remember what organization she was with – was doing a study on the effects of solitary confinement on us inmates. I don't even know what came out of that. I wanted to see her conclusions, but I was never shown a report, or a paper, and I don't know if recommendations were ever made to improve our situation. Better not to expect anything from these kind of interviews. (SS, 52, in prison 10 years)

Despite interviewee SS's concern, agencies or institutions that proceed with such prison investigations – either on their own initiative or with a government mandate – do, in fact, provide the CSC with recommendations most of the time. The problem resides in the CSC's attitude towards such recommendations.

To illustrate the CSC's intransigency to change, I examine the result of external oversight on two long-lasting and thorny correctional issues: women in prison and the use of administrative segregation. These two examples are particularly relevant for the issue of age-related policy reform. Like some of the old-age policy suggestions in this book, reform ideas centred on the needs of female prisoners and on administrative segregation were based on the principle that tough-on-crime policies are not effective across prison groups, that they have little benefit for public safety, and that punitive responses to what is perceived as dangerous behaviour should be replaced with other types of interventions. However, task forces and committees have been created for numerous other correctional problems, and their recommendations have also rarely been implemented.[7]

In 1990, the government-appointed Task Force on Federally Sentenced Women (TFFSW) issued their *Creating Choices* report.[8] This report followed decades of mandated research on women prisoners that essentially had no practical consequences.[9] *Creating Choices* reflected on the needs of federally incarcerated women and attempted to produce a correctional approach that would respond specifically to the unique needs of women. At the time, the penal approach to women was seen by many as repressive and of little consequence to their rehabilitation and reintegration. The report's goal was to create a framework that would respond to those concerns.

Aside from government agencies, representatives of other stakeholders, including Aboriginal women and former prisoners, sat on the task force and voiced their opinions. The recommendations of the TFFSW centred on certain key principles such as empowerment, meaningful choices for women, respect and dignity, a supportive environment, and a shared responsibility between the CSC, other stakeholders, and the women themselves for their reintegration into the community.[10] The government firmly agreed to implement the recommendations. However, as Hannah-Moffat observed in her book on penal governance, "when the state concedes a right, structural arrangements for that right to be implemented do not necessarily follow."[11] The implementation committee refused to work with independent stakeholders, such as the Elizabeth

---

7   See e.g. Ministry of the Solicitor General, *Task Force on Aboriginal Peoples in Federal Corrections* (Ottawa: Ministry of the Solicitor General, 1998); David Mullan, *Review of the CCRA Complaints and Grievance System* (Ottawa: Correctional Service of Canada, 2010); Sandra Ka Hon Chu et al, *Under the Skin: A People's Case for Prison Needle and Syringe Programs* (Toronto: Canadian HIV/AIDS Legal Network, 2010), online: http://sagecollection.ca/en/system/files/undertheskin-eng.pdf.

8   Canada, Task Force on Federally Sentenced Women, *Creating Choices: The Report of the Task Force on Federally Sentenced Women* (Ottawa: Ministry of the Solicitor General, 1990), online: https://www.csc-scc.gc.ca/women/toce-eng.shtml [TFFSW].

9   Kelly Hannah-Moffat, *Punishment in Disguise: Penal Governance and Federal Imprisonment of Women in Canada* (Toronto: University of Toronto Press, 2001) at 134–5 [Hannah-Moffat].

10   TFFSW, *supra* note 8.

11   Hannah-Moffat, *supra* note 9 at 137.

Fry Societies, and, despite implementing some of the recommendations, it failed to do so according to the spirit in which they were written.

For example, while the CSC dressed its policies in a progressive framework, prisons continued to punish women rather than help them.[12] In her book, Hannah-Moffat provides concrete examples of such failures: healing lodges were created but they were not made available to everyone who needed them; in time, the lodges began to look increasingly like prisons as opposed to alternative correctional intervention centres; the infamous Prison for Women (P4W) in Kingston was not shut down; the CSC did not significantly increase its role in helping women reintegrate into the community; and women's prisons continued to be placed in isolated locations.[13] Hannah-Moffat maintains that the recommendations of the task force are largely seen nowadays as "unachievable ideals," and, "while the benevolent rhetoric of empowerment and healing embodied in *Creating Choices* has permeated correctional discourses, the more sinister and punitive disciplinary reality of 'corrections' persists."[14]

In 1999, another report, *Whatever Happened to the Promises of Creating Choices: Federally Sentenced Maximum Security Women*, written by Sky Blue Morin,[15] reflected on the results from *Creating Choices*. It concluded that the recommendations in regard to Aboriginal women had not been implemented and that the goals had not been reached; women had not been empowered, offered meaningful choices, or placed in supportive environments. Punitive responses continued to be the main answer to the behaviour of Aboriginal women who were still placed in maximum security institutions in large numbers. Moreover, as discussed at the beginning of this chapter, the Management Protocol, a highly oppressive security tool disproportionately targeting Aboriginal women, was introduced in 2003. Thus, the evidence-based recommendations of the TFFSW failed under the CSC's preference for punitive policies.

After the TFFSW's report was issued, a new federal legal framework came into effect. The *Corrections and Conditional Release Act (CCRA)*[16] contains a significant number of prisoners' rights, provides for better oversight and an improved grievance system, significantly recognizes the

---

12 Kelly Struthers Montford, "Transforming Choices: The Marginalization of Gender-Specific Policy Making in Canadian Approaches to Women's Federal Imprisonment" (2015) 27:2 CJWL/RFD 284 at 287 [Struthers Montford].

13 Hannah-Moffat, *supra* note 9 at 144–5.

14 *Ibid* at 177–8.

15 Sky Blue Morin, *Whatever Happened to the Promises of Creating Choices: Federally Sentenced Maximum Security Women* (Ottawa: Correctional Service of Canada, 1999).

16 *CCRA*, supra note 1; *Corrections and Conditional Release Regulations*, SOR/92-620 [*CCRR*].

unique needs of women prisoners, and mandates programs respectful of Aboriginal cultures and traditions. However, neither the recommendations of the TFFSW nor this novel legislation helped to significantly improve the lives of incarcerated women.

In 1994, after a violent incident against some women at the P4W in Kingston, Madame Justice Louise Arbour was appointed by the government to head a Commission of Inquiry into Certain Events at the Prison for Women (Arbour Commission).[17] The findings of the commission reiterated many of the concerns of the TFFSW. It provided evidence that the recommendations were not implemented in the spirit in which they were made, and that the prevailing approach to incarcerated women remained highly punitive, traumatizing, and outside the law. The events that led to the creation of this commission are in stark contrast to the TFFSW's goal of decreasing security and punitive responses to incarcerated women and placing them in supportive environments. During this particular 1995 incident at P4W in Kingston, prisoners were placed in segregation for long periods of time with little oversight, stripped naked by a special handling team, maced, and left in cold cells with the windows open overnight. At that time, not only had the TFFSW set very different goals for incarcerated women, but the law had also been reformed, and numerous rules and procedures were in place to supposedly prevent such actions. However, Arbour noted that "the applicable law or policy in a given situation appeared unknown or easily forgotten and ignored."[18] Arbour focused many of her recommendations on the need to have substantial oversight over decisions taken by prison administrators, on accountability, and on due process to protect prisoners' rights. She also made extensive recommendations for creating a better grievance system and improving oversight for the use of administrative segregation.

Some of the Arbour Commission's recommendations were subsequently implemented. For example, P4W was finally shut down five years later after a handful of prisoners were again incarcerated in semi-solitude for the last two years of its existence. Little to no development was made, though, in terms of the grievance procedure, which was key to protecting prisoners' rights, oversight, and accountability. Neglect and abuse of power, as criticized in the Arbour Report, as well as the failure to empower women to make their own choices, remained key issues in prisons for women, together with improper reintegration programs,

---

17 Louise Arbour, *Commission of Inquiry into Certain Events at the Prison for Women in Kingston* (Ottawa: Public Works and Government Services of Canada, 1996) [Arbour Report].

18 *Ibid.*

insufficient community resources, and the separation of mothers and young children.[19]

The Arbour Report points out the government's failure to improve systemic problems relating to women in prison. For example, for two decades prior to the incidents at P4W, Michael Jackson had documented the abusive use of administrative segregation. In his 1983 book *Prisoners of Isolation*, Jackson criticized the deferential nature of the regional reviewers of segregation decisions, which led to an overuse of solitary confinement with devastating effects on prisoners.[20] Two decades later, Arbour's assessment showed that little had changed in terms of the use of segregation and the process that leads to it.

As a result of the concerns Arbour raised, the government put together a Task Force on Administrative Segregation in 1996–1997. Independent experts (including author Michael Jackson) were appointed as part of this task force. Two of its key recommendations were that segregation decisions needed to be independently adjudicated and a segregation advisory committee needed to be created.[21] The CSC outright refused to consider these essential suggestions. As Jackson later documented, the CSC did not make the report available to staff, prisoners, or the public. Jackson's follow-up documents to the Commissioner of the CSC on the recommendations of the task force were met with indifference and resistance.[22] Little reasoning was provided for such resistance, and what was offered mainly revolved around the need to maintain security. Two years after the completion of the task force's work, Jackson reported on three prisoners who had experienced segregation. He observed that the effects of not having an independent adjudicator were drastic: staff members cared about the relationships they had with each other and would not take the side of a prisoner in any situation. As long as segregation decisions were internally adjudicated, staff relationships would always influence the outcome. Among other issues noted by Jackson are the following: the corresponding guidelines in the Draft Administrative Handbook were not observed; prisoners did not enjoy the procedural

---

19 Hannah-Moffat, *supra* note 9 at 198. See also Ivan Zinger, "Human Rights Compliance and the Role of External Prison Oversight" (2006) 48:2 CJCCJ 127 at 129–30 [Zinger, "Human Rights Compliance"].

20 Michael Jackson, *Prisoners of Isolation: Solitary Confinement in Canada* (Toronto: University of Toronto Press, 1983).

21 Public Safety Canada, *Commitment to Legal Compliance, Fair Decision and Effective Results: Task Force Report Reviewing Administrative Segregation* (Ottawa: PSC, 1997).

22 For an account of CSC's reception of the task force's recommendations, see Michael Jackson, *Justice Behind the Walls: Human Rights in Canadian Prisons* (Vancouver: Douglas & McIntyre, 2002) at 386–9 [Jackson, *Justice Behind the Walls*].

safeguards that guaranteed that they receive three days' notice of the hearing and written documentation; and hearings were not recorded.[23]

Other agencies have completed annual reports showing how some of the problems addressed by the previously discussed commissions continue to persist. For example, the Working Group for Human Rights in 1997 (Yalden Report),[24] the Standing Committee on Justice and Human Rights in 2000,[25] the Cross-Gender Monitoring Project in 2000,[26] and the Canadian Human Rights Commission in 2003[27] each undertook their own evaluations of the use of administrative segregation. Their recommendations, including the chief need for independent administrative segregation decision-making, were also ignored. The reports of the Canadian Association of Elizabeth Fry Societies (CAEFS) also show that the goals set out in *Creating Choices* have never been met and that many of the Arbour Commission's recommendations remain on paper only. To date, the CAEFS reports show that women, and in particular Aboriginal women, continue to be placed in high security environments. Administrative segregation continues to be overused with devastating effects on the well-being of these prisoners.[28] In addition, the work of the OCI, discussed later in this chapter, shows that issues such as women's conditions of confinement and the use of segregation have not improved, and the law thus continues to be disregarded on these and other matters.

Worse, activists noted the CSC's tendency to pick and choose the recommendations that serve its set agenda. For example, during the Harper government years (2006–2015), the popular "tough-on-crime" agenda was pushed forward, and prison policies were taken to reflect it. Ivan Zinger, then executive director of the OCI, criticized the fact that the recommendations informing CSC policies originated from committees supporting the government's agenda.[29] For example, in 2007, a

---

23 *Ibid* at 395–432.

24 Maxwell Yalden, *Human Rights and Corrections: A Strategic Project* (Ottawa: CSC, 1997).

25 House of Commons, Standing Committee on Justice and Human Rights, *A Work in Progress: The Corrections and Conditional Release Act* (Ottawa: Public Works and Government Services Canada, 2000) [*A Work in Progress*].

26 Therese Lajeunesse et al, *Cross Gender Monitoring Project, Third and Final Annual Report*, submitted to the Correctional Service of Canada (Ottawa: CSC, 2000).

27 Canadian Human Rights Commission, *Protecting Their Rights: A Systemic Review of Human Rights in Correctional Services for Federally Sentenced Women* (Ottawa: CHRC, 2003), online: https://www.chrc-ccdp.gc.ca/eng/content/protecting-their-rights-systemic-review-human-rights-correctional-services-federally.

28 See the annual reports of the Canadian Association of Elizabeth Fry Societies, online: http://www.caefs.ca/feature/annual-report/.

29 Ivan Zinger, "Human Rights and Federal Corrections: A Commentary on a Decade of Tough on Crime Policies in Canada" (2016) 58:4 CJCCJ 609, https://doi.org/10.3138/cjccj.2016.E06 [Zinger, "Human Rights and Federal Corrections"].

CSC review panel produced a report called *A Roadmap to Strengthen Public Safety*[30] (Sampson Report), which presented a skewed profile of the prison population (which was allegedly becoming increasingly dangerous) and thus justified increased security measures. The findings were discredited in 2009 by the Jackson and Stewart report[31] and by numerous OCI findings to the contrary.[32] For example, the Sampson Report did not note the increase in the number of vulnerable (that is, older or mentally ill) prisoners.[33] Nonetheless, the government has consistently used that report to justify its security-based decisions. The recommendations of the Sampson Report are also in stark contrast to the findings of previous task forces, such as the TFFSW and the Arbour Commission. Struthers Montford noted that *A Roadmap* is a gender-neutral document that essentially cancels the women-centred correctional recommendations made a decade prior by the TFFSW[34] and reinforces the use of increased security instead of a more supportive environment. Still, the government chose to implement the Sampson recommendations despite claiming that the *Creating Choices* goals are still at the centre of its policies.

Confronted with this pattern, it is not surprising that the participants in my study conveyed doubt regarding the success of my or anyone else's recommendations to change current policies and decisions, and introduce adequate health care services, infrastructure, and programming for senior inmates.

> It's not that they purposefully harm us. It's just indifference on their part for our fate. That's hard to fix. (AB, 53, in prison 9 years)

Office of the Correctional Investigator

> In the almost twenty years since I have been in prison, I called the Correctional Investigator many times, mostly for health care services concerns. Nothing ever happened, nothing ever changed. (AE, 57, in prison 17 years)

---

30 CSC Review Panel, *A Roadmap to Strengthening Public Safety*, Catalogue No. PS84-14/2007E (Ottawa: Public Works and Government Services Canada, 2007).

31 Michael Jackson & Graham Stewart, *A Flawed Compass: A Human Rights Analysis of a Roadmap to Strengthening Public Safety* (2009), online: http://www.justicebehindthewalls.net/resources/news/flawed_Compass.pdf.

32 See e.g. Canada, Office of the Correctional Investigator, *Annual Report, 2009–2010* (Ottawa: OCI, 2010) at 51, online: http://www.oci-bec.gc.ca/cnt/rpt/pdf/annrpt/annrpt20092010-eng.pdf [OCI 2009–2010].

33 Zinger, "Human Rights and Federal Corrections," *supra* note 29 at 8.

34 Struthers Montford, *supra* note 12, at 288.

As mentioned, the government mandates investigations by task forces or commissions, but they generally take place in response to specific events, which raises significant doubts about the CSC's commitment to the law. The Arbour Commission, for example, was called after excessive force was used against women. Task forces have also been struck in response to continued pressure or threats of legal action from scholars and activists, as was the case with the TFFSW and the Task Force on Administrative Segregation.

In order to identify violations in a timely manner, however, external monitoring of the CSC's activity needs to happen on an ongoing basis. Canada has a federal prison ombudsman, the Correctional Investigator, tasked with monitoring how prisoners' rights are being respected and enforced behind bars. The Office of the Correctional Investigator is a governmental agency, independent from the CSC, which makes regular assessments of how prisoners' rights are being upheld. The OCI was created in 1973 as a result of the riots that took place at Kingston Penitentiary in which eighteen officers were killed and parts of the institution itself were destroyed. After the riot, prisoners were transferred to Millhaven Penitentiary, where eighty-six of them were assaulted by correctional officers as retribution. A royal commission of inquiry was appointed to look into these events, and, based on its recommendations, the OCI was created to oversee the correctional system and improve accountability.[35]

The OCI's mandate can be found in the *CCRA*,[36] which confirmed OCI's access to correctional institutions and the CSC's obligation to respond to all OCI reports.[37] The OCI is directly responsible to the Minister of Public Safety, the same minister in charge of the CSC. The OCI has discretion regarding its investigation and can review CSC policies and procedures associated with individual complaints, based on notice from an individual, the Minister of Public Safety, or on its own initiative.[38] The OCI also has the power to review everything from policy to operational decision-making by staff,[39] and its interventions have a double purpose. On one hand, the OCI attempts to bring redress to the individual by negotiating at the institutional level. On the other hand,

---

35 Howard Sapers & Ivan Zinger, "The Ombudsman as a Monitor of Human Rights in Canadian Federal Corrections" (2010) 50:5 Pace L Rev 1511 at 1517–18 [Sapers & Zinger].

36 *CCRA, supra* note 1, ss 157–96.

37 CSC's historic passivity regarding the OCI's policy recommendations is documented by Jackson, *Justice Behind the Walls, supra* note 22 at 576–83.

38 *CCRA, supra* note 1, s 170 (1)–(2).

39 *Ibid,* s 167.

starting from the complaints, it can identify systemic issues and make corresponding recommendations.

Sapers and Zinger described the process the OCI goes through in addressing a complaint. First, the OCI attempts to deal with the complaint at an institutional level. If that fails, it moves up to the regional and national levels. If that fails as well, it presents the Commissioner of the CSC with a report. If, in OCI's opinion, the Commissioner does not properly address the matter, the OCI will send the matter to the Minister of Public Safety and, through the minister, to Parliament. The OCI may also include the matter in one of its annual or special focus reports.[40] The *CCRA* ensures that the OCI has unlimited and direct access to information for its investigations, from premises to files to witnesses.[41] For example, Sapers and Zinger report that for the year 2008–2009, the OCI resolved 2,000 complaints through "immediate response" (that is, information, assistance, or referral), and over 4,000 resulted in an inquiry or investigation.[42]

The enhanced access to information on the ground presents a great advantage for the OCI's investigations. Its power extends to complaints that perhaps would not find their way to a court. However, the OCI's redress power is limited to non-binding recommendations to the CSC or to Parliament. Compliance with such recommendations is instead dictated by the agency's moral force and standing. The OCI's investigations have resulted in numerous public reports that provide valuable inside information to citizens. The reports also contributed, over time, to pressuring the CSC to improve some of its policies.

Unfortunately, not unlike the attitude towards recommendations coming from task forces and commissions, the CSC's attitude towards OCI's reports is historically defensive and resistant. In his book, *Justice Behind the Walls*, Michael Jackson provides an early history of the uneasy relationship between the OCI and the CSC.[43] The first OCI report came out in 1973–1974, and, as early as 1978, the OCI published criticism of how the CSC responded to its recommendations. Specifically, the OCI noted the wardens' and the Commissioner's tendencies to back their own staff at any cost, "a practice which makes the job of the Correctional Investigator more difficult than it should be."[44] From then on, each report of the

---

40 Sapers & Zinger, *supra* note 35 at 1520.

41 *CCRA, supra* note 1, s 172.

42 Sapers & Zinger, *supra* note 35 at 1521.

43 Jackson, *Justice Behind the Walls, supra* note 22 at 576–81.

44 Canada, Office of the Correctional Investigator, *Annual Report, 1977–1978* (Ottawa: OCI) at 3, as cited in Jackson, *Justice Behind the Walls, supra* note 22 at 576.

OCI contained criticisms regarding how the CSC implements the OCI's chief recommendations, including recommendations on double bunking, the grievance procedure, treatment of women, and administrative segregation.[45]

When faced with the growing needs of elderly prisoners, the CSC's track record is of equal concern. For the last few years, the OCI has documented the increasingly pressing needs of elderly prisoners. While this issue is newer compared to some of the outstanding problems it previously raised, the response to aging-related recommendations thus far has been consistently unsatisfactory. In its 2010–2011 report, the OCI recommended, for the first time, the creation of appropriate accommodations for elderly prisoners, appropriate programs and medical treatment, staff trained in gerontology and palliative care, and adequate release programs.[46] The CSC responses to these recommendations were of the following nature:

> OCI RECOMMENDATION 6: *I recommend that the Service develop a more appropriate range of programming and activities tailored to the older offender, including physical fitness and exercise regimes, as well as other interventions that are responsive to the unique mobility, learning, assistive and independent living needs of the elderly inmate.*
>
> CSC RESPONSE: Upon admission, all older offenders and those with self-care needs undergo a functional assessment, which measures their ability to perform daily living activities. Results of this assessment influence further

---

45   See e.g. Canada, Office of the Correctional Investigator, *Annual Report, 1984–1985* (Ottawa: Supply and Services Canada, 1985) at 19–20, as cited in Jackson, *Justice Behind the Walls, supra* note 22 at 578; Canada, Office of the Correctional Investigator, *Annual Report, 1994–1995* (Ottawa: Supply and Services, 1995) at 57, as cited in Jackson, *Justice Behind the Walls, supra* note 22 at 581; Canada, Office of the Correctional Investigator, "Shifting the Orbit: Human Rights, Independent Review and Accountability in the Canadian Corrections System," Discussion Paper by Todd Sloan (Ottawa: OCI, 2004), online: http://www.oci-bec.gc.ca/cnt/rpt/pdf/oth-aut/oth-aut20040629-eng.pdf [OCI, "Shifting the Orbit"]; Canada, Office of the Correctional Investigator, "A Preventable Death" (Ottawa: OCI, 2008) at 22, 25, online: http://www.oci-bec.gc.ca/cnt/rpt/pdf/oth-aut/oth-aut20080620-eng.pdf [OCI, "A Preventable Death"]; Canada, Office of the Correctional Investigator, *Annual Report, 2013–2014* (Ottawa: OCI, 2014) at 19, online: http://www.oci-bec.gc.ca/cnt/rpt/pdf/annrpt/annrpt20132014-eng.pdf [OCI 2013–2014]; Canada, Office of the Correctional Investigator, *Annual Report, 2014–2015* (Ottawa: OCI, 2015) at 26, online: http://www.oci-bec.gc.ca/cnt/rpt/pdf/annrpt/annrpt20142015-eng.pdf [OCI 2014–2015].

46   Canada, Office of the Correctional Investigator, *Annual Report, 2010–2011* (Ottawa: OCI, 2011) at 25, online: http://www.oci-bec.gc.ca/cnt/rpt/pdf/annrpt/annrpt20102011-eng.pdf [OCI 2010–2011].

health related consultations as well as special needs for accommodation and services. Throughout the inmate's sentence he/she is assessed in terms of their ability to function in their environment.

OCI RECOMMENDATION 9: *I recommend that the Service prepare a national older offender strategy for 2011–12 that includes a geriatric release component as well as enhanced post-release supports.*
CSC RESPONSE: CSC will continue to implement the framework that is already in place to ensure appropriate release planning for offenders, including geriatric offenders. As part of the planning process, when indicated, a functional assessment is completed by health care services and identified areas of concern are taken into consideration in the development of an individualized release plan. For example, a functional assessment might suggest the need for a certain type of accommodation.[47]

Since then, the challenges presented by older prisoners and the little corresponding progress made by the CSC have been addressed in OCI reports with regularity.

The Service's overall response to my findings and six recommendations is both contradictory and disappointing. The CSC appears satisfied that a functional health care assessment of individual inmates aged 50 and over is sufficient; there are no plans to move forwards with developing a comprehensive, integrated national older offender strategy. The health and safety concerns of aging inmates detailed in the report, including victimization, mobility and assistive living needs, learning, correctional and vocational programming and palliative care, do not appear to be a priority.[48]
   My 2010–11 Annual Report contained a special focus on the issues and challenges facing aging/older offenders in federal prisons. At that time, the older offender population (age 50 and older) represented fewer than 20 per cent of the total inmate population. Today, the proportion of the inmate population over the age of 50 is just under 25 per cent, an overall increase of nearly one-third in the last five years alone ... As these trends accelerate and intensify, the Service is struggling to keep pace with their implications.[49]

---

47 Correctional Service of Canada, "Response of the Correctional Service of Canada to the 38th Annual Report of the Correctional Investigator 2010–2011" (Ottawa: CSC, 2011), online: https://www.csc-scc.gc.ca/publications/ci10-11/index-eng.shtml.
48 Canada, Office of the Correctional Investigator, *Annual Report, 2011–2012* (Ottawa: OCI, 2012) at 26, online: http://www.oci-bec.gc.ca/cnt/rpt/pdf/annrpt/annrpt20112012-eng.pdf [OCI 2011–2012].
49 OCI 2014–2015, *supra* note 45 at 10.

As I have previously reported, the rising number of natural cause and/or premature death behind bars requires answers and some clear public policy direction. Federal penitentiaries were never intended to serve as hospitals or hospices. The Office continues to believe that there are better, safer and less costly options in managing an age cohort that poses the least risk to public safety yet is among the most expensive to incarcerate.[50]

There are various reasons for the CSC's historic non-responsiveness to external recommendations. Zinger, the current correctional investigator, recently identified a number of reasons based on both the CSC responses to reports and the general political environment.[51] As such, he suggested that a tough-on-crime and alarmist agenda brings votes, and this agenda is often incompatible with a thorough protection of human rights. He also stated that, in accordance with such a view and regardless of evidence to the contrary as to its efficiency, the CSC disproportionately invests in security to the detriment of other more rehabilitative and therapeutic programs that can assist prisoners.[52] Also, when austerity measures are taken, cuts are made to sectors other than security and salaries.[53] The disproportionate emphasis on security originates from skewed prisoner profiles (for example, it is said that the number of violent offenders has increased, but the increase in the number of vulnerable prisoners is ignored),[54] from aging infrastructure that makes it difficult to supervise prisoners in a more relaxed manner,[55] and from a reluctance to endorse new technology in areas other than security.[56] In addition, the CSC continues to emphasize the use of weapons and physical force in its officers' training rather than people skills and moving the officers towards a more dynamic and engaged security system.[57]

Corrections is a particularly difficult area in which to exercise oversight and to hold individuals or groups accountable. It would be tempting to conclude that these mechanisms do not work properly and to settle for what they can do, without further pushing for strengthening their oversight role. However, as Zinger suggested, oversight mechanisms such as

---

50 Canada, Office of the Correctional Investigator, *Annual Report, 2015–2016* (Ottawa: OCI, 2016) at 12, online: http://www.oci-bec.gc.ca/cnt/rpt/pdf/annrpt/annrpt20152016-eng.pdf [OCI 2015–2016].

51 Zinger, "Human Rights and Federal Corrections," *supra* note 29 at 10–13.

52 *Ibid* at 8.

53 *Ibid.*

54 *Ibid* at 10–13.

55 *Ibid* at 13.

56 *Ibid* at 14.

57 *Ibid* at 11.

the OCI are most needed at full strength in an environment where politicians tend to capitalize on tough-on-crime agendas regardless of their impact on public safety and where a culture of disrespect for the law and repeat human rights violations reigns.[58]

Where To?

Enhancing OCI's Oversight Strength

As I have endeavoured to show in this book, a gap exists between what aging prisoners require by way of health care and the currently available prison services. Faced with novel information, the CSC, as the power delegated by the government, should be the organization to act on the information and adjust its policies accordingly.

It must be noted that the OCI began addressing the issue of aging seven years ago, when the problem was less acute. Unfortunately, its recommendations have been largely ignored. This type of response is characteristic of how the CSC deals with both the OCI and with recommendations from other governmental or non-governmental inquiries. As mentioned, the issues identified in the 1970s, 1980s, and 1990s continue to fill the pages of recent reports. Unfortunately, aging prisoners, like those interviewed for this study, do not have time to wait for policy changes, and their number continues to increase at a rapid rate.

When envisioning ways in which policy reform for the elderly can be achieved, I agree with those who support the activities of the OCI and of different task forces and commissions. Their work is crucial in ensuring that democratic values are upheld behind bars and throughout the reform process. Their examinations allow us to identify issues that would otherwise be far from the public eye. However, the authority of such agencies, especially of the OCI, needs to be strengthened. As it stands, the OCI is not always effective, and its ability to produce real change in the lives of individuals like this study's participants is questionable. This ineffectiveness is not the fault of the OCI itself, but, rather, the way it is set up, the limitations of its mandate, and the flaws in our democratic system that have been perpetuated by the government and Parliament's attitude towards external prison oversight.

Parkes and Pate explain in their study that, for an oversight mechanism to be functional, it needs to be truly independent, accessible to prisoners, and have the power to order meaningful and enforceable remedies.[59] The

---

58 Zinger, "Human Rights Compliance," *supra* note 19 at 127.
59 Parkes & Pate, *supra* note 4 at 267.

OCI appears to be accessible to prisoners, but its independence limitations and its inability to enforce its recommendations seriously detract from its efficiency. Some immediate steps should be taken, then, to ensure that this prison oversight mechanism has the ability to protect human rights in prison and that its recommendations lead to meaningful reform.

First, the OCI needs greater independence in accordance with its role as a prison ombudsman. Currently, the OCI is responsible to and only has access to Parliament through the Minister of Public Safety. Without the minister's support, the OCI cannot make representations to either the House of Commons or the Senate. However, the Minister of Public Safety is also the minister responsible for federal corrections. While the two governmental agencies are separate, the same minister is in charge of both bodies, which significantly affects their perceived independence and the work that they do. The Minister of Public Safety has a history of not getting involved in the relationship between the OCI and the CSC, and the minister is thus often highly deferential to the decisions made by the Commissioner of the CSC. The minister has never pressured the CSC to respond positively to the OCI's recommendations or to reform CSC policies, even when they were ostensibly illegal.[60] This deferential stance is hardly surprising, as the policies the OCI often criticizes are, in fact, supported by governmental policies. It is unlikely that a minister would take action against the government's own interests. These examples illustrate why someone in charge of an agency cannot also be in charge of the organization that monitors that agency's compliance with the law.

In 2000, the House of Commons Standing Committee on Justice and Human Rights conducted the *CCRA* five-year review. The CSC's non-compliance with the OCI's recommendations was a central issue. Sensing the little support that the OCI received from the then Solicitor General and Parliament, the committee recommended that the OCI simultaneously submit its reports to the Solicitor General, Parliament, and the Standing Committee on Justice and Human Rights.[61] The Solicitor General flatly rejected the proposal.

Considering that in the years since 2000, the Minister of Public Safety (formerly called the Solicitor General) has not been more impartial or supportive of the OCI's work, there is no longer room for compromise. To preserve its independence, the OCI should be responsible to Parliament alone and no longer be under the supervision of the Minister of Public Safety. Keeping the current relationship between the ombudsman and Parliament indirect is counter-productive and significantly limits the

---

60 See e.g. OCI, "Shifting the Orbit," *supra* note 45 at 21.
61 *A Work in Progress, supra* note 25.

information exchange between the two institutions, as well as the OCI's ability to plead for parliamentary accountability and interventions that could shift illegal government policies.

Second, the OCI needs further tools to help enforce its recommendations, especially when these pertain to illegal practices. Some reform in the legal status of the OCI would thus be beneficial. The OCI could be granted the authority to create two types of rulings: a set of recommendations for good practices and a set of mandatory and binding "recommendations." Thus, where the OCI finds human rights violations by policies and procedures, it should have the authority to require that the CSC change them. To respect the CSC's delegated power, the OCI could also make non-mandatory recommendations as to the direction the reform should take, but ultimately allow the CSC to decide how the reform would look as long as it brings the policies back under the law. This way, the impact of the OCI investigations would be of significant consequence for human rights.

Third, the OCI should be given standing to bring cases to court. It often happens that individual complaints receive no resolution because of the CSC's refusal to work with the OCI. Also, recommendations pertaining to serious systemic issues are often not implemented. In such cases, the OCI, either on behalf of a prisoner or on its own initiative, should be able to request a court to rule on the legality of the CSC's decisions or policies. Unlike the OCI's recommendations, court decisions are much easier to enforce. The OCI's access to court would also address part of other task forces' and commissions' problems with the CSC's non-responsiveness. The OCI has often supported and replicated the findings of independent commissions of inquiry and monitored the implementation of their recommendations. By adopting third party commissions' findings as its own, the OCI would be able to challenge in court the refusal of the CSC to comply with the recommendations of those commissions.

Alternatively, a specialized administrative tribunal could be created to resolve conflicts between the OCI and the CSC, and rule on a policy's legality where the two institutions do not agree. This suggestion is not new: in 1996 the Correctional Investigator himself suggested that a specialized administrative tribunal could mediate this relationship. According to the Correctional Investigator, the tribunal would be created with the following attributes:

a [...] with the authority to compel the Correctional Service compliance with legislation and policy governing the administration of the sentence and to redress the adverse effects of non-compliance, and

b that access to the tribunal be provided for in those instances where if within a reasonable time after receiving a recommendation from the Correctional Investigator pursuant to s. 179 of the *Corrections and Conditional Release Act*, the Commissioner of Corrections takes no action that is seen as adequate or appropriate.[62]

Michael Jackson supported this OCI recommendation, arguing that a specialized tribunal, or a specialized division of an existing tribunal (for example, the Canadian Human Rights Tribunal), would develop specialized expertise in both administrative and judicial remedies relevant to the correctional system; be able to render enforceable decisions; and have the authority to deal with both individual complaints and systemic issues. Given the significant limitations of the internal grievance procedure discussed in the next chapter, Jackson also took the OCI's recommendation a step further. He proposed that, while the main focus of the tribunal would be to deal with unresolved issues originating from the OCI's statutory mandate, prisoners should also be able to bring forward claims directly if they are of general interest to prisoners.[63] In the years since that recommendation, the CSC's attitude has only reinforced the need for a court or a specialized tribunal to mediate the relationship between the OCI and the CSC. Without such an institution, the OCI's recommendations will continue to be practically unenforceable, and the CSC will continue to ignore them with impunity.

OPCAT Ratification as a Framework for Oversight Reform

Many of the previously proposed reforms to the Canadian oversight mechanisms, and especially to the OCI, could be achieved through Canada's signing of the United Nations (UN) *Optional Protocol*[64] *to the Convention against Torture* (OPCAT).[65]

The OPCAT created an international prison oversight mechanism, the Subcommittee for the Prevention of Torture (SPT), with a mandate to visit national places of detention in the state members and draft annual recommendations for each state. Its recommendations are based on the rights protected by the *Convention against Torture*, crucial in ensuring

---

62 Canada, Office of the Correctional Investigator, *Annual Report, 1995–1996* (Ottawa: OCI, 1996) at 2. The same proposal was made almost a decade later in OCI, "Shifting the Orbit," *supra* note 45 at 32.

63 Jackson, *Justice Behind the Walls*, *supra* note 22 at 587–8.

64 *Optional Protocol to the Convention against Torture and Other Cruel, Inhuman or Degrading Treatment or Punishment*, UNGA A/Res/57/199, 2002 [OPCAT].

65 *Convention Against Torture and Other Cruel, Inhuman or Degrading Treatment or Punishment*, 10 December 1984, 1465 UNTS (entered into force 26 June 1987, ratification by Canada 24 July 1987) [CAT].

the basic well-being of incarcerated individuals. Despite having ratified the *Convention*, Canada has not signed the OPCAT. In 2016, the government announced that Canada had begun the process of ratifying the OPCAT.[66] However, three years later, at the time this book went to press, there was uncertainty regarding the progress Canada has made towards that ratification.[67]

The OPCAT came into force in 2006 and has been signed by about one-third of the countries party to the *Convention against Torture*.[68] It lays out a two-tier monitoring system to be implemented in all state members. One tier is comprised of an international mechanism, the SPT. The second tier is formed by a national preventive mechanism (NPM), which would function as a national independent institution and receive training and advice from the SPT.[69]

In addition to the structure, what is unique about the system is the philosophy behind its operations. Unlike most other regional mechanisms, the SPT and corresponding NPMs are not set up to receive complaints of inhuman treatment behind bars or to respond to human rights violations. Rather, their goal is to make visits to places of detention and, based on these visits, to advise and make recommendations for measures that would help prevent such violations.[70] Thus, what the OPCAT essentially does through its mechanisms is offer a way to translate human rights into action, and adds meaning to the states' prevention obligations under the *Convention against Torture*.[71] Thus, signing the OPCAT has a powerful symbolic significance in terms of commitment to the values promoted by the international documents.[72]

The OPCAT also has practical benefits for human rights protections. The duties of the SPT are thus to visit detention places in member states,

---

66 Canadian Civil Liberties Association, "Canada to Join Critical Anti-torture Protocol" (3 May 2016), online: https://ccla.org/canada-to-join-critical-anti-torture-protocol.

67 Canada OPCAT Project, "Canada's OPCAT Progress to Come under Renewed UN Scrutiny" (October 2018), online: https://canadaopcatproject.ca/2018/10/12/committee-against-torture-shadow-briefing-paper.

68 Rachel Murray et al, *The Optional Protocol to the UN Convention Against Torture* (New York: Oxford University Press, 2011) at 163.

69 Christine Bicknell & Malcolm Evans, "Monitoring Prisons: The Increasingly Complex Relationships Between International and Domestic Frameworks" in Tom Daems & Luc Robert, eds, *Europe in Prisons: Assessing the Impact of European Institutions on National Prison Systems* (London: Palgrave Macmillan, 2017) 11 at 12 [Bicknell & Evans].

70 *Ibid* at 15.

71 See *CAT, supra* note at 65, arts 2, 3, 16. For a full list of what the states' obligations are, see Natalie Pierce, "Implementing Human Rights in Closed Environments: The OPCAT Framework and the New Zealand Experience" (2014) 31 Law Context: A Socio-Legal J 154 at 170–1 [Pierce].

72 Pierce, *supra* note 71 at 162.

make recommendations for improving conditions of detention, ensure cooperation with other international mechanisms for human rights protection, assist with the creation of NPMs, and continue to work with and assist NPMs.[73] The NPM in most countries is built on an ombudsman plus model, which means that the agency is attached to existing independent prison monitoring agencies (the Office of the Correctional Investigator in Canada, for example). In this way, the powers of the existing ombudsman are enlarged in order to have the legal capacity mandated by the OPCAT. The NPM's function can be fulfilled within the pre-existing agency either through a discrete office or by being dispersed across the agency. Some jurisdictions have had to create different bodies within an agency in order to deal with both federal and regional levels.[74]

Though still in its early days, the system has proven efficient. The OPCAT's two-tier system reflects local structures and requires a uniform level of human rights protections. Because the NPMs are local, they have more access to local prisons than an international body would and are mindful of the idiosyncrasies within the jurisdiction in which they function. On the other hand, the NPMs benefit from training and advice from the SPT. Unlike a local agency, the SPT draws examples from similar jurisdictions, accumulates best practices from around the world, and, through its continuous dialogue with NPMs and states, enables pragmatic solutions.[75]

Countries that have signed the OPCAT have provided positive feedback overall. A study conducted across member states reported that countries with a strong commitment to human rights or pre-existing regional mechanisms were more likely to have ratified the OPCAT. Also, countries acknowledged that their record of human rights abuses among prisoners was instrumental in their decision to ratify the OPCAT, which was seen as a way to gain knowledge and strategies to solve the problem.[76] A number of other reasons for ratification were mentioned: developed countries wanted to set an example and encourage other countries to sign; some countries mentioned not wanting to be or be perceived as complacent in the fight against torture; some countries pointed out their desire to promote an international standard for the fight against torture; some countries invoked the history of past abuses and their desire for future protection; and many countries noted their desire to focus on ways to ensure durable prevention that can stand through the different governments that may come and go.[77] In terms of

---

73 Murray et al, *supra* note 68 at 90.
74 Bicknell & Evans, *supra* note 69 at 14–15.
75 Murray et al, *supra* note 68 at 172–3.
76 *Ibid* at 166.
77 *Ibid* at 168–9.

effects, studies in New Zealand noted that, from the 2013–2014 report written by the local NPM, sixty-five out of eighty recommendations had been fully implemented, and, upon its following visit, the SPT found that New Zealand was doing well in terms of human rights in detention places. The study noted that the OPCAT system forced the government to update its list of places of detention and make information about all of them publicly available, ensuring a uniform standard of conditions of confinement in all of those places. The study noted that the visits of the STP and the NPM acted as a deterrent for bad governmental behaviour and encouraged more commitment and investigative dialogue between different actors engaged in corrections.[78]

Another New Zealand study, completed five years after the country signed the OPCAT, noted that the strength of oversight was significantly increased and the strength of the pre-existing oversight mechanism was enhanced. An identified advantage was the guideline and self-assessment tool provided to the local NPM (built within an existing oversight mechanism) by the SPT. This guideline allowed the local agency to evaluate its own performance in terms of strategies, visit planning, prevention of reprisals, constitutional and legal issues, systematizing experiences, and annual reports. These factors led to notable improvements to custody conditions and treatment, and to policies and practices, through independent but constructive relations with the detention agencies.[79]

In the United Kingdom, the NPM was also attached to the pre-existing local oversight mechanisms, Her Majesty's Inspectorate of Prisons (HMIP). While concerns had been raised regarding how the two would manage to work together, recent studies have noted that this coordination adds a level of complexity and forces the institutions to collaborate. Even though the relationship between the institutions is often uncomfortable and unclear, seemingly, this uncomfortable dynamic has led to increased vigilance and greater accountability.[80]

In relatively short order, the OPCAT has become a symbol for a country's dedication to implementing human rights in its detention centres. Countries that have ratified the OPCAT have been shown to have

---

78 Judy McGregor, "The Challenges and Limitations of OPCAT National Preventive Mechanisms: Lessons from New Zealand" (2017) 23:3 Austl J H R 351 at 356–7.

79 Pierce, *supra* note 71 at 203–4.

80 Nicola Padfield, "Monitoring Prisons in England and Wales: Who Ensures the Fair Treatment of Prisoners?" (2017) 70:1 Crime Law Soc Change 57, online: https://doi.org/10.1007/s10611-017-9719-x. See also Anne Owers, "Comparative Experiences of Implementing Human Rights in Closed Environments: Monitoring for Rights Protection" (2014) 31 Law Context: A Socio-Legal J 209.

higher awareness of shortcomings and a desire to improve, as well as a robust history of already utilizing oversight mechanisms. Thus, the fact that Canada has not signed the OPCAT, despite being a signatory to the *Convention against Torture*, is telling. Committing to the values without committing to the means of implementing those values amounts to very little. Also, in practical terms, some evidence shows that the OPCAT, through its two-tier system, leads to an enhancement of the local oversight mechanisms. Thus, creating an NPM within or affiliated to the OCI that benefited from the SPT's advice and training would create a stronger system of independent supervision, which may help overcome some of the current issues facing the OCI. The OCI itself has repeatedly affirmed[81] that signing the OPCAT would be a significant step – both symbolically and practically – in the advancement of prisoners' rights.[82]

Conclusion

As Zinger has argued, the more enclosed an environment is, the more a government stands to gain from its tough-on-crime policies (regardless of their actual impact on public safety), and the longer its history of human rights violations, the greater is the need for enhanced external supervision and oversight.[83]

The CSC's refusal to allow for substantial oversight and implement external recommendations from stakeholders, including the statutorily mandated Office of the Correctional Investigator, makes it extremely difficult for meaningful policy reforms to occur without substantial external intervention. This situation is particularly worrisome for older prisoners who need significant reform. Under these circumstances, substantial and sustainable prison reforms meant to advance the protection of incarcerated individuals in general, and older prisoners in particular, need to include a reform of the oversight mechanisms, particularly of the OCI's role and powers. The recommendations provided in this chapter are thus a starting point to strengthen both external oversight and accountability in Canadian prisons. In addition, a good way to ensure

---

81 Zinger, "Human Rights Compliance," *supra* note 19 at 136–7; Sapers & Zinger, *supra* note 35 at 1527–8; Canada, Office of the Correctional Investigator, *Annual Report, 2007–2008* (Ottawa: OCI, 2008) at 45, online: http://www.oci-bec.gc.ca/cnt/rpt/pdf/annrpt/annrpt20072008-eng.pdf.

82 For the importance of an international oversight prison mechanism based on a convention, see e.g. Sandra Lehalle, Pierre Landreville, & Jean-Paul Céré, "Le Comité européen de prévention de la torture: Mécanisme de contrôle des établissements de détention" (2006) 48:2 CJCCJ 223, https://doi.org/10.3138/cjccj.48.2.223.

83 Zinger, "Human Rights Compliance," *supra* note 19 at 135.

such strengthening and to implement many of the reforms would be to ratify the OPCAT and implement its two-tier oversight mechanism.

However, one should not simply wait for such oversight mechanisms to transform the CSC into an open and collaborative institution. As was the case two decades ago, Justice Arbour's words still ring true: "[T]here is little hope that the Rule of Law will implement itself in the correctional culture without assistance and control from the Parliament and the courts."[84] Thus, to bring the CSC under the rule of law, substantial prisoner access to tribunals and courts must be improved. This topic will be addressed in the next two chapters.

---

84   Arbour Report, *supra* note 17 at 182.

Chapter Five

Correcting Wrongs and Pushing for Reform through Administrative Boards and Tribunals

In this chapter I review the different administrative actions that elderly incarcerated individuals could use to claim their rights before an administrative board or tribunal, as well as their option to challenge the decisions of these agencies in court. I will look at the current limitations of such actions, the (still) deferential attitude of courts towards the administration of prisons, and the potential of certain actions, when successful, to bring about both individual and systemic redress and correct that which the government refuses to do.

Three avenues will be discussed in particular: the internal grievance procedure, which is guaranteed by the *Corrections and Conditional Release Act* (*CCRA*) and its related regulation, the *Correctional and Conditional Release Regulations* (*CCRR*), and generally needs to be exhausted before a prisoner has access to the courts; the judicial review in the Federal Court of decisions made based on the grievance process; and the complaint process before the Canadian Human Rights Commission and Tribunal, based on the *Canadian Human Rights Act* (*CHRA*). What the administrative avenues have in common is that, when working, they can provide significant relief for a range of violations, they are free of charge, and they do not require a high level of legal knowledge. On paper at least, these avenues appear more accessible to applicants than court proceedings.

The Internal Administrative Grievance Procedure

The more you complain, the more they [the officers] hate you. And they can make your life really hard. (AB, 53, in prison 9 years)

Status Quo

Once John finished detailing his problems and the difficulties he had in accessing health services or medical devices, I asked him: "So what do you do when you can't obtain what you need?" He said:

> Well, each inmate has what's called a CO2, like a copper [officer] who is responsible directly for that prisoner. Like a parole officer but for problems in prison. They say if I have problems I need to take them to the CO2. Yeah, that doesn't do any good. My CO2 doesn't care. I rarely even see him. It's really just a title, he doesn't do anything. And then I can talk to my parole officer. I actually see my parole officer because I have scheduled appointments. And if I want an appointment I can generally get one. My previous parole officer at Frontenac was great, very helpful. She got me the day parole when my wife passed. This one now is useless. When I told her I can't get my knee braces and I can't stand at work without them, she said, "How old are you? I am your parole officer, not your baby sitter."

I asked him what's next. After he talks to all these people and he still does not get what he needs or he feels that he has been wronged, what does he do?

> Nothing. I am in prison, what can I do? ... Well, I guess I can write a complaint ... Shit lot of good that would do.

I started asking him about the complaint system. Like most other prisoners I talked to, John was well acquainted with the prison grievance system. Prisoners have forms they can fill out when they have an issue or a complaint. Once completed, grievance forms are reviewed by the warden. John said that prisoners have access to legislation and if they want, they can say "that this and that in the legislation was not respected. Some people spend a lot of time writing those complaints. Doesn't matter. It's not like someone reads them."

John said that in the decades he had been in prison, he had written a number of formal complaints in different institutions. He said that not once had anything been solved. He could not remember everything he complained about, but he recalled the more recent issues: not being allowed to visit his dying wife and not receiving pillows to help with his circulation problems. John said that it took a very long time to hear back. In fact, he received the answer to his day pass request over one year after he filed it, by which time his wife had already passed. He was unsure what happened to the pillow request. John said all he wanted now was to be released, so he did not bother with complaining anymore. He mentioned that he used to be seen as a troublemaker, and he believed that label was partly because he had been more aggressive in writing complaints.

The grievance procedure is the main tool, together with the Office of the Correctional Investigator (OCI), for prisoners to challenge conditions of confinement and treatment. For the most part, prisoners do not have direct access to a court. Rather, for claims of non-compliance with prison law, such as *CCRA* provisions, prisoners must first exhaust the internal grievance process and then, if dissatisfied with the answer received from the Commissioner of the Correctional Service of Canada (CSC) at the last level of adjudication, they can challenge the decision in the Federal Court.

The grievance system is an internal administrative procedure that connects the individual with senior officials in the institution and potentially at the headquarters, and it allows for the prisoners to inform these officials of improper conditions in the institutions and breaches of prisoners' rights. It is an easy way to ensure that officers are held accountable and that prisoners' rights and entitlements are respected, as per legal and policy provisions. Unlike filing a complaint in court, the grievance procedure does not require any specific legal knowledge or legal representation, and it is free of charge.

The grievance procedure is regulated in the *CCRA*:

Grievance procedure

90 There shall be a procedure for fairly and expeditiously resolving offenders' grievances on matters within the jurisdiction of the Commissioner, and the procedure shall operate in accordance with the regulations made under paragraph 96(u).

Access to grievance procedure

91 Every offender shall have complete access to the offender grievance procedure without negative consequences.[1]

Further, the *CCRR* provides that when a prisoner is dissatisfied with the decision or action of a staff member, the prisoner may file a complaint with the staff supervisor. The supervisor should provide the prisoner with a written and reasoned response.[2] If the supervisor refuses to review the decision or the prisoner is dissatisfied with the answer, they may file a grievance with the head of the institution or the Commissioner

---

1   *Corrections and Conditional Release Act*, SC 1992, c 20, ss 91, 92 [*CCRA*].

2   *Corrections and Conditional Release Regulations*, SOR/92-620, s 74 [*CCRR*].

(if the prisoner is complaining about the head of the institution).[3] If dissatisfied with the decision of the head of the institution, the prisoner may complain to the Commissioner.[4] At all levels, the prisoner is entitled to written and reasoned responses.[5]

This administrative system is not unique to Canada. In fact, most jurisdictions have some form of grievance system. For instance, the state of California has an almost identical grievance system to the Canadian one: the prisoner must completely exhaust the administrative process before they have access to courts, and the process itself has three levels, from institutional to headquarters.[6] A recent comprehensive study of the Californian grievance process has been conducted by Calavita and Jenness, based on interviews with prisoners, officers, and other staff, as well as on reviews of grievances and responses to those grievances. In their analysis, a number of themes emerged in regard to how the grievances are received and replied to. For instance, most of the grievances were unsuccessful, even though the data suggested that the complaints were not frivolous.[7] Most prisoners in their study (73 per cent) had filed a grievance at least once, the leading grounds being living conditions and inadequate health care.[8]

Most prisoners feared retaliation from staff when filing a complaint.[9] The interviews with staff revealed that these fears were not unfounded, and they helped explain the low rate of success. Officers portrayed prisoners as "deceiving and instinctively and reflexively dishonest," liars, emotionally incapable of telling the truth, "hyper insecure," "with an instinctive ability to manipulate information."[10] The backlash against people filing grievances was consistent: they were seen as narcissistic, "they suffer and want others to suffer as well."[11] Officers complained that the number of grievances had got out of hand, that the grievances were frivolous: they maintained that prisoners complain because they can, "for attention or to buck the system."[12] A widespread view held that the person filing a complaint does not accept responsibility for the actions that landed them in prison, and people writing complaints are violating

---

3 *Ibid*, s 75.

4 *Ibid*, s 80.

5 *Ibid*, ss 74(3), 78, 80(3).

6 Kitty Calavita & Valerie Jenness, *Appealing to Justice: Prisoner Grievances, Rights, and Carceral Logic* (Oakland, CA: University of California Press, 2015) at 55–6.

7 *Ibid* at 130.

8 *Ibid* at 56.

9 *Ibid* at 75.

10 *Ibid* at 103.

11 *Ibid* at 104.

12 *Ibid* at 108.

the rules of prison logic.[13] The study found that inmate appeal decisions have repercussions in terms of medical treatment for prisoners, release dates, conditions of confinement, yard time, food quality, and the fulfilment of a variety of daily needs.[14] As the officers put it – complaining leads to the prisoner losing credibility.[15]

Calavita and Jenness's findings related to officers' attitudes help contextualize the experiences of those interviewed for my study. In turn, the latter are consistent with those of the prisoners interviewed by Calavita and Jenness.[16] In my study, of the 70 per cent who reported filing a grievance at one point or another during their stay in prison, less than 10 per cent reported some positive outcome as a result. Most participants said they complained about health care: delays, lack of medication or devices, refusal to be scheduled for an appointment with a specialist, and other similar issues. They also complained about the manner in which their families were treated when visiting and about spending long periods in administrative segregation. The waiting time for a response was between six months and two years.

Prisoners generally perceived the grievance process as futile, as something not taken seriously by authorities. As pointed out, Calavita and Jenness identified this perception as a major theme: officers themselves actually confirmed that they did not take grievances seriously.[17] The attitude of prisoners in my study towards the grievance procedure was well summarized by one participant:

> Everything in prison is going through the motions. Does anyone believe that filing a grievance will solve anything? No. Maybe in the beginning, but people who spent some time inside know better. Do people still make complaints? Of course. There isn't anything else you can do. Some people suck it up and do their time. When you're a lifer like myself, all I do is do my time. I don't know if I am getting out. So I file grievances just to remind them I am still here. They won't do anything for me, but at least they should remember I exist. (KK, 55, in prison 24 years)

Many hardened lifers, indeed, did not care much about consequences. However, consistent with the findings of Calavita and Jenness, a set of individuals did note that staff members are never supportive of prisoner

---

13 *Ibid* at 106.
14 *Ibid* at 120.
15 *Ibid* at 121.
16 *Ibid* at 63.
17 *Ibid* at 106–9.

grievances, that they are labelled "whiners" if they complain, and that this label often makes its way into their official files. *CCRA*'s guarantee of no negative consequences for those accessing the procedure, therefore, is not meaningful.

> Yes I filed grievances [because they wouldn't let me call my daughter]. Not anymore. They go on record and they come back to bite you. (DD, 52, in prison 5 years)

Some prisoners may make vexatious complaints. However, numerous prisoners, especially in the group I interviewed (like the ones Calavita and Jenness interviewed in California), have serious and urgent concerns about their health, both physical and mental. Their complaints are not frivolous. According to those I interviewed, not only do their complaints go unaddressed, they have not elicited so much as an acknowledgment that there is a deficiency inside the prison system. When you consider that some of these grievances constitute breaches of *CCRA* provisions, the implications of this practice are quite shocking.[18]

While the problems of the aging are somewhat novel to penitentiaries, their fairly recent emergence is not why the grievance system has failed this group. Rather, the grievance procedure has been systematically criticized by courts, scholars, and lawyers for decades and deemed incapable of holding the CSC accountable.[19]

In her 1996 report reviewing the events that took place at the Prison for Women (P4W) in Kingston in 1994, Justice Arbour also reviewed the effectiveness of the grievance procedure. Despite being reformed and given a new statutory basis in the *CCRA* in 1992, the procedure was harshly criticized in the report. Justice Arbour noted that all the events under review by her commission had been at one point on the desks of CSC staff in the form of grievances from the incarcerated women. Some of these complaints were never answered, even though they included serious allegations regarding the use of force, conditions in segregation, cross-gender search, body cavity search, and other such issues. Those who did receive an answer often faced unacceptably long delays and, in a number of cases, the responses they received came from an inappropriate person. There was also no system in place to prioritize the complaints according to their urgency, and even the urgent ones were caught in the net of bureaucracy. Arbour also criticized the prevailing

---

18 See discussion in chapter three.
19 Michael Jackson, *Justice Behind the Walls: Human Rights in Canadian Prisons* (Vancouver: Douglas & McIntyre, 2002) at 576–93.

practice by which senior officials and the Commissioner almost uncon-
ditionally sided with the officers against whom the complaint was made,
the inmate's version of events was always seen as doubtful, and admission
of error was regarded by the CSC as an admission of defeat.[20] Arbour
emphasized the importance of a functioning grievance system in maintaining the rights of prisoners, the rule of law, and the integrity of the
CSC. She suggested that all grievances be reviewed either directly by the
Commissioner or by an independent third party.[21]

Perhaps unsurprisingly, the Arbour recommendations were not implemented. In 2000, the OCI acknowledged that the CSC had failed
to implement the recommendations and that the grievance system was
still hampered by excessive delays and a lack of accountability from the
CSC.[22] In 2004, in its discussion paper "Shifting the Orbit," the OCI recommended that binding arbitration be created at the third level of the
grievance process, given its marked inefficiency and the CSC's clear lack
of impartiality.[23]

In 2005, the Supreme Court of Canada (SCC) itself reflected on
the serious limitations of the prison grievance procedure. In *May v
Ferndale*,[24] the SCC confirmed prisoners' concurrent access to directly
file a *habeas corpus* complaint[25] in a provincial court for certain matters
instead of exhausting the internal grievance procedure and filing for
judicial review in Federal Court. In justifying the need for direct access
to provincial courts, the SCC noted the most significant faults of the
grievance system, which rendered it highly inefficient: the policies of the
Commissioner are left to be reviewed by internal boards and agents who
are subordinated to the Commissioner; the *CCRA* and *CCRR* do not contain any grounds on which grievances can be reviewed or any remedies;

---

20 Louise Arbour, *Commission of Inquiry into Certain Events at the Prison for Women in
    Kingston* (Ottawa: Public Works and Government Services Canada, 1996) at 150–1
    [Arbour Report].

21 *Ibid* at 257.

22 Canada, Office of the Correctional Investigator, *Annual Report, 1999–2000* (Ottawa:
    OCI, 2000), online: http://www.oci-bec.gc.ca/cnt/rpt/pdf/annrpt/annrpt19992000-
    eng.pdf.

23 Canada, Office of the Correctional Investigator, "Shifting the Orbit: Human Rights,
    Independent Review and Accountability in the Canadian Corrections System,"
    Discussion Paper by Todd Sloan (Ottawa: OCI, 2004) at 39, online: http://www.oci-
    bec.gc.ca/cnt/rpt/pdf/oth-aut/oth-aut20040629-eng.pdf [OCI, "Shifting the Orbit"].

24 *May v Ferndale Institution*, 2005 SCC 82, [2005] 3 SCR 809 at paras 63–72 [*May*].

25 *Habeas corpus* applications are nonetheless limited to violations of rights that restrict
    the individuals' remainder liberty, generally through the use of solitary confinement
    or transfer to more restrictive forms of security. *Habeas corpus* applications and direct
    access to provincial courts are discussed in chapter six.

and the decisions themselves are not legally enforceable, which calls into question the fairness of the procedure.

The SCC's decision did not achieve more than the *CCRA* did. In 2006, Parkes and Pate criticized the grievance system as being far from a mechanism for oversight and accountability. Based on the work of the Canadian Association of Elizabeth Fry Societies (CAEFS), Parkes and Pate reported findings similar to the ones presented in this book. Numerous women were reluctant to use the grievance system because of potential repercussions; sometimes complaints were handled by the very person whose decision was being challenged; and one was "hard pressed to find a prisoner who [had] faith in this decision-making power."[26] The authors also provided an example from the Fraser Valley Institution, where virtually none of the *CCRA* guarantees were respected. A prisoner who had filed a sexual harassment complaint was not allowed to retain a copy of the investigation's findings or of the response. She was simply informed that her complaint was unfounded. The CAEFS looked into the process and found that the staff who supported the prisoner's claims had not been interviewed and their statements were not considered in the investigation. Even after the CAEFS and the OCI intervened, the CSC did not change its decision, and the staff member in question returned to work.[27] The same year, based on statistics from the OCI, Zinger called the grievance process "ineffective, bureaucratic, and costly" and argued that it did not solve the problems of prisoners who were not housed in accordance with the law or policy.[28]

During the 2007 investigation into the death of Ashley Smith while in custody, the grievance procedure was once again at the centre of the OCI's criticism. As it turned out, Ms Smith had filed seven complaints in August 2007, some of which were answered only after her suicide in October 2007. To take one example, she requested hygienic items and was denied on the basis that she did not properly use them.[29]

As a result of such events, in 2010 the CSC appointed David Mullan to review the grievance procedures and make recommendations for improvement. Not unlike the OCI, Mullan found that the system was ineffective and bureaucratic. He recommended that resources be dedicated

26 Debra Parkes & Kim Pate, "Time for Accountability: Effective Oversight of Women's Prisons" 48:2 CJCCJ 251 at 270–1 [Parkes & Pate].

27 *Ibid* at 260.

28 Ivan Zinger, "Human Rights Compliance and the Role of External Prison Oversight" 48:2 CJCCJ 127 at 136 [Zinger, "External Oversight"].

29 Howard Sapers, Correctional Investigator of Canada, *A Preventable Death* (Ottawa: OCI, 2008) at 11, online: http://www.oci-bec.gc.ca/cnt/rpt/pdf/oth-aut/oth-aut20080620-eng.pdf.

to solving grievances in a timely manner at the institutional level. He also recommended that each maximum and medium security institution appoint an independent mediator to deal with the grievances. He suggested that there be a grievance coordinator clerk to sort the grievances based on their urgency.[30] Some of his recommendations were incorporated in *An Act to Amend the Corrections and Conditional Release Act (vexatious complainants)*, which passed in 2013.[31] However, the most important recommendations, chiefly the ones dealing with independent mediation, prioritization of grievances, and dedication of more resources, were not adopted.

In spite of this report, the grievance process did not improve in terms of efficiency or effectiveness. In 2012, Justice Mactavish allowed an application for judicial review of a decision of the Assistant Commissioner made in response to a grievance of a prisoner who claimed that the CSC did not fulfil its statutory obligation to provide a fair and expeditious procedure to prisoners' grievances because of systemic delays in the internal grievance process.[32] The application was allowed because the Assistant Commissioner failed to understand and address "the nature and scope of the problem of systemic delay in the grievance process"[33] identified in the applicant's grievance. Also, in a handful of instances, the Federal Court noted that "where there are urgent, substantial matters and an evident inadequacy in the grievance procedure, the Court may exercise its discretion to hear an application."[34] Thus, recognizing the significant flaws in the grievance process, the Federal Court agreed to hear the applications without the grievance process being exhausted first. However, the ultimate outcome was not necessarily more successful.[35]

In its *Annual Report, 2014–2015*, the OCI noted that the number of grievances was on the rise, reaching 32,340 yearly. Hence, there was a growing backlog and prolonged, systemic delays, especially at the national level. In January 2015, the CSC's compliance rate with the statutory provision in terms of timeliness was 30 per cent overall and 13 per cent for priority grievances. The wait time for a reply was often over one year. The OCI recommended that the Ministry of Public Safety conduct a compliance audit of the CSC's legal obligations to provide

---

30 David Mullan, *Report of External Review of Correctional Service of Canada Offender Complaints and Grievance Process* (Ottawa: CSC, 13 July 2010) [Mullan]. For another example of failures of the system, see Parkes & Pate, *supra* note 26 at 259.

31 *An Act to amend the Corrections and Conditional Release Act (vexatious complainants)*, SC 2013, c 3.

32 *Spidel v Canada (AG)*, 2012 FC 958 at para 1.

33 *Ibid* at para 84.

34 *McMaster v Canada (AG)*, 2008 FC 647 (FCTD).

35 *Ibid*; *Gates v Canada (AG)*, 2007 FC 1058.

accessible, fair, and expeditious resolution to prisoner grievances.[36] Finally, in 2016, Zinger indicated that, despite the malfunctions of the grievance system, the budgetary cuts undertaken by the Conservative government (2006–2015) included cuts to the funding of the internal grievance procedure.[37] These cuts have been maintained post-2015 by the Liberal government. Thus, there is no indication that the CSC has any plans to reform the system.

To summarize, the internal inmate complaint and grievance system is, according to the *CCRA*, the first and main remedial tool for prisoners whose needs are not met by the services available. It is intended to mediate the conflict between prisoners and staff, to provide oversight over officers' actions and decisions, to help maintain policies in line with the law, and to hold the CSC accountable. However, its long-criticized failures to achieve these goals are engrained in its very design. As Parkes and Pate noted, an accountability mechanism needs to be independent, accessible, and provide enforceable remedies.[38] At present, the internal grievance procedure does none of these things.

First, the procedure is internal, and thus the CSC is left to review its own policies and possibly make decisions that have negative consequences for its staff. However, as Arbour put it, "the CSC does not have the capacity to accept error and accountability."[39] This issue was a major theme in the California study. Calavita and Jenness looked into why, despite serious complaints being dismissed as frivolous, the rate of decision reversal at another appeal level of the grievance was minimal. Based on the interviews and the review of the grievances, they concluded that the consistency could be explained by team loyalty, professional collegiality, importance of rank, and deference to ground-level staff.[40] The authors found informal mechanisms in place to ensure the consistency between decisions at different levels: reprimand for deviations, "shallow decision-making" based on stereotypes of prisoner appellants, us versus them mentality, and inter-organizational communication.[41] Thus, as long as the procedure remains internal, regardless of its different levels of appeal, this system will fail.

---

36 Canada, Office of the Correctional Investigator, *Annual Report, 2014–2015* (Ottawa: OCI, 2015) at 31–2, online: http://www.oci-bec.gc.ca/cnt/rpt/pdf/annrpt/annrpt20142015-eng.pdf.

37 Ivan Zinger, "Human Rights and Federal Corrections: A Commentary on a Decade of Tough on Crime Policies in Canada" (2016) 58:4 CJCCJ 609 at 610, https://doi.org/10.3138/cjccj.2016.E06 [Zinger, "Human Rights and Federal Corrections"].

38 Parkes & Pate, *supra* note 26 at 266–72.

39 Arbour Report, *supra* note 20 at 151.

40 Calavita & Jenness, *supra* note 6 at 136.

41 *Ibid* at 137.

Second, the extent to which the procedure is truly open to prisoners is questionable. As shown both by my study and by Parkes and Pate's,[42] prisoners are often threatened and intimidated into not filing or withdrawing complaints. Also, since prisoners have very little to gain from this ineffective and time-consuming process, it can hardly be said that they have substantial access to redress. Finally, the grievance procedure has no remedies attached to it and no mechanisms to enforce even positive decisions. Thus, the grievance procedure not only has no potential to address systemic problems – it also has very little strength to address even individual concerns.

Where To?

These issues are of particular concern for the aging prison population, which is the focus of this book. As discussed in chapter three, some of the *CCRA* standards are not upheld by the practices that create older prisoners' conditions of confinement. The usefulness of having standards and rights guaranteed by legislative provisions is virtually cancelled because prisoners do not have immediate access to courts, and the grievance system to which they have formal access is slow and inefficient.

Some scholars and activists have suggested that enhanced access to courts for prisoners is mandatory if the CSC is to be brought back under the rule of law.[43] While filing complaints directly to court may have significant benefits in terms of the independence of adjudication and enforceability of remedies, it may be unrealistic to expect that courts can manage all types of prisoner complaints themselves. Thus, what is needed is a functioning administrative system in which prisoners can file complaints free of charge, with little legal complications.

In the past, other authors have made suggestions to improve the grievance system. Justice Arbour suggested that all grievances be heard by the Commissioner.[44] The sad truth is that, at the national level, grievances appear to be the most mishandled, and the Commissioner is no less inclined to side with officers than lower officials are.[45]

---

42 Parkes & Pate, *supra* note 26 at 260.
43 See e.g. Arbour Report, *supra* note 20; Parkes & Pate, *supra* note 26; Jackson, *Justice Behind the Walls*, *supra* note 19.
44 Arbour Report, *supra* note 20 at 257.
45 This situation has been noted in Arbour's own report (Arbour Report, *supra* note 20 at 150–1), as well as in other reports; see e.g. OCI, "Shifting the Orbit," *supra* note 23 at 39. See also Calavita and Jenness discussing the same trend in their jurisdiction, *supra* note 6 at 136.

The OCI,[46] backed by Jeremy Patrick,[47] has suggested that a specialized administrative tribunal be created. As discussed in the previous section, I think such a tribunal would be valuable in helping the OCI to fulfil its mandate and force policy reform where needed. Jeremy Patrick envisioned the OCI receiving complaints from prisoners, making a triage, and sending the most significant to this tribunal.[48] Michael Jackson also imagined such a tribunal fulfilling a double role: mediating the relationship between the OCI and the CSC, and having the discretionary capacity to receive complaints directly from prisoners and address "the most serious."[49] Finally, in 2003, the Canadian Human Rights Commission addressed the possibility of an independent administrative tribunal with the power "to compel the Correctional Service to comply with legislation and policy governing the administration of sentences, and to redress the negative effects of non-compliance."[50] The commission suggested that this tribunal should have jurisdiction to accept complaints from both prisoners and prisoner advocates for systemic matters. Moreover, it suggested that this tribunal could be part of an existing structure such as the Canadian Human Rights Tribunal.[51]

I support Justice Arbour's second recommendation,[52] similar to one made by Mullan,[53] that an independent adjudicator be present in each institution. I suggest that the grievance procedure be maintained as it is, but that the position of an independent chairperson, similar to the one for disciplinary hearings,[54] be created in all penitentiaries. This person's only responsibility should be to adjudicate grievances, and they should be aided by an independent clerk who would prioritize the most urgent grievances. The independent adjudicator should have the power to declare when an individual's rights have been breached and to make recommendations regarding the individual (if they should be released out of segregation, be given the medication needed, be transferred to the hospital, or other appropriate actions).

---

46 OCI, "Shifting the Orbit," *supra* note 23 at 39.
47 Jeremy Patrick, "Creating a Federal Inmate Grievance Tribunal" (2006) 48:2 CJCCJ 287 [Patrick].
48 *Ibid* at 296.
49 Jackson, *Justice Behind the Walls, supra* note 19 at 588.
50 Canadian Human Rights Commission, *Protecting Their Rights: A Systemic Review of Human Rights in Correctional Services for Federally Sentenced Women* (Ottawa: CHRC, 2003) at 67, online: https://www.chrc-ccdp.gc.ca/eng/content/protecting-their-rights-systemic-review-human-rights-correctional-services-federally [CHRC, *Protecting Their Rights*].
51 *Ibid.*
52 Arbour Report, *supra* note 20 at 257.
53 Mullan, *supra* note 30.
54 *CCRR, supra* note 2, s 24.

Arbour and Mullan both refer to this position as an independent "mediator," who would mediate the conflict between the CSC and the prisoner. Like Parkes and Pate, I do not think mediation has a place in the prison environment.[55] In a space where one party holds all the power and the other is completely at its mercy, there can be no mediation. Equally, the presence or absence of rights or respect for the rule of law cannot be mediated or negotiated. What is needed is an independent adjudicator with the power to decide which CSC actions and decisions have breached which statutory rights, and who can order the CSC to cease that kind of action.

If independent adjudication is deemed too costly, at the very least, it should exist at the last level of the grievance process. As Jackson put it, "if the grievance process is underpinned by the possibility of independent binding adjudication, the incentive to resolve grievances at an early stage will ensure that only the exceptional case proceeds beyond there."[56]

For the enforceability of its decisions, the independent chairperson ought to have access to court, which could render an order. A similar process is in place to enforce the settlement decisions of the Human Rights Commission: both the commission and the interested parties can apply for an order to the Federal Court.[57]

Alternatively, an administrative tribunal could be created to hear prisoners' grievances (either fully independent or part of an existing structure, such as the Human Rights Tribunal) to which all prisoners would have access to file grievances. It is unclear if this tribunal would be a faster or more efficient avenue than an institutional independent chairperson, but it may carry more guarantees of impartiality. Needless to say, prisoners should be able to apply for judicial review in court if unsatisfied with the decision of either the independent chairperson or the tribunal.

Regardless of the direction taken, in order to be truly meaningful without having to rely exclusively on courts for remedies, the adjudication of grievances must become independent from the CSC. As Patrick observed, the CSC is the only governmental agency (even though, in terms of use of force, it is second only to the police) that does not have an external board in place to review complaints against its members.[58] This lack of oversight has been proven to foster partiality, unfairness, mistrust, and lawlessness.

---

55 Parkes & Pate, *supra* note 26 at 278.
56 Jackson, *Justice Behind the Walls, supra* note 19 at 601.
57 *Canadian Human Rights Act*, RSC 1985, c H-6, s 48(3) [*CHRA*].
58 Patrick, *supra* note 47 at 288.

Judicial Review of Grievance Decisions

> When you write a complaint they just ignore you. I really want to take them
> to court to see if they can ignore that. It's just so complicated, especially that
> I don't have access to internet. I am studying in our law library here, but
> I feel the internet would be more useful. (RR, 53, in prison 8 years)

Status Quo

In December 2016, I participated in a meeting organized by Legal Aid
Ontario, together with lawyers and representatives of different organizations interested in the protection of prisoners' rights: Queen's Prison Law
Clinic, CAEFS, John Howard Society, Ontario Human Rights Commission,
and others. As part of their five-year prison law strategy, Legal Aid Ontario
decided to fund two test cases in which the lack of appropriate health care
services for elderly prisoners would be challenged. Test cases are legal
suits in which murky areas of the law are tested in court in an attempt to
find an avenue to gain recognition and protection for the clients' rights.

The issue of prisoner entitlement and rights, for all its recent developments, continues to be a hard sell in courts. The issue of the specific needs and accommodation that elderly prisoners are facing is yet
to be raised in a court. The brainstorming during the meeting revolved
around what the best type of legal challenge would be if a lawyer were
to challenge the lack of timely medical services, painkillers, appropriate
infrastructure, safe environment, and other accommodations as defined
by older prisoners' needs. Someone suggested that the client be asked to
write a grievance and claim that his *CCRA* rights to essential health care
"at an acceptable level of the profession"[59] were breached. As mentioned,
CCRA-based claims must first exhaust the internal grievance procedure
before access is given to apply to judicial review by a court. Once the
client's grievance was rejected by the Commissioner of the CSC, they
would be able to file a complaint in the Federal Court by way of judicial
review. Thus, the claim would be based in the *CCRA* by way of judicial
review. This avenue is an attractive way to seek court protection because,
as others have noted,[60] *CCRA*-entrenched rights are prison specific and
thus are perhaps more amenable to court review than other types of
rights that apply to prisoners, such as rights under the *Canadian Charter
of Rights and Freedoms* (*Charter*). Nonetheless, the second this otherwise

---

59   *CCRA, supra* note 1, s 80.
60   Jackson, *Justice Behind the Walls, supra* note 19 at 58.

sensible suggestion was made, all the lawyers in the room exclaimed, "Not the Federal Court!"

This anecdote summarizes the experience numerous seasoned prison lawyers have had with judicial review and speaks volumes to the success rate for prisoners seeking judicial redress once they have been failed by the grievance process. Access to the courts is essential for the protection of rights, as courts are the only institutions sufficiently independent and capable of rendering enforceable remedies and forcing the rule of law upon other agencies. Thus, even where an agency, such as an administrative board or tribunal, has a statutory delegated decision-making power for purposes of expertise and expediency, its final decision can generally be judicially reviewed or appealed in court. Judicial review has been defined as "the judicial avenue by which courts supervise the powers delegated to statutory, subordinated decision-makers."[61] In cases brought forward by the participants in my study, a range of correctional decisions would be made by the CSC and its agents, as per the power delegated to them through the *CCRA*.[62] In terms of court supervision, these decisions are subject to review by a federal court, pursuant to section 18 of the *Federal Court Act*.[63] Nonetheless, historically, this judicial oversight mechanism has proved to be of limited use in protecting prisoners' interests.

Since 1979 when the first case expanding judicial review for prisoners was rendered, the system has improved. Before 1979, courts adopted a hands-off approach regarding prison decisions, practices, and policies. In 1979, in *Martineau (2)* the court stated that prisoners were owed a duty to act fairly. Thus, judicial review was expanded to decisions made by prison authorities and the remedy of *certiorari* (to quash an impugned decision) was rendered available "whenever a public body has the power to decide any matter affecting the rights, interests, property, liberty of any person."[64] While this decision was to be applied only for "the most severe injustice," likely arising as a result of procedural issues, its implications soon transcended questions of procedure and moved into the realm of the competing interest of liberty, self-interest, and administrative exigency. Prisoners would from thereon have the ability to challenge administrative decisions on procedural and non-procedural grounds.[65]

---

61 David Cole & Allan Manson, *Release from Imprisonment: The Law of Sentencing, Parole and Judicial Review* (Toronto: Carswell, 1990) at 40 [Cole & Manson].

62 *CCRA*, *supra* note 1, s 90.

63 *Federal Court Act*, RSC, 1985, c F-7, s 18.

64 *Martineau v Matsqui Institution Inmate Disciplinary Board* (1979), [1980] 1 SCR 602 [*Martineau No. 2*].

65 Cole & Manson, *supra* note 61 at 63.

The *Pezim*[66] and *Southam*[67] decisions introduced three standards upon which a court would assess an administrative decision: patently unreasonable and reasonableness *simpliciter* (which entailed different levels of deference) and correctness. The latter standard entailed no deference, and the court would assess whether or not the administrator reached the right decision. After *Dunsmuir*,[68] two standards are left: reasonableness (which is a "qualitative inquiry into matters such as justification, transparency, and intelligibility and ... assesses the decision within a set of acceptable outcomes"[69]) and correctness (which allows for no deference towards the administrator). Even before *Dunsmuir*, correctness was often used to assess purely legal questions, matters of jurisdiction, and the constitutionality of certain practices. Prison cases would often be assessed under the reasonableness standard, and the history of judicial review is one of very high deference to correctional authorities.

There have been few occasions in which a correctional decision was deemed to be unreasonable.[70] Recently, the Federal Court reached such a finding when reviewing a decision on a disciplinary matter.[71] Beyond the fact that the prisoner appellant was successful, the case is notable because the Federal Court found the following:

> This Court has noted that in circumstances where an administrative decision is important to the affected person, affects the liberty of the affected person, is a liability determination drawing upon legal standards rather than executive policy, or is constrained by narrowing statutory language, this Court may afford the administrative decision-maker a narrower margin of appreciation. In other words, review may be somewhat more intense.[72]

Though they maintained the reasonableness standard, the Federal Court found that the decision of the chair on that disciplinary matter must be scrutinized "with some strictness."[73]

The *Sharif* decision is in stark contrast with most of the other judicial review cases coming out of the prison context. Another recent case is telling, not only about the state of the grievance system, but also about

---

66 *Pezim v British Columbia (Superintendent of Brokers)*, [1994] 2 SCR 557.
67 *Canada (Director of Investigation and Research) v Southam Inc*, [1997] 1 SCR 748.
68 *Dunsmuir v New Brunswick*, 2008 SCC 9, [2008] 1 SCR 190.
69 Allan Manson et al, *Sentencing and Penal Policy in Canada: Cases, Materials, and Commentary*, 2nd ed (Toronto: Emond Montgomery, 2008).
70 *Tehrankari v Canada (Correctional Service)* (2000), 38 CR (5th) 43 (FCTD).
71 *Sharif v Canada*, 2018 FCA 205 [*Sharif*].
72 *Ibid* at para 11.
73 *Ibid* at para 12.

the Federal Court's reluctance to supervise it. Jeffrey Ewert sought judicial review of the final decision on his grievance in which he complained about how his interregional transfer had been conducted. His judicial review was denied, but the court noted: "The applicant's grievance was received on January 12, 2015, and the response is dated March 31, 2017, that is over two years later. This is clearly beyond sixty days, and despite undue circumstances, I see no justification for this. However, the time delay did not have a determinative effect on the result which is overall an acceptable outcome."[74]

Moreover, even in cases where the decision assessed had a constitutionality component and thus the standard utilized on judicial review was correctness, the courts often deferred to the judgement of the correctional authorities.[75] To make matters worse, in 2012 the SCC decided, in *Doré v Barreau du Québec*, that administrative decisions regarding the constitutionality of practices as opposed to statutes (matters broaching on *Charter* "values" as opposed to *Charter* rights) were henceforth to be reviewed based on the lower reasonableness standard.[76] In the case of elderly prisoners, what may be problematic and perhaps called into question is not so much the legislation, but rather the prison practices and decisions (such as the practice of segregating mentally ill prisoners, prohibiting widely used and efficient painkillers, housing disabled prisoners in inappropriate accommodations, forcing prisoners to stand for hours outside to pick up medication). If any of the prisoners were to challenge the constitutionality of such practices in court, following an unfavourable decision resulting from the grievance process, the court's assessment would now be made on a reasonableness standard.[77] Prison and administrative law scholars have criticized *Doré* as inconsistent with

---

74 *Ewert v Canada (AG)*, 2018 FC 47. This decision was later overturn by the Federal Court of Appeal: *Ewert v Canada*, 2018 FCA 175.

75 See e.g. *Fitzgerald v William Head Institution*, [1994] BCJ No 1534 (BCSC); *Légère v Canada* (1997), 133 FTR 77 (TD); *Harms v Canada (Correctional Service)* (2000), 195 FTR 144 (TD); *Boudreau v Canada (AG)*, [2000] FCJ No 2016 (TD); *Durie v Canada (AG)* (2001), 201 FTR 8 (TD); *Dupras v Kent Institution*, 2001 FCT 632; *William v Canada (Correctional Service)*, [1993] 1 FC 710, 15 Admin L Rev (2d) 83 (FCA); *Forrest v Canada (Solicitor General)* (1998), 154 FTR 22 (TD); *Steele v Stony Mountain Institution* (1991), 45 BCLR (2d) 273, 76 CR (3d) 307 (CA); *Fieldhouse v British Columbia* (1995), 40 CR (4th) 263, 98 CCC (3d) 207 (BCCA); *Lord v Canada*, 2001 FCT 397.

76 *Doré v Barreau du Québec*, 2012 SCC 12.

77 It is worth noting that practices that can be proven to be legislative policies because they encompass norms of general application will be treated akin to legislation (*Great Vancouver Transport Authority v Canadian Federation of Students – British Columbia Component*, 2009 SCC 31) and thus the correctness standard will still apply.

administrative and constitutional law,[78] leading some to question if *Doré* is in fact "good law."[79]

Finally, aside from the courts' high levels of deference towards administrators, there are other reasons to explain why judicial review in a Federal Court has had limited success. As summarized in *May v Ferndale*, a judicial review process is lengthy, the Federal Court is not locally accessible to all prisoners, the onus to prove the error of the administrator's decision is fully on the appellant, and the Federal Court has full discretion to deny remedy.[80] These shortcomings are perhaps why, while important, judicial review is likely the least useful court procedure for prisoners compared to avenues such as the *Charter* or *habeas corpus* applications discussed in the next chapter.

Where To?

In 1997, Justice Arbour suggested that there is a need for a more vigorous court intervention in order "to regain control of the legality of a sentence."[81] She thus recommended that prisoners have direct access to court when bringing forward their grievances. Parkes and Pate supported this position, arguing that courts present better guarantees of independence and broader remedial powers than tribunals and administrative boards. They conceded that, if an administrative tribunal is created to review grievances, for example, then judicial review of its decisions is mandatory.[82]

I agree that broader court access, both formally and substantially, is needed for prisoners. As I will argue in the next chapters, there is a need to improve the substantial access of prisoners to superior courts, in terms

---

78 Audrey Macklin, "Charter Rights or Charter-Lite? Administrative Discretion and the Charter" (2014) 67:2 SCLR 561; Mark D. Walters, "Respecting Deference as Respect: Rights, Reasonableness and Proportionality in Canadian Administrative Law" in Hanna Wilberg & Mark Elliott, eds, *The Scope and Intensity of Substantive Review: Traversing Taggart's Rainbow* (Oxford: Hart Publishing, 2015) 195; Lisa Kerr, "Easy Prisoner Cases," (2015) 71 SCLR (2d) 235.

79 The Honourable Justice David Stratas, "The Canadian Law of Judicial Review: A Plea for Doctrinal Coherence and Consistency" (2016) 42:1 Queen's LJ 27 at 33–4. See also *Loyola High School v Quebec (AG)*, 2015 SCC 12, [2015] 1 SCR 613, where three out of seven SCC judges did not even mention *Doré* in their minority opinion.

80 *May, supra* note 24 at paras 65–71. A similar point regarding the limitations of challenges brought though judicial review in the Federal Court was also made in previous cases, such as *R v Miller*, [1985] 2 SCR 613 at 640–1 [*Miller*]; *Steele v Stony Mountain Institution*, [1990] 2 SCR 1385 [*Steele*].

81 Arbour Report, *supra* note 20 at 195.

82 Parkes & Pate, *supra* note 26 at 275–6.

of *Charter* challenges, *habeas corpus*, and civil claims. In terms of griev-ances based on breaches of statutes or policies, it would be preferable if they were brought directly before a provincial superior court. Not only would this route circumvent a lengthy and ineffective administrative pro-cess, these courts are better placed to review prison matters (in terms of local accessibility, expertise in *Charter* and criminal justice matters, and expediency).[83]

In realistic terms, this proposal may not be possible, and, as argued earlier, if grievances are to be maintained at the administrative level, an independent chairperson or an administrative tribunal whose decisions can be challenged in court must be created to hear prisoners' claims. Concomitantly, the standard of review for decisions made by these au-thorities or by correctional agents should be modified, either by courts or through legislation. In arguing for heightening the standard of review, Jackson suggested that prison decision-makers are nothing like regular administrative boards and tribunals, who are generally owed deference. The latter are called upon to decide questions of law and to exercise their understanding on the body of jurisprudence. However, the CSC and its agents have proven time and again that they lack any understand-ing of the law.[84] In this context, the high deference offered to prison ad-ministrators by courts may be misplaced.[85] A body that has continuously used its so-called expertise to escape the rule of law and shown no regard for individual rights has forfeited its authority.

I thus suggest that in all situations where prison decisions have been made regarding a prisoner's right, including decisions made in response to a prisoner grievance, and especially if these decisions continue to be made by internal CSC agents, the judicial standard of review will need to be correctness. That could perhaps be achieved by passing legislation inserting a statutory right of appeal on a correctness basis. It may be equally helpful if the Federal Court boosted the expected standard in its case law, but it is unlikely that this adjustment would happen in a way that relied wholly on the source of the decisions on review. Thus, one can only hope that requiring the Federal Court to assess prison decisions on a correctness basis, regardless of their nature, would send a forceful message to the judges that their active input and supervision is not only desired but needed.

---

83 See e.g. *May*, *supra* note 24 at paras 62–70.

84 Jackson, *Justice Behind the Walls*, *supra* note 19 at 600.

85 On the problems raised by the deference of courts to corrections based on expertise, see Lisa Kerr, "Contesting Expertise in Prison Law" (2014) 60:1 McGill LJ 43.

Finally, it would be useful if Federal Court judges dealing with such judicial review applications could benefit from intensive training on matters pertaining to imprisonment and punishment. Their expertise on these cases has been repeatedly questioned by the SCC.[86] Such training might also help reverse the Federal Court's tendency to defer to the expertise of prison administrators without undertaking in-depth analyses of the applications.

Canadian Human Rights Commission and Tribunal

I think I heard of it [Human Rights Commission and Tribunal], maybe I heard people talking or saw it on TV. But I didn't know they can help us. Is it like a court? (AE, 57, in prison 17 years)

Canadian human rights law has developed steadily for the last four decades, and has been built around the idea that discrimination affects not only individuals but the well-being of the society in general. The structure built to guard against discrimination has sometimes been seen as a model for other jurisdictions.[87] There are a number of human rights agencies, but the ones particularly pertinent for the present discussion are the Canadian Human Rights Commission and its corresponding Tribunal.

The Canadian Human Rights Commission (CHRC) has been mandated by the *Canadian Human Rights Act* (*CHRA*)[88] to act as a human rights watchdog and, more specifically, to research, raise awareness, and speak out on any matter regarding human rights in Canada.[89] Legislators and scholars often refer to matters under the CHRC's jurisdiction as "human rights" in general, but in reality the essence of both the statute and the CHRC's work is anti-discrimination law.[90] That said, in time, the areas covered by the CHRC have developed towards a broader understanding of discrimination. Thus, the law has progressed from recognizing only direct discrimination to incorporating substantive equality

---

86 *Miller, supra* note 80; *Steele, supra* note 80; *May, supra* note 24.

87 Alison Harvison Young, "Keeping the Courts at Bay: The Canadian Human Rights Commission and Its Counterparts in Britain and Northern Ireland: Some Comparative Lessons" (1993) 43:1 UTLJ 65 at 65–6.

88 *CHRA, supra* note 57, ss 26–38.

89 Canadian Human Rights Commission, *2016 Annual Report* (Ottawa: CHRC, 2016) at 69, online: https://www.chrc-ccdp.gc.ca/eng/content/annual-report-2016 [CHRC 2016].

90 Dominique Clement, "Renewing Human Rights in Canada" (2017) 54:4 Osgoode Hall LJ 1311 at 1313 [Clement].

(including unintentional discrimination and sexual harassment)[91] and to recognizing intersectionality of discrimination.[92] Presently, the discrimination dealt with through these mechanisms generally must arise in the context of employment or service provision,[93] may be direct or indirect, and is not premised on treating everyone the same.[94] The prohibited discrimination grounds under *CHRA* are "race, national or ethnic origin, colour, religion, age, sex, sexual orientation, gender identity or expression, marital status, family status, genetic characteristics, disability and conviction for an offence for which a pardon has been granted or in respect of which a record suspension has been ordered."[95]

The work of the CHRC has revolved around receiving complaints and providing advice to individuals affected by these types of discrimination.[96] The way the system is set up, the CHRC receives information and formal complaints from individuals or agencies acting on behalf of individuals (such as union and social justice organizations).[97] The system is founded on the idea that discrimination is often inadvertent and based on misunderstanding, hence dialogue is key.[98] Thus, if the CHRC finds that the complaint may be warranted, it will try to direct the complaint towards alternative dispute resolution mechanisms. If no agreement is reached, and when warranted, the CHRC may refer a case to the Canadian Human Rights Tribunal (CHRT).[99] Only a very small portion of the complaints (for example, 41 out of 1,488 in 2016,[100] and 6 per cent between 1988 and 1998[101]) make it before the CHRT.[102]

The CSC is a federal institution that provides services to people under its control. As such, it squarely fits within the CHRC's authority.[103] One could easily envision situations where certain policies or practices of the CSC create an adverse effect on older people because of their age

---

91 Dianne Pothier, "Adjudicating Systemic Equality Issues: The Unfulfilled Promise of Action Travail des Femmes" (2014) 18 CLELJ 177 at 178 [Pothier].
92 Clement, *supra* note 90 at 1314.
93 *CCRA, supra* note 1, ss 5–9.
94 Clement, *supra* note 90 at 1319.
95 *CHRA, supra* note 57, s 3(1).
96 *Ibid* ss 4–5; *Report of the Canadian Human Rights Act Review Panel* (Ottawa: Canadian Human Rights Act Review Panel, 2000) at 8, online: http://publications.gc.ca/collections/Collection/J2-168-2000E.pdf [*CHRA* Review Panel].
97 *Ibid* at 59.
98 Clement, *supra* note 90 at 1328.
99 CHRC 2016, *supra* note 89 at 45.
100 *Ibid* at 45.
101 *CHRA* Review Panel, *supra* note 96 at 26.
102 For a description of the complete complaint process, see *ibid* at 12–18.
103 *CHRA, supra* note 57, s 5.

or disability. In fact, discrimination based on disability formed 60 per cent of the complaints received by the CHRC in 2016, which makes it the most frequent grounds for discrimination brought before the commission.[104] The individuals interviewed for this book mentioned a host of medical problems associated with aging: chronic conditions (cancer, arthritis, lung problems, digestive issues), chronic pain, increased need for emergency care, mental disability (depression, dementia), terminal illness, physical disability, and risk of falls.[105] Thus, the blanket application of certain CSC practices and policies could be challenged for having a harsher effect on older people and for creating disproportionate hardship on this group compared to younger individuals who are less likely to encounter the same rates of chronic illness and disability. Examples of practices and policies that could potentially be challenged based on sections 3 and 5 of the *CHRA* include the following:

- older individuals with disabilities hosted in non-accessible locations, with long walking distances, with stairs, and in double-bunked cells, which adds stress on their bodies and exposes them to injuries by falling
- painkillers restricted to Tylenol 3 for all types of chronic pain (per the *CSC National Drug Formulary*[106]), despite its limited efficiency, leaving 50 per cent of elderly individuals who are experiencing pain in terrible physical and mental distress
- prisoners required to line up outdoors, standing, often for up to an hour, to pick up medication (the practice in three institutions), which enhances their chronic pain, some of their diseases, and further exposes them to younger prisoners who cut in line
- nurse not available on-site 24/7, resulting in the wait time to see a nurse being generally three days, regardless of the issue, which leads to symptoms of chronic diseases not being treated in a timely fashion

---

104 CHRC 2016, *supra* note 89 at 57.
105 Gerontology medical literature widely associates these problems with aging. See e.g. Christine K. Cassel, Jarvey J. Cohen, & Eric B. Larson, *Geriatric Medicine: An Evidence-based Approach* (New York: Springer, 2003) at 361–5, 509, 921; James A. Blackburn & Catherine N. Dulmus, *Handbook on Gerontology: Evidence-based Approaches to Theory, Practice, and Policy* (Hoboken, NJ: Wiley, 2007); M. McKenna et al, "Assessing the Burden of Disease in the United States Using Disability-Adjusted Life Years" (2005) 28:5 AJPM 415 [McKenna et al]; F.C. Andrade, "Measuring the Impact of Diabetes on Life Expectancy and Disability-Free Life Expectancy among Older Adults in Mexico" (2010) 65B:3 J Gerontol B Psychol Sci Soc Sci 381; C. Jagger et al, "The Burden of Diseases on Disability-Free Life Expectancy in Later Life" (2007) 62:4 J Gerontol A Biol Sci Med Sci 408 [Jagger et al].
106 Correctional Service of Canada, *National Drug Formulary* (Ottawa: CSC, 2013). This document was obtained through an *Access to Information Act* request in April 2016.

- lack of systemic palliative care, which leaves terminally ill prisoners in pain, afraid, vulnerable, and in inhumane end-of-life circumstances (CSC Palliative Care Guidelines)[107]
- lack of access to compassionate release, despite some people's proximity to death, and the inability of prison facilities to care for those who are terminally ill
- lack of seniors-only units, which brings a higher risk of abuse from younger prisoners
- lack of properly trained caregivers, which leads to prisoners with disabilities being abused and neglected
- lack of medical diets, appropriate and differentiated based on disease, which leads to people in need starving or being forced to eat food that worsens their diseases (see CD "Food Services" and SOP "Food Services – Central Feeding")[108]
- blanket prohibition of orthopaedic pillows and mattresses, and the discretionary option of the warden to allow for other items, whether paid for or not, such as braces, orthopaedic shoes, walking aids, hearing aids, and other such appliances (*National Essential Healthcare Framework*);[109] for many age-related chronic conditions, these items make a significant difference, and thus, should be considered essential health care, available free of charge, as per *CCRA* section 80[110]

Without going into the details and merits of such challenges in individual cases, it appears that numerous participants to the study would have, *prima facie*, a basis for complaining of discriminatory treatment based in section 5 of the *CHRA*. As mentioned, individuals who wish to challenge their treatment based on this act can make a formal application to the CHRC. The commission investigates, and if it finds that there is merit to such a claim, together with the complainant, it can file a complaint with the CHRT.[111]

---

107 Correctional Service of Canada, *Palliative Care and End of Life Care in Canadian Federal Institutions Guideline* (Ottawa: CSC, 2009). This document was obtained through an *Access to Information Act* request in April 2016.

108 Correctional Service of Canada, "Food Services," Commissioner's Directive No. 880 (Ottawa: CSC, 21 February 2000), online: https://www.csc-scc.gc.ca/lois-et-reglements/880-cd-eng.shtml; Correctional Service of Canada, "Food Services – Central Feeding," Standard Operating Practices No. 880-01 (Ottawa: CSC, 21 February 2000), online: https://www.csc-scc.gc.ca/politiques-et-lois/880-1-sop-eng.shtml.

109 Correctional Service of Canada, *National Essential Healthcare Framework* (Ottawa: CSC, 23 July 2015). This document was obtained in April 2016 through an *Access to Information Act* request.

110 *CCRA, supra* note 1, s 80.

111 CHRC 2016, *supra* note 89 at 69.

Some very clear advantages can be seen for following the route of a human rights complaint with the CHRC and, potentially, the CHRT. First, this avenue is highly accessible, as it is free of charge.[112] Second, it does not require legal representation or sophisticated legal knowledge. Because the complaint is filed with the commission first, the commission is the one that undertakes an investigation at its own expense. While the complainant will generally have to represent themselves if the matter comes before the tribunal, they will still receive some prior support from the commission in preparation for this stage.[113] Third, if the case makes it to the CHRT, the decisions of the tribunal have the potential not only to provide redress to the individual claimant but also to lead to policy reform, and thus to affect systemic change. The ability to provide systemic remedies was confirmed by the SCC in 1987, in a case filed by Action Travail des Femmes.[114] The SCC recognized that some forms of discrimination are systemic, and granting an immediate remedy to the individual will not solve the contextual situation that led to it. Hence, systemic remedies are envisioned as prospective remedies directed at destroying the pattern of discrimination; they aim to improve the situation of the discriminated group in the future.[115]

A number of cases before the CHRT have since been granted systemic remedies. For example, in 2010 the tribunal ordered a significant policy change in a case against Elections Canada. In *Hughes v Elections Canada* (EC),[116] the tribunal concluded that the complainant was discriminated against based on disability, because some polling stations (such as the complainant's station) were situated in non–barrier-free locations. The CHRT ordered compensation for the individual, as well as policy changes to be implemented within twelve months. These changes included disability training for employees, the creation of a verification procedure for the accessibility of locations on the day of the event, the provision of sufficient signage on-site, and the installation of a procedure for receiving complaints about lack of accessibility. This reform was to be supervised by the commission, and the EC was to report back to the tribunal with progress made. The tribunal remained seized until after the following general election.[117]

The ability of the CHRT to provide systemic remedies is particularly important in the prisoner context. Potential breaches of rights are

112   *Ibid* at 69.
113   *CHRA* Review Panel, *supra* note 96 at 47–8.
114   *Action Travail des Femmes v Canadian National Railway Co,* [1987] 1 SCR 1114.
115   Pothier, *supra* note 91 at 178–81.
116   *Hughes v Elections Canada,* 2010 CHRT 4.
117   See also *Nkwazi v Correctional Service of Canada,* [2011] CHRD No I, where systemic remedies were granted upon a finding that the CSC's employment practices were discriminatory. But see *Moore v British Columbia (Ministry of Education),* 2005 BCHRT 580,

created by systemic policies that fail to account for age-related vulnerabilities and heightened needs. Thus, to produce real change, the remedy would need to go beyond the complaint, which rarely happens as a result of the internal grievance procedure or its corresponding judicial review. For example, in 2001 the CHRT heard a case called *Kavanagh v Canada*,[118] based on a complaint of discrimination against a transsexual prisoner. The case was successful in part, and the tribunal found that two policies of the CSC were problematic. First, the CSC required male prisoners, pre-sex change surgery, to be placed in male institutions. Second, the CSC provided a blanket prohibition for sex assignment surgeries. It argued that the surgery was not "essential health care" (as per section 80 of the *CCRA*). The CHRT found that the requirement for all male prisoners to be placed in male institutions discriminated against individuals who identified as transsexuals and did not get the chance to undergo sex assignment surgery. It also found that the blanket prohibition of the surgery was discriminatory because no other medical procedure was strictly prohibited by CSC policies. The tribunal noted, based on evidence, that some individuals underwent significant distress without the surgery, and thus, in certain cases, the sex assignment procedure could constitute "essential health care" and would need to be provided free of charge. In other cases, the surgery would need to have the same status as other non-essential health care procedures (when, for cost, the procedure could be available in the right circumstances). The decision of the CHRT was groundbreaking. The tribunal ordered the CSC to modify its policies regarding transsexual individuals. It ordered that the CSC render policies in which it recognizes the vulnerability of transsexual individuals and their need for accommodation. It also ordered that, in consultation with the CHRC, the CSC modify its policies regarding sex assignment surgery over a six-month period. Moreover, the CHRT ordered the CSC to file copies of its new policy with the tribunal within six months and retained jurisdiction over outstanding issues. It is exactly this type of discussion regarding what medical services count as essential for a particular group in specific life circumstances, and how the CSC policies require reform to provide accommodation for these people, that would help fill the void in which older prisoners currently find themselves.[119]

---

54 CHRR D/245, where the systemic remedies granted by the Tribunal were invalidated by the BCSC (*British Columbia v Moore*, 2008 BCSC 264) in a decision upheld by the BCCA (*British Columbia v Moore*, 2010 BCCA 478).

118 *Kavanagh v Canada (AG)* (2001), 41 CHRR 119 (CHRT) [*Kavanagh*].

119 While groundbreaking, the case did not fully solve the issues of transgender prisoners, who continue to face significant hurdles in having their needs met. The *Kavanagh* decision itself received some criticism in the transgender literature for not going far enough

One potential limitation of human rights challenges is that the *CHRA* contains provisions that allow the CHRC to attempt to reconcile the two parties.[120] In a settlement, the two parties reach a common agreement.[121] The complainant will receive some money, generally less than what they would receive in court. As mentioned, because of this structure, few cases make it before the CHRT. The settlements are secret: they are not re-ported, do not constitute precedent, and have no systemic ramifications. The external review of the *CHRA* in 2000 strongly recommended that complainants have direct access to file complaints with the tribunal.[122]

The settlements are supervised by the CHRC, however, which arguably makes them fairer than the settlements between parties to a court case. In a regular out-of-court settlement, there is no third party to super-vise the negotiation. The other advantage of a human rights settlement, compared to an out-of-court one, is that the commission sometimes negotiates some systemic provisions in the settlement. The provisions of a settlement can be enforced by order of the Federal Court.[123] For example, after the events surrounding the 1994 incidents at P4W in Kingston, an organization called Women for Justice filed a complaint with the CHRC. After a year-long investigation, the commission found women were discriminated against in CSC facilities based on sex, and that their conditions were worse than those of men. In the conciliation decision, the commission recommended that the CSC create programs and facilities substantively equivalent to those for men, and that it hire women in policy and senior management positions.[124]

---

to protect transgender people. On these issues, see e.g. Rebecca Mann, "The Treatment of Transgender Prisoners, Not Just an American Problem: A Comparative Analysis of American, Australian, and Canadian Prison Policies Concerning the Treatment of Transgender Prisoners and a 'Universal' Recommendation to Improve Treatment" (2006) 15 Law & Sex 91; Vancouver Prison Justice Committee, "Transgender Prisoners in Canada" (July 2007), online: http://www.vcn.bc.ca/august10/downloads/trans_prisoners_july2007.pdf; Kyle Kirkup, "How Ontario's Prisons Pioneered Sensitivity to Transgender Inmates" *TVO.org* (26 January 2016), online: https://tvo.org/article/current-affairs/shared-values/how-ontarios-prisons-pioneered-sensitivity-to-transgender-inmates; Kyle Kirkup, "Gender Dysphoria and the Medical Gaze in Anglo-American Carceral Regimes" in Jennifer Kilty & Erin Dej, eds, *Containing Madness: Gender and 'Psy' in Institutional Contexts* (London: Palgrave Macmillan, 2018) 145.

120 *CHRA*, *supra* note 57, s 47; CHRC 2016, *supra* note 89 at 69; *CHRA* Review Panel, *supra* note 96 at 26.

121 *CHRA*, *supra* note 57, s 48.

122 *CHRA* Review Panel, *supra* note 96 at 34, 36–47.

123 *CHRA*, *supra* note 57, s 48(3).

124 Kelly Hannah-Moffat, *Punishment in Disguise, Penal Governance and Federal Imprisonment for Women in Canada* (Toronto: University of Toronto Press, 2001) at 135–6.

The disadvantage of prisoner challenges stopping at the CHRC (because they were settled, or because the commission simply reported on those prison matters[125] without referring them to the CHRT, or because the commission dismissed them) is that the tribunal is not given the chance to build its expertise in this field and to set precedents through its case law. For example, from the fourteen challenges brought by different complainants before the CHRT and registered on CanLII against the Correctional Service of Canada, only seven have a prisoner complainant.[126] The other ones were brought forward by CSC employees regarding discrimination in the workplace,[127] a field in which the tribunal has more expertise.[128]

Indeed, the importance of the CHRT and the CHRC's expertise has been noted in terms of enforcement of remedies. Pothier noted that the tribunal has expertise in discrimination but often lacks expertise in the particular context in which the case occurs. If the respondent is cooperating, this deficiency may not matter, and the general guidelines for implementation of systemic remedies may be enough. However, if the respondent is not cooperating, it is very difficult to supervise the implementation of systemic remedies based on general principles.[129] Thus,

---

125 In 2001, CAEFS and Native Women's Association of Canada requested that the CHRC conduct a systemic review on the discrimination of incarcerated women (CHRC, *Protecting Their Rights, supra* note 50). While the investigation was praised, some of the women involved were critical of how CHRC followed up on its recommendations. It did not appear that the report had a great overall impact in correctional policies regarding incarcerated women. For a review of the investigative process and a critique of its outcome, see Gayle Horii, Debra Parkes, & Kim Pate, "Are Women's Rights Worth the Paper They Are Written On? Collaborating to Enforce the Human Rights of Criminalized Women" in Gillian Balfour & Elizabeth Comack, eds, *Criminalizing Women: Gender and (In)justice in Neoliberal Times* (Halifax: Fernwood Publishing, 2006) 302 at 302–22.

126 *Boucher v Canada (Correctional Service)*, 1988 CanLII 4489 (CHRT); *Kavanagh, supra* note 118; *Pochay v Correctional Service of Canada*, 2008 CHRT 45 (CanLII); *Collins v Correctional Service of Canada*, 2010 CHRT 33 (CanLII); *Starblanket v Correctional Service of Canada*, 2013 CHRT 28 (CanLII); *Pelletier v Correctional Service of Canada*, 2013 CHRT 26; *Desmarais v Correctional Service of Canada*, 2014 CHRT 5.

127 *Uzoaba v Canada (Correctional Service)*, 1994 CanLII 1636 (CHRT); *Nkwazi v Correctional Service of Canada*, 2001 CanLII 38287 (CHRT) (this is one of the few cases involving this complainant); *Baptiste v Canada (Correctional Service)*, 2001 CanLII 5801 (CHRT); *Wiseman v Canada (AG)*, 2009 CHRT 19; *Bélanger v Correctional Service of Canada*, 2009 CHRT 36; *Bélanger v Correctional Service of Canada & Union of Canadian Correctional Officers*, 2010 CHRT 30; *MacEachern v Correctional Service of Canada*, 2014 CHRT 4.

128 CHRC 2016, *supra* note 89 at 51; most of the complaints have been from an employment context (over 70 per cent). The report also states that the major focus of the Commission, and thus, of the Tribunal, lies in employment equity: *ibid* at 58.

129 Pothier, *supra* note 91 at 207.

another potential limitation of the system is that the systemic remedies offered by the tribunal may be difficult to enforce.[130]

That said, agencies such as the Prisoners' Legal Services (PLS) – part of the West Coast Prison Justice Society (WCPJS) – have recognized the importance of human rights challenges in protecting prisoner rights. The PLS has repeatedly advised and helped prisoners to bring human rights challenges;[131] in a few cases, when the CHRC dismissed these challenges, it successfully appealed the dismissal before the Federal Court on behalf of the prisoner claimant. For instance, in 2010, the PLS successfully represented a prisoner whose complaint was dismissed by the commission. The prisoner had mental disabilities and had spent extensive time in segregation where he often engaged in self-harming.[132] In 2013, the PLS won a judicial review filed on behalf of a prisoner whose ADHD medication was discontinued when he was transferred to maximum security. He was placed in segregation for about three years because he could not control his behaviour without medication. His human rights complaint had been dismissed by the CHRC. The Federal Court found that the investigation had been inadequate and re-sent the matter to the commission.[133] Another PLS success is worth noting, as it is closely related to the older prisoners' concerns. In 2008, the PLS filed a human rights complaint on behalf of a prisoner who was placed in a cell accessible only by stairs. The PLS successfully filed for interim relief in Federal Court, which affirmed the need to accommodate prisoners who are in uniquely vulnerable positions.[134] Also, according to the WCPJS website, the PLS has two ongoing related human rights challenges. One of them, currently before the commission, challenges the discriminatory policies of the CSC against transgender prisoners.[135] While this challenge was still ongoing at the time of writing, it has already resulted in a positive development. In January 2018, the PLS, together with the CSC and the CHRC, released a joint statement on changes to the accommodation of transgender prisoners.[136] The second challenge is a judicial review filed

---

130 *Ibid* at 178.
131 For the work the Prisoners' Legal Services does on behalf of prisoners in need of legal advice and support, including a list of cases it has been involved in, see West Coast Prison Justice Society, https://prisonjustice.org.
132 *Tekano v Canada (AG)*, 2010 FC 818.
133 *Brazeau v Canada (AG)*, 2013 FC 545.
134 *Drennan v Canada (AG)*, 2008 FC 10.
135 West Coast Prison Justice Society, "Transgender Prisoners," online: https://prisonjustice.org/transgender-prisoners-2/.
136 See CSC, CHRC, & PLS, "Joint News Release: Changes to the Way Transgender Offenders Are Accommodated in Canada's Federal Prison System," 31 January 2018, online:

in Federal Court against the CHRC for denying human rights protection to prisoners without immigration status.[137]

Perhaps because of work such as that of the PLS, prisoner challenges reaching the CHRT appear to have picked up since 2010 compared to the decade prior. An example of a successful case before the tribunal was *Collins v Correctional Service of Canada (2010)*.[138] In that case, the tribunal found that the rule obliging prisoners to stand to count discriminated against the complainant who, because of his disability and chronic pain, had difficulty standing. While it initially rejected Collins's request, once the complaint was filed with the CHRT, the CSC granted him an exemption from standing. In addition, the tribunal also granted the complainant compensation for pain and suffering. However, in this case, the orders of the CHRT did not contain any systemic provisions.

Recently, some very promising complaints have been brought forward as a result of the CHRC's investigation. Evidence of such complaints can be found in the CHRT's decisions on some procedural technicalities, generally to limit the scope of the complaint or to order the release of some necessary documentation for the commission's investigation. For example, in 2013 a complaint was brought by a prisoner relating to the CSC's restriction of pipes and smudging practices in its institutions.[139] In 2014, two claims were made – one by a male, the other by a female prisoner – against the CSC's practices and policies that discriminate against people with mental disabilities and fail to accommodate their needs.[140] Mental illness is a very common ground of discrimination seen before the commission and the tribunal. According to the CHRC's 2016 report, 48 per cent of all complaints based on disability (which was the leading ground for complaints overall) were based on mental illness.[141]

In my own study, I found that the rate of mental illness among older individuals was very high.[142] Thus, an argument could be made that the inadequate mental health care reported by participants (such as

---

https://prisonjustice.org/joint-news-release-changes-to-the-way-transgender-offenders-are-accommodated-in-canadas-federal-prison-system/.

137 *Tan v Canada (AG)*, 2018 FCA 186.

138 *Collins v Correctional Service of Canada*, 2010 CHRT 33.

139 *Pelletier v Correctional Service of Canada*, 2013 CHRT 26.

140 *Desmarais v Correctional Service of Canada*, 2014 CHRT 5; *Starblanket v Correctional Service of Canada*, 2014 CHRT 29.

141 CHRC 2016, *supra* note 89 at 57.

142 In addition, the medical literature confirms that many of the mental illnesses the participants in the study identified (such as chronic depression, anxiety, dementia, and severe memory loss) are often associated with aging: McKenna et al, *supra* note 105; Jagger et al, *supra* note 105.

the use of segregation to manage illness or the limited availability of mental health services in some institutions) disproportionately impacts the older population, and some of the practices of the CSC were, *prima facie*, discriminatory towards older prisoners with mental illnesses. It is easy to see how a decision of the CHRT on this matter would have the potential to reform CSC health care policies and constitute a positive precedent for a potential claim from older prisoners. However, the procedural hearings were not followed by any decisions as to the merits of these claims. The absence, years after the decisions on procedure were released, of a decision of this nature (or of those such as *Brazeau* and *Tekano*, which were returned to the commission by the Federal Court after the intervention of the PLS) reinforces the limits of a human rights challenge for such systemic, highly important issues. These matters were either settled, likely with no consequences to the larger, systemic problems, or a decision on the merits is to come, which speaks to the significant delays in the CHRT's adjudication process.[143]

Regardless of the potential limitations, the Canadian Human Rights Commission and Tribunal are likely underutilized. The commission, in particular, has proven to be of help and support for prisoner claimants who otherwise have very limited access to legal aid and lawyers.[144] Cases like *Kavanagh* show that the CHRT does not shy away from analysing the CSC's medical practices and policies and from qualifying essential health care depending on the particularities of a certain group. Ultimately, the desired outcome of a claim based on age discrimination is the recognition of aging people as a vulnerable group in need of accommodation, both in terms of infrastructure and medical services, and an obligation of the CSC to reform its policies to that end.

Conceivably, in the years to come, older prisoners will forward their complaints to the CHRC. Even if most of the complaints end up settling under the commission's supervision, even one CHRT decision regarding accommodation for older people may be enough to result in real change.

---

143 Patrick mentions that the delays in adjudicating grievances are to be found across most administrative boards and tribunals, including the Human Rights Commission, where the duration from the moment a claim was filed with the commission to a final decision, potentially of the Tribunal, was 25.3 months: Patrick, *supra* note 47 at 294. On the significant backlogs that the Commission and Tribunal have faced, see Clement, *supra* note 90 at 1319. In *CHRA* Review Panel, *supra* note 96 at 26–7, the panel noted that between 1991 and 1995 the Commission's backlog was in the range of 62 per cent to 72 per cent.

144 The issues surrounding access to legal aid, as well as the difficulties related to bringing a court challenge absent legal support, will be explored in the chapter six.

Conclusion

Administrative remedial mechanisms have numerous limitations, mainly surrounding their guarantees of independence and impartiality, their potential to enforce the remedies they render, and the delays in adjudication. However, the advantage they present cannot be denied: they are straightforward processes and do not require as much money or legal knowledge as court proceedings. In the case of the CHRT, the remedies granted can also be systemic, and the complainant receives support with their application from the CHRC. In addition, the problems that administrative boards present can be mitigated by ensuring that their decisions can be challenged in court.

Unfortunately, prisoners do not have a high rate of success, either through administrative boards or on judicial review. Even though their rights are entrenched in legal frameworks, the remedial systems fail to resolve their often serious complaints. In a system in which grievances are independently assessed and courts exercise non-deferential oversight, people like John and Eric would be able to trust that their complaints, based on *CCRA* or existing policies, would be heard. For example, John would be able to claim that his unique diet is part of essential care for his diabetes, and its absence offends section 80 of the *CCRA*. An individual who is disabled and has no choice but to use stairs could challenge their placement in such an institution based on the *CCRA*, which requires accommodation for special needs groups. Similarly, individuals deprived of mental health care on a regular basis (for example, in institutions where only suicidal people have access to a psychiatrist) can complain that the guarantees of access to acceptable mental health treatment are not met. Equally, people deprived of appropriate pain management could attempt to claim that at their stage of the disease, appropriate pain management is "essential health care." Tylenol 3 as a one-size-fits-all solution is not an acceptable community standard of the profession. Similarly, based on sections 3 and 5 of the *CHRA*, older prisoners would be able to challenge a multitude of the discriminatory prison policies before the CHRC and, potentially, the CHRT.

The problem lies in enforcing these provisions due to the malfunctioning of the internal grievance procedure, the deference of the Federal Court to prison administrators, and the – sometimes deserved – mistrust surrounding the effectiveness of the CHRC. As others have suggested, this situation, together with the CSC's resistance to the recommendations of the OCI and external task forces, justifies a more aggressive court intervention in prison matters. Unfortunately, prisoner court challenges, as I will explain in the next chapter, have not been much more successful in protecting prisoners' rights and producing systemic change. In order to trigger change in such circumstances, we need to do more than just enhance prisoners' access to courts. We need to change the attitude of the agents involved regarding the place of prisoners in society, the validity of their rights, and the roles and duties of the agents themselves in protecting those rights. If reformed, the grievance procedure and the Human Rights Commission and Tribunal, with the corresponding judicial review possibilities, could prove to be accessible and useful avenues to bring about individual redress and perhaps, especially in the case of the tribunal, to determine a change in the correctional policies that affect older prisoners. These administrative avenues cannot and should not replace prisoner direct access to court. However, they should be effective in complementing it, particularly where systemic change is needed.

Chapter Six

Correcting Wrongs and Pushing for Reform through Courts

Courts offer constitutionally entrenched guarantees of impartiality and independence that no administrative tribunal can offer.[1] Also, courts can and should get involved in overseeing prison matters in a more substantive way than simply reviewing decisions made by administrative boards and tribunals. As explained, the prisoner cannot challenge the breach of prison statutes directly in court, only through the administrative grievance system and, subsequently, through judicial review in the Federal Court. However, the prisoner, when injured, can sue the CSC for damages in a court of law. Equally, the prisoner can bring a *Charter* or *habeas corpus* challenge (both human rights constitutional claims at their core) directly to a provincial superior court.

To some, access to justice has a double meaning. On one hand, it is seen as practical access to courts: the availability of lawyers, resources needed to claim rights in a court of law, legal information, and so on.[2] More recently, scholars have shifted attention to the substantive meaning of access to justice: the general fairness of the system, the possibility of helping individuals achieve a good life, and access to courts in a manner that advances the claimants' cause and gives them access to just outcomes.[3] Having a right on paper is only as good as the mechanism

---

1 See e.g. Debra Parkes & Kim Pate, "Time for Accountability: Effective Oversight of Women's Prisons" (2006) 48:2 CJCCJ 251 [Parkes & Pate].

2 See e.g. Faisal Bhabha, "Institutionalizing Access-to-Justice: Judicial, Legislative and Grassroots Dimensions" (2007) 33 Queen's LJ 139 [Bhabha]; Constance Backhouse "What Is Access to Justice?" in Julia Bass, W.A. Bogart, & Frederick Zemens, eds, *Access to Justice for a New Century: The Way Forward* (Toronto: Law Society of Upper Canada, 2005) 113; Trevor W.C. Farrow, "What Is Access to Justice?" (2014) 51:3 Osgoode Hall LJ 958 at 970–2 [Farrow].

3 Farrow, *supra* note 2 at 972. See also Sarah Buhler, "The View from Here: Access to Justice and Community Legal Clinics" (2012) 63 UNBLJ 427 [Buhler].

that enforces that right. For instance, older individuals may be statutorily and constitutionally entitled to infrastructural accommodation, better health care services, and, generally, age-sensitive conditions of confinement and release options. Thus, the government may have an obligation to reform their prisons to ensure a uniform respect for the entitlements of their charges. But, if courts are unwilling to enforce prisoners' rights and ensure that institutions tend to prisoners' basic needs, incarcerated individuals are *de facto* left on the outside of the justice system, and their stated rights are meaningless. Being left on the outside of the justice system, for prisoners, also often means being left on the outside of a real chance for institutional reform. As Arbour noted two decades ago, courts are the only means left to bring the rule of law behind prison walls in a systemic manner, because "there is nothing to suggest that the Service is either willing or able to reform without judicial guidance and control."[4]

Access to courts is not easy for an incarcerated individual. The need to strengthen courts' role in upholding prisoners' rights has long been demanded by legal academics.[5] For decades, courts shied away from holding prison administrators accountable, confirming the Foucauldian theory:

> It is ugly to be punished, but there is no glory in punishing. Hence that double system of protection that justice has set up between itself and the punishment it imposes. Those who carry out the penalty tend to become an autonomous sector; justice is relieved of responsibility for it by a bureaucratic concealment of the penalty itself.[6]

Kerr notes that, while there are signs that this situation may now be changing, historically, courts have only agreed to review issues surrounding the quantity of the sentence, and not its quality.[7] Thus, while

---

4 Louise Arbour, *Commission of Inquiry into Certain Events at the Prison for Women in Kingston* (Ottawa: Public Works and Government Services Canada, 1996) at 198 [Arbour Report].

5 *Ibid*; Michael Jackson, *Justice Behind the Walls: Human Rights in Canadian Prisons* (Vancouver: Douglas & McIntyre, 2002) [Jackson]; Allan Manson, "Solitary Confinement, Remission and Prison Discipline" (1990) 75 CR (3d) 356 [Manson, "Solitary Confinement"]; Mary E. Campbell, "Revolution and Counter-revolution in Canadian Prisoners' Rights" (1996) 2 Can Crim L Rev 285 [Campbell]; Parkes & Pate, *supra* note 1; Lisa Kerr, "Contesting Expertise in Prison Law" (2014) 60:1 McGill LJ 43 [Kerr, "Contesting Expertise"]; Allan Manson, "Scrutiny from the Outside: The Arbour Commission, the Prison for Women, and the Correctional Service of Canada" (1996) 1 Can Crim L Rev 321 at 334–7 [Manson, "Scrutiny"].

6 Michel Foucault, *Discipline and Punishment: The Birth of Prison*. Translated by Alan Sheridan (New York: Vintage Books, 1995; original, Paris: Gallimard, 1975) at 10.

7 Lisa Kerr, "Easy Prisoner Cases" (2015) 71 SCLR (2d) 235 at 236 [Kerr, "Easy Prison Cases"].

decisions and practices that may directly prolong the sentence would be reviewed, judges would generally defer to the wisdom of administrators whenever the issue of conditions of confinement occurred. Kerr notes that the barrier between quantity and quality in a sentence is arbitrary. In fact, issues such as overcrowding, disciplinary measures, lack of programming, and lack of appropriate health care may lead to individuals not being able to fulfil their conditions for early release or may render them poorly equipped to survive in the community upon release. Thus, "it is difficult to modulate the concern with fitness and deserve in the judicially imposed sentences with the power of the prison officials to modulate the punishment in the course of its administration"[8] without active court oversight.

It is becoming increasingly clear that prison reform must start with reform in the willingness of courts to take back responsibility over sentencing.[9] Judicial oversight on how rights are upheld during incarceration is crucial to ensuring the continued legality of the sentence. Deference to the wisdom of prison administrators has typified the last few decades, a period also marked by prisoner rights abuses, unfulfilled promises of reform, and a notorious passivity of Parliament and government to take note of these issues. In the words of Louise Arbour, "[i]f anything emerges from this inquiry, it is the realization that the Rule of Law will not find its place in corrections by 'swift and certain disciplinary action' against staff and inmates. The Rule of Law has to be imported and integrated ... from the other partners in the criminal justice enterprise, as there is no evidence that it will emerge spontaneously."[10] Thus, not only will all prison rules and measures need to be respectful of the rule of law, and to yield to prisoners' rights,[11] but courts also need to intervene and uphold prisoners' rights as they reflect on the quantity and the quality of the sentence being served. As the historic accounts in the previous chapters show, legal rules and declaration of rights such as those in the *Charter* and the *CCRA* are important but not sufficient. Progress and long-lasting prison reform can only be gained through the creation of ongoing mechanisms for oversight and accountability.[12] As Justice LeBel put it in *May v Ferndale*, "[t]imely judicial oversight, in which provincial superior courts must play a concurrent if not predominant role, is still necessary to safeguard the human rights

---

8 *Ibid* at 246.

9 Arbour Report, *supra* note 4 at 195.

10 *Ibid* at 180.

11 *Ibid* at 179.

12 Campbell, *supra* note 5 at 296.

and civil liberties of prisoners, and to ensure that the rule of law applies within penitentiary walls."[13]

With their guarantees of independence and impartiality, power to grant redress, and expanded ability to render remedies that can lead to change, courts' enhanced willingness to oversee the implementation of rights in prison would be the single most important catalyst for both institutional reform and improvement of the non-judicial prison oversight mechanisms. In the previous chapter, I touched upon the remedial potential of the Federal Court on judicial review following negative decisions pursuant to the administrative grievance system. While important, the Federal Court and the grievance system appear to be poorly equipped to offer consistent protection to prisoners. It is now time to reflect in more depth on the potential benefits of direct court intervention (as opposed to following an administrative adjudicative process), in particular provincial superior court, in order to protect older incarcerated individuals and to advance their rights, either under the form of access to release or to better, more accommodating conditions of confinement. The first sections of this chapter are dedicated to prisoners' substantive access to justice and, particularly, to how legal action can and should ensure that older prisoners, as disadvantaged individuals and group, can find in courts a haven for just outcomes and fulfilment of their age-based needs. The last section addresses the practical or procedural barriers that prisoners in general, and older prisoners in particular, have in accessing courts and, by consequence, in achieving meaningful recognition of rights and needs fulfilment.

Charter Challenges

Status Quo: Potential and Limitations of Prisoner Charter Challenges

The entrenchment of the *Canadian Charter of Rights and Freedoms* (*Charter*) in the Canadian Constitution[14] marked a significant moment in the advancement of prisoners' rights. While the *Charter* does not contain any specific reference to prisoners, they often fall squarely within the groups specifically protected by the *Charter*. For instance, some rights apply to "every individual," or "everyone,"[15] whereas the democratic or mobility rights, for instance, apply to "citizens."[16]

---

13 *May v Ferndale Institution*, 2005 SCC 82, [2005] 3 SCR 809 [*May*].

14 *Canadian Charter of Rights and Freedoms,* Part I of the *Constitution Act, 1982,* being Schedule B to the *Canada Act 1982* (UK), 1982, c 11 [*Charter*].

15 *Ibid,* ss 2, 7, 12, 15.

16 *Ibid,* ss 3, 6.

The enactment of the *Charter* created hopes for a new culture of respect for prisoner rights within the correctional environment and expectations that the rule of law would be brought behind bars: "the biggest benefit flowing from a constitutionally entrenched Charter of Rights and Freedoms is not to be found in the litigation it spawns, but rather in the climate and culture of respect it creates amongst both government and citizens for fundamental human rights and freedoms."[17] In this respect, it is worth noting the *Charter*'s influence on the drafting in 1991 of the *Corrections and Conditional Release Act* (*CCRA*),[18] the expansive prison legislation to specifically ensure that prisoners retain all rights and privileges, that only the least restrictive measures shall be used against individuals, and that a formal grievance process for prisoners is in place.[19]

While the *Charter*'s influence on this legislation was a great advancement for prisoners' rights, it fell short of delivering the enhanced protection it promised. First, respect for the law, including the *Charter*, does not, as discussed in chapter three, come naturally in the prison environment without court intervention. The government has consistently failed to reform its policies in accordance with the legal norms and respect for prisoners' rights, and has often sought legislative loopholes that would allow it to enact policies to advance its agenda.[20] Second, litigation based on the *Charter* played an important role, but "the intermittent, exceptional, and delayed nature" added limits to its capacity to achieve the compliance of the correctional rules and practices with the law and the Constitution.[21]

In fairness, *Charter*-based litigation made a significant contribution to expanding the protection of prisoners' procedural rights. Thus, the duty to act fairly, recognized in *Martineau*,[22] was enhanced by the protection offered by section 7 to the right to life, liberty, and security of the person and the right not to be deprived thereof except in accordance with the principles of fundamental justice.[23] For instance, in *Howard*, the Federal Court of Appeal expanded the duty to act fairly to the right of the prisoner to be represented by counsel in a disciplinary hearing, because "the right-enhancing effect of the *Charter* thus greatly increases the ambit of protection afforded."[24] The court also reinforced the importance of the

---

17 Jackson, *supra* note 5 at 63.
18 *Ibid*; Campbell, *supra* note 5 at 321.
19 Campbell, *supra* note 5 at 321.
20 See e.g. *ibid* at 324.
21 *Ibid* at 304.
22 *Martineau v Matsqui Institution Inmate Disciplinary Board* (1979), [1980] 1 SCR 602 [*Martineau No. 2*].
23 *Charter*, *supra* note 14, s 7.
24 *Howard v Presiding Officer of the Inmate Disciplinary Court of Stony Mountain Institution*, [1984] 2 FC 642 (CA) at 681 [*Howard*].

preservation of *Charter* rights in prison: "all that is not immediately necessary must yield to the fullest exigencies of liberty."[25] In other cases, a violation of a procedural right under section 7 was found where the disciplinary charge was not sufficiently articulated,[26] in some cases of involuntary transfers, or where the prisoner was not informed about the content of the allegations against him.[27]

However, despite *CCRA* and case law assertions that prisoners do not lose rights because of incarceration, looking at the *Charter* litigation, particularly where substantive rights were involved, it appears that is not quite so.

First, a number of *Charter* rights have been diminished in the prison context. For instance, under section 8 the individual has the right to be free from unreasonable search and seizure. However, most prisoner claims brought forward on this basis have been rejected.[28] Even where a breach of section 8 was found, the state generally was able to justify it under section 1.[29] Section 1 allows for legislation to be rendered in violation of other *Charter* provisions if such violation is "demonstrably justifiable in a democratic society."[30]

Second, the standards used to assess prisoner *Charter* challenges appear to be lower than in other cases. Lisa Kerr has observed,[31] for instance, that many courts tend to find a justification for *Charter* breaches under section 1 for blanket security reasons. While a strenuous test, known as the *Oakes* test,[32] must be met in order for a breach to be found justifiable, in some prison cases no particular explanation or test was undertaken. Rather, the judge provided such justifications as "there are reasonable limitations in the prison context on rights previously enjoyed."[33]

Third, and connected to the second point, courts have a history of refusing to conduct a full investigation into a *Charter* prison claim, deferring to the expertise of the administrators even before reaching the section 1

---

25   *Ibid* at 688.
26   *Storry v William Head Institution*, 139 FTR 122, [1997] FCJ No. 1768 (TD) [*Storry*]; *Fitzgerald v William Head Institution*, [1994] BCJ No. 1534, [1994] BCWLD 1982 (SC) [*Fitzgerald*].
27   *DeMaria v Canada (Regional Transfer Board and Warden of Joyceville Institution)* (1988), 62 CR (3d) 248 at 254, [1988] 2 FC 480 (TD) [*DeMaria*].
28   *Weatherall v Canada (AG)*, [1993] 2 SCR 872, 23 CR (4th) 1; *Warriner v Kingston Penitentiary*, [1991] 2 FC 88, 39 FTR 285, [1991] FCJ No. 1116 (TD).
29   See e.g. *R v Sutherland* (1997), 120 Man R (2d) 125, [1997] MJ No. 390 (QB) [*Sutherland*].
30   *Charter*, *supra* note 14, s 1.
31   Kerr, "Contesting Expertise," *supra* note 5 at 56–7.
32   *R v Oakes*, [1986] 1 SCR 103 [*Oakes*].
33   *Maltby v Saskatchewan (AG)* (1982), 143 DLR (3d) 649 at 655, 2 CCC (3d) 153 (Sask QB) [*Maltby*]; see also, more recently, *R v Farell*, 2011 ONSC 2160, 85 CR (6th) 247.

justification analysis. Debra Parkes points out that such frugal investigations are hallmarks of *Charter* analysis regardless of the section on which the claim was brought, be it section 7,[34] section 11(h) and the right not to be punished twice,[35] section 12 and the right to be free from cruel and unusual treatment and punishment,[36] or section 15 and the right to equal treatment. Courts often forfeited established case analysis frameworks and accepted, without inquiry, the evidence provided by correctional services, especially when decisions that impact conditions of confinement were at issue.

For instance, courts have in the past utilized explanations commonly considered under section 1 (which comes into play only once a breach has already been established) at the deciding phase of the case to reach the conclusion that a breach did not occur.[37] In addition, the standards used are sometimes not appropriate readings of the *Charter*: the court in *Aziga* required that conditions in segregation must be a manifested violation of the right, or else courts would be simply second guessing prison administrators. The "manifested violation" has never been part of any *Charter* test.[38] Another example that outraged prison activists was *Shubley*,[39] where the Supreme Court of Canada (SCC) stated that solitary confinement with restricted diet and opportunity for fresh air was not of true "penal consequence," and thus section 11 did not apply to the case. No in-depth inquiry or analysis of what might constitute "penal consequences" in the particular context was undertaken. Instead, the court deferred to the administrators' assertion that since disciplinary offences were not criminal offences, the punishment they attracted was not penal, and thus a section 11 review was not warranted.[40]

---

34 Debra Parkes, "A Prisoners' Charter? Reflections on Prisoner Litigation under the Canadian Charter of Rights and Freedoms" (2006) 40:2 UBC L Rev 629 at 670–1 [Parkes, "Prisoners' Charter"]. See *Piche v Canada (Solicitor General)* (1984), 17 CCC (3d) 1 (FCTD), aff'd (1989), 47 CCC 495 (CA) [*Piche*] (double-bunking); *Williams v Canada (Commissioner of Corrections)*, [1993] FCJ No. 646 (TD) [*Williams*]; *Protective Custody Inmates, Kent Institution v Kent Institution* (1991), 2 WDCP (2d) 193, [1991] FCJ No. 221 (TD) [*Protective Custody Inmates*]; *Sweet v Canada* (1999), 249 NR 17, [1999] FCJ No. 1539 (CA) [*Sweet*] (compulsory urinalysis).

35 *R v Shubley*, [1990] 1 SCR 3, 74 CR (3d) 1 [*Shubley*].

36 *Piche*, *supra* note 34.

37 *R v Aziga* (2008), 78 WCB (2d) 410, 2008 CanLII 39222 (ONSC); *Fieldhouse v Canada* (1994), 33 CR (4th) 346, [1994] BCJ No. 1807 (SC), aff'd (1995), 40 CR (4th) 263, [1995] BCJ.No. 975 (CA). See also Allan Manson's criticisms of the court's deference to prison administrators in *Fieldhouse*: Allan Manson, "*Fieldhouse* and the Diminution of Charter Scrutiny" (1994) 33 CR (4th) 358.

38 Kerr, "Contesting Expertise," *supra* note 5 at 61.

39 *Shubley*, *supra* note 35.

40 Kerr, "Contesting Expertise," *supra* note 5 at 62; Parkes, "Prisoners' Charter," *supra* note 34 at 652; Manson, "Solitary Confinement," *supra* note 5 at 356.

Fourth, even when claims were successful, courts sometimes held back on the remedies that they granted. For instance, *Maurice* was the most remarkable prison case on freedom of conscience.[41] Maurice challenged the policy that denied him a vegetarian meal, granted solely on religious grounds. However, he strongly believed that eating animals was wrong. He won the case, but the court stopped short of requiring a change in policy. Thus, the decision had no systemic effect, and the policy remained in effect for everyone else except Maurice. Similarly, most of the successful section 7 cases on procedural grounds failed to lead to systemic improvements.[42]

All of this is bad news for a group of vulnerable prisoners in need of strong court intervention to protect their interests and advance their rights through systemic change. And yet, the *Charter* remains one of the key rights-rendering mechanisms for any individual. In a case commentary,[43] Allan Manson explained the role of courts in monitoring prison activity. He described imprisonment as a state institution, which, as any institution, is a tool through which the state interacts with the community it governs. The *Charter*, he argued, obliges courts to examine the shape of institutions and ensure that their administration conforms to the practices the *Charter* protects.[44] Arbour, in her report, expressed faith not only that courts and *Charter* litigation can bring systemic change better than any other avenue but, indeed, that absent judicial intervention no prison reform would take place.[45] Commenting on the Arbour Report, Manson stated that "the members of the judiciary should take Arbour's opinions to heart; otherwise government appointed review is just a self-justifying cliché."[46]

While courts are still somewhat inconsistent in their approach to prison legal claims in general, and *Charter* ones in particular, this inconsistency is not a reason to stop seeking individual and systemic remedies in court. Doing so would mean accepting that the most important recourse of protection against the state is not available to prisoners. Moreover, the scholarly push for a better judicial approach towards prison matters has not been completely fruitless, and there are signs of further change.

For instance, for twenty years the only significant, substantive *Charter* win for prisoners was *Sauvé*.[47] In 2002, through a *Charter* challenge, the

---

41 *Maurice v Canada (AG)*, 2002 FCT 69, 210 DLR (4th) 186 [*Maurice*].
42 Parkes, "Prisoners' Charter," *supra* note 34 at 643.
43 Manson, "Solitary Confinement," *supra* note 5 at 356.
44 *Ibid.*
45 *Arbour Report*, *supra* note 4 at 198.
46 Manson, "Scrutiny," *supra* note 5.
47 *Sauvé v Canada (Chief Electoral Officer)*, 2002 SCC 68, [2002] 3 SCR 519 [*Sauvé*].

SCC decided that prisoners have the right to vote, and the legislative provisions to the contrary were repealed. It was indeed a huge victory that led to real change behind bars. The court clearly stated that prisoners' rights are rights, not privileges, and that they continue to exist as long as they are compatible with incarceration. Moreover, the court stated that under section 1 the state is allowed to bring justification for legislative limitations of rights.[48] However, the court should not automatically defer to the administration, but rather apply a robust inquiry into these justifications, under the *Oakes* test, just as it would do in any other case.[49]

Some legal scholars argued that this victory was exceptional. It involved a non–prison-related legislation and had little to do with distribution of correctional resources. In short, it was not part of the correctional administration preference. The win was "low hanging fruit."[50] On the other hand, the case illustrated that courts are considerably less likely to defer to prison administration when there is equal expert evidence brought forward by both sides and not just by the state.[51]

The issue of evidence is clearly connected to that of deference to administration. Parkes has remarked on the difficulty of collecting evidence from behind bars, particularly for issues that may be systemic. On one hand, most of the research studies that generate scientific data and deliver expert witnesses are commissioned by the CSC. On the other hand, access to existing evidence may be expensive to get or not readily available, especially when the individual is not represented (as many are not, because they cannot afford a lawyer).[52] In some cases, prisoners lost specifically because they were not able to gather the evidence needed to show systemic or individual discrimination.[53]

While the availability of evidence in *Sauvé* may be pinned on the fact that something other than a correctional policy was at issue, in recent years things appear to have shifted even more towards typical prison matters. In 2010, a challenge was brought in *Bacon* to the use of solitary confinement, and the claimant won.[54] The case was successful because of the testimony of a renowned psychologist, who was able to bring significant

---

48 *Ibid* at para 7.
49 *Ibid* at paras 12–16.
50 Kerr, "Contesting Expertise," *supra* note 5 at 76; Parkes, "Prisoners' Charter," *supra* note 34 at 640; Efrat Arbel, "Contesting Unmodulated Deprivation: Sauvé v Canada and the Normative Limits of Punishment" (2015) 4:1 Can J HR 121.
51 Kerr, "Contesting Expertise," *supra* note 5 at 76.
52 Parkes, "Prisoners' Charter," *supra* note 34 at 667.
53 *Crowe v Canada* (1993), 63 FTR 177, [1993] FCJ No. 424 (TD); *Schemmann v Canada (Correctional Service)* (1995), 96 FTR 154, [1995] FCJ No. 786 (TD).
54 *Bacon v Surrey Pretrial Services Centre*, 2010 BCSC 805, [2010] BCWLD 8074 [*Bacon*].

empirical evidence to the effects of solitary confinement in general, and on the claimant in particular. The court emphasized that the prison's justifications need to be considered in light of specific qualitative features of the confinement and the effects it has on the individual.[55] The remedy in this case was individual, but the case itself opened the door to courts assessing solitary confinement as part of *Charter* challenges, and the expectation is that soon enough courts will require that the provisions in the *CCRA* allowing for indefinite administrative segregation will be struck down.[56]

In 2013, in *Inglis*,[57] a prisoner challenged the discontinuation of the mother-child program in British Columbia's prisons. The prison conducted no risk assessment of the program before discontinuing it and had no evidence of any risks. On the other hand, the claimants, supported by a number of intervenors, brought in multiple expert witnesses to present scientific evidence demonstrating the benefits of the program. The claimant won, and the remedy was systemic: the decision was quashed, and the mother-child program was reintroduced in the province.

Similarly, in *Strikiwsky*, the lack of methadone programs in prison was challenged under sections 7, 12, and 15 of the *Charter*. The case was settled outside the court, but the large amount of empirical evidence accrued led to a settlement that had a systemic effect: henceforth, methadone was made accessible in all prisons.[58]

Two recent challenges to the use of solitary confinement registered some success in lower courts and constitute promising steps forward in terms of the willingness of courts to consider *Charter* challenges. First, the Ontario Superior Court held that lack of appropriate oversight of the decision to segregate individuals constituted a breach of section 7 of the *Charter*.[59] While a positive step, this decision clearly did not go far enough: it barely mentioned any evidence of the effects of segregation on individuals, found no violation of section 12, and did not deem independent oversight to be a constitutional requirement.

A bigger *Charter*-based success in the prison context was registered in January 2018. The BC Civil Liberties Association (BCCLA) and John Howard Societies brought challenges in court to the use of solitary

55   *Ibid.*

56   Kerr, "Contesting Expertise," *supra* note 5 at 82.

57   *Inglis v British Columbia (Minister of Public Safety)*, 2013 BCSC 2309, 237 ACWS (3d) 380 [*Inglis*].

58   *Strikiwsky v Stony Mountain Institution* (2000), 193 FTR 59, [2000] FCJ No. 1404 (TD) [*Strikiwsky*]. Parkes, "Prisoners' Charter," *supra* note 34 at 651.

59   *Corporation of the Canadian Civil Liberties Association v R*, 2017 ONSC 749. This case, at the time the manuscript went to press, is under appeal.

confinement as cruel and unusual treatment and punishment under section 7, section 12, and section 15. The BC Supreme Court decided in favour of the complainants, heavily relying on significant social science evidence.[60] The court stated that the *CCRA* provisions on solitary confinement violate section 7 because they allow for prolonged, indefinite isolation; there is no independent review of the decision to place individuals in segregation; and prisoners have no right to counsel at segregation review decisions.[61] The provisions also violate section 15 because they allow for the segregation of mentally ill individuals,[62] and they have a discriminatory effect on Indigenous prisoners,[63] but not on women.[64] However, the court found that section 12 was not violated.[65] While arguably one of the greatest prison litigation successes, we cannot ignore that, even though the court accepted the evidence regarding the devastating effects solitary confinement has on the individual,[66] it did not find the practice to be cruel and unusual under section 12 but rather that segregating someone is "defensible" for upwards of fifteen days and perhaps even beyond that.[67]

Similarly, in *R v Ewert*,[68] the SCC accepted evidence that the risk assessment tools used by the Correctional Service of Canada (CSC) may produce inaccurate results for Indigenous prisoners, and may lead to over classification and thus to a significant restriction of an individual's residual liberty. The court also accepted evidence regarding the systemic discrimination against Indigenous prisoners and applied a section 15 *Charter* analysis to find a breach of the CSC statutory duty under section 24 of the *CCRA*.[69] Nonetheless, the SCC refused to find any *Charter* violations, either under section 7 or under section 15.[70]

---

60 *British Columbia Civil Liberties Association v Canada (AG)*, 2018 BCSC 62 at paras 160–254 [*BCCLA*]. BCSC invalidated a number of *CCRA* provisions that the trial judge deemed to be in violation of the *Charter* but suspended its declaration of invalidity to provide time for the federal government to make changes to the legislation. On appeal, the British Columbia Court of Appeal extended the suspension of the declaration of invalidity until 28 June 2019 (though the substance of the appeal had not yet been decided at the time of writing): *British Columbia Civil Liberties Association v Canada (AG)*, 2019 BCCA 5.

61 *Ibid* at paras 88–177.

62 *Ibid* at para 522.

63 *Ibid* at para 191.

64 *Ibid* at para 463.

65 *Ibid* at para 270.

66 *Ibid* at paras 247–51.

67 *Ibid* at paras 230–2.

68 *R v Ewert*, 2018 SCC 30 [*Ewert*].

69 *Ibid* at paras 64–7.

70 *Ibid* at paras 68–79.

Despite cases like *Ewert*, some of the other recent *Charter* litigation has led scholars to be more optimistic about the chances of future claims provided substantial empirical evidence is available. Kerr has suggested that cases such as *Bacon* and *Inglis* highlight a fact that has been apparent since *Sauvé*, if not before: the main question that courts must untangle when faced with a prison *Charter* challenge is, "[I]s this right compatible with incarceration?" This question must be answered based on evidence and not by automatically deferring to the preference of administrators.[71] In this context, perhaps studies like the present book or the health studies recently conducted by medical researchers[72] will open the door to further independent investigations and consolidate the evidence needed to prove that improper conditions of confinement and health services may, in fact, be systemic breaches of rights and worthy of court consideration, especially since most of the other rights-conferring mechanisms appear ill equipped to respond to these current correctional problems.

Some scholars continue to believe that the *Charter* is inherently individualistic and that, even when *Charter* litigation is successful, the remedy does not lead to substantive, systemic change. For instance, constitutional law scholar Benjamin Berger argues that "one of the hallmarks of the *Charter*'s individualism is its difficulty in taking cognizance of rights claims and social policy measures that seek to empower groups or institutional contexts that lead to the full enjoyment of the human goods that the Constitution purports to protect."[73] While most successful prison *Charter* challenges indeed fall short of a systemic solution, an increasing number of disadvantaged groups have found protection in the *Charter* way beyond the claimant's individual rights. Aside from *Inglis* and the more recent *BCCLA* case imposing a change to the solitary confinement provisions and policies, outside of the prison context courts have, for example, upheld under the *Charter* the rights of sex workers[74] and the right to assisted dying.[75] Both cases relied on large amounts of empirical

---

71 Kerr, "Contesting Expertise," *supra* note 5 at 87.
72 See e.g. Fiona Kouyoumdjian et al, "Health Status of Prisoners in Canada: Narrative Review" (2016) 62:3 Can Fam Physician 215; Fiona Kouyoumdjian & Andrée Schuler, "Research on the Health of People Who Experience Detention or Incarceration in Canada: A Scoping Review" (2015) 15 BMC Public Health 419; Samantha Green, Jessica Foran, & Fiona Kouyoumdjian, "Access to Primary Care in Adults in a Provincial Correctional Facility in Ontario" (2016) 9:1 BMC Res Notes 131.
73 Benjamin L. Berger, *Law's Religion: Religious Differences and the Claims of Constitutionalism* (Toronto: University of Toronto Press, 2015) at 72 [Berger].
74 *Canada (AG) v Bedford*, 2013 SCC 72, [2013] 3 SCR 1101 [*Bedford*].
75 *Carter v Canada (AG)*, 2015 SCC 5, [2015] 1 SCR 331 [*Carter*].

research showing the dangers the legislation posed to the security of specific groups of people.[76]

One may argue that only remedies offered under section 52[77] – when the rights are breached through legislation – have the potential to produce systemic effects. In such cases, a common remedy is to declare the offending provisions unconstitutional. Thus, these provisions cannot continue to be applied, which benefits everyone who previously was caught under the unconstitutional provisions. Such was the case in *Bedford* and *Carter* and, indeed, in *Sauvé* and *BCCLA*.

As it happens, with a few exceptions, the offensive acts in prison are often non-legislative. They are often prison practices, rules, and decisions that breach rights. Such was the decision not to offer methadone or the decision to withdraw the mother-child program. Similarly, a host of decisions that negatively impact older individuals may be seen as non-legislative: the requirement to line up for hours to pick up medication, lack of painkillers, withholding medical items and devices, failure to provide psychiatric care, and other such practices. When a breach is found in such cases, remedies are granted under section 24. Some remedies under section 24 have indeed been individualized. For instance, in *Maurice*, the prison was required to grant Maurice the vegetarian meal he asked for, but this requirement applied solely to the claimant.[78] Nonetheless, under section 24(1), courts are entitled to grant "any remedy that they see fit,"[79] including a systemic remedy. *Inglis* is significant in that the remedy obliged the provincial correctional service to reintroduce the mother-child program for all prisoners similarly situated to the claimant.[80] More generally, in a remarkable section 24(1) case, the court not only granted a systemic remedy through which it ordered the defendant to build a French-language school, but it also retained jurisdiction over monitoring the building of the school. The SCC affirmed the trial judge's remedy.[81]

Thus, a remedy affecting systemic change is possible under the *Charter*, both under section 52 and under section 24. While *Charter* litigation in and of itself cannot bring about the reform needed for older prisoners, courts' willingness to frame more matters related to conditions

---

76 For a detailed description of the systemic potential of individual *Charter* challenges, see *Canadian Bar Association v HMTQ*, 2006 BCSC 1342 at paras 70–85 [*CBA*].

77 *Charter*, *supra* note 14, s 52.

78 *Maurice*, *supra* note 41.

79 *Charter*, *supra* note 14, s 24(1).

80 *Inglis*, *supra* note 57.

81 *Doucet-Boudreau v Nova Scotia (Minister of Education)*, 2003 SCC 62, [2003] 3 SCR 3 [*Doucet-Boudreau*].

of confinement as human rights matters would send a clear signal to legislators and administrators that a comprehensive reform cannot be delayed. Perhaps once the rule of law is more vigorously pushed through prison doors by court decisions, prison administrators will be more inclined to respect it without constant external intervention. Perhaps also courts will follow the current trend of inclusiveness towards prisoners' rights and to what constitutes a prisoner's right and embark on a more expansive use of their ability to grant remedies under section 24(1). The words of Parkes aptly express this hope and expectation: "With the lack of legislative attention to calls for independent oversight and effective remedies for violating prisoners' rights, the second quarter century of *Charter* litigation may see courts emboldened to take a greater role at the remedial stage."[82]

In reality, absent an active court that pushes through its decisions for the implementation of rights, the *Charter* will remain partially meaningless in the prison context. Thirty-five years after the enactment of the *Charter*, it is now clear that the spirit of legality with which the *Charter*, by its mere presence, was to infuse state action will not happen in prison. While I agree that constitutional litigation is a last resort avenue, the time to aggressively resolve to such last resort mechanisms has arrived.

Challenging the Treatment of Older Prisoners under the Charter

> Suing them [CSC] is the only way to get anything. But you need patience because they will try to wear you down. (AO, 57, in prison 20 years)

The data collected for this study suggest there may be some issues regarding compliance of the policies or their implementation with the constitutional human rights framework. Three *Charter* sections come specifically to mind, and the data now beginning to emerge could help lead to successful challenges brought forward by older individuals.

First, section 12 guarantees everyone's right to be free from cruel and unusual treatment and punishment.[83] Though underused in practice, this section has been the only one interpreted to apply specifically to conditions of confinement,[84] and courts held that, where certain conditions are so grossly disproportionate as to outrage the standard of decency, they may be found to be unconstitutional. Practices that include having prisoners wear badly stained underwear, exposing prisoners to

---

82 Parkes, "Prisoners' Charter," *supra* note 34 at 675.

83 *Charter, supra* note 14, s 12.

84 *R v Smith*, [1987] 1 SCR 1054 [*Smith*].

prolonged periods of segregation with little fresh air,[85] or the use of re-
straining suits[86] were found, in the circumstances, to violate section 12.

A number of situations described in this book may lead us to question
whether perhaps the conditions of confinement for older individuals
amounts to cruel and unusual treatment, given that some of these circumstances may have a devastating effect on their health. Each claim would
need an individual assessment based on an analytical framework, but, *prima
facie*, considering the purpose of this section, numerous situations would
appear to be feasible candidates for such a challenge. Having data to point
to a systemic issue would add significant credibility to the challenge.[87]

Nonetheless, the standard for section 12, gross disproportionality, is,
without a doubt, very onerous, so much so that, despite section 12 being the only *Charter* section specifically rendered to apply to conditions
of confinement, Parkes has argued that the analyses for potential challenges to conditions of confinement have generally been made under
section 7[88] (though not very successfully). This approach may explain
why so many section 12 prison cases have failed.[89]

While some of the newly collected data may satisfy even the current
section 12 standard, I have argued elsewhere that, when it comes to conditions of confinement, maintaining such a high standard may in fact
not be justified.[90] Section 12 was deemed to apply to two distinct situations: to challenge a sentence rendered by a judge or a minimum sentence prescribed by law, and to challenge conditions of confinement.[91]
The grossly disproportionate standard and the criteria to determine it
were all rendered in cases pertaining to sentences.[92] In fact, in *Smith*,
Justice Lamer explained the need to have such a high standard by arguing that other more "trivial" sentence illegalities can be dealt with
by appealing the sentence,[93] and that the standard ensures judges and

---

85 *Trang v Alberta (Edmonton Remand Centre)*, 2010 ABQB 6 [*Trang*].

86 *Munoz v Alberta (Edmonton Remand Centre)*, 2004 ABQB 769 [*Munoz*].

87 Kerr, "Contesting Expertise," *supra* note 5 at 74–5; Parkes, "Prisoners' Charter," *supra*
    note 34 at 667.

88 Parkes, "Prisoners' Charter," *supra* note 34 at 658.

89 *Collin v Kaplan* (1982), 143 DLR (3d) 121, 2 CRR 352 (FCTD); *R v KRP*, [1994]
    BCJ No. 2405 (Prov Ct); *Maltby*, *supra* note 33; *Soenen v Edmonton Remand Centre*
    (1983), 48 AR 31, 3 DLR (4th) 658 (QB); R v Chan, 2005 ABQB 615; *R v Olson*
    (1987), 62 OR (2d) 321, [1987] OJ No. 855 (CA), aff'd [1989] 1 SCR 296.

90 Adelina Iftene, "Unlocking the Doors to Canadian Older Inmate Mental Health
    Data: Rates and Potential Legal Responses" (2016) 47 Intl J L Psychiatry 36 [Iftene,
    "Unlocking the Doors"].

91 *Smith*, *supra* note 84.

92 *Ibid*; *R v Ferguson*, 2008 SCC 6; *R v Smickle*, 2014 ONCA 49; *R v Nur*, 2015 SCC 15.

93 *Smith*, *supra* note 84.

lawmakers are not simply "second guessed."[94] While this explanation may be true for sentences, where many other oversight mechanisms are available (appeals for sentences rendered by judges, for example, or public accountability for laws passed by Parliament through a transparent process), it is hardly the case for prison conditions of confinement.

If section 12 is also to apply to the quality of the punishment and not just the quantity, as prescribed by case law,[95] a different framework needs to be developed for conditions of confinement. Decisions and practices that determine conditions of confinement are normatively and conceptually different from sentencing decisions or a law, and they do not benefit from the same oversight and accountability mechanisms. Maintaining such a high standard due to reluctance to "second guess" the administrators is yet another sign of unfaltering deference. Judges enjoy guarantees of impartiality and independence; lawmakers have been voted into office by citizens. Administrators carry none of these characteristics, and the exercise of enhanced judicial oversight over their actions is not only permissible, it is also required in order to maintain the rule of law in all state institutions.

Allowing the assessment to be made on a standard such as "deliberate indifference"[96] or "minimal level of impairment"[97] would enhance courts' oversight over conditions of confinement and render section 12 truly feasible for the protection of prisoners whose conditions are significantly harsher than what their sentences require. If courts revisited the standard they apply for evaluating conditions of confinement under section 12, we might see an increase in successful challenges and thus a significant push towards a more systemic prison reform.[98]

Second, section 7 states that "everyone has the right to life, liberty, and security of the person and the right not to be deprived thereof except in accordance with the principles of fundamental justice."[99] This section has

---

94 *Ibid.*

95 *Ibid; Trang, supra* note 85; *Munoz, supra* note 86.

96 This standard is used in the United States for claims made based on the 8th amendment, corresponding to section 12 of the *Charter. Estelle v Gamble,* 429 US 97 at 104 (1976).

97 This standard is used by the European Court of Human Rights for claims made on art 3 of the *European Convention for Human Rights and Freedoms: Valasinas v Lithuania,* No. 44558/98, [2001] VIII ECHR 385; *Dougoz v Greece* (1998), No. 40907/98, [2001] II ECHR 255.

98 The grossly disproportionate standard has been criticized in relation to its application to sentences as well. See e.g. Allan Manson, "Arbitrary Disproportionality: A New Charter Standard for Measuring the Constitutionality of Mandatory Minimum Sentences" (2012) 57 SCLR 173; Kent Roach, "Searching for Smith: the Constitutionality of Mandatory Sentences" (2001) 39:2/3 Osgoode Hall L Rev 367; Debra Parkes, "The Charter's Minimal Impact on Mandatory Minimum Sentences" (2012) 57 SCLR 149.

99 *Charter, supra* note 14, s 7.

produced the most litigation by far, and it has been useful in protecting prisoners' procedural rights,[100] but significantly less so in its response to substantive claims.[101] In the past, in non–prisoner-related contexts, section 7 was used to protect substantive rights where legislation indirectly limited access to medical care[102] and ministerial decisions restricted access to health care,[103] endangering life and security of the person in a manner incompatible with the principles of fundamental justice.

I have argued elsewhere that certain prison conduct, either through directives, decisions, or ongoing practices, harms older people in a manner that violates section 7.[104] In that context, I focused on several examples: the use of segregation for mentally ill prisoners, allowed or even prescribed by a series of Commissioner's Directives (CDs);[105] the insufficient number of medical personnel, in particular mental health specialists, caused by hiring decisions of the CSC regional directors;[106] prisoners being forced to stand daily in line, sometimes outside, to pick up medication due to the positioning of the pill-dispensing windows;[107] a lack of appropriate medical diets deriving from highly restrictive CDs and Standard Operating Practices regulating food services;[108] restricted

---

100 See e.g. *Pickard v Mountain Institution* (1994), 30 CR (4th) 399, 75 FTR 147 (FCTD); *Storry, supra* note 26; *Fitzgerald, supra* note 26; *DeMaria, supra* note 27; *Howard, supra* note 24.

101 *Piche, supra* note 34; *Williams, supra* note 34; *Protective Custody Inmates, supra* note 34; and *Sweet, supra* note 34.

102 *Chaoulli v Quebec (AG)*, 2005 SCC 35 [*Chaoulli*].

103 *Canada (AG) v PHS Community Services Society*, 2011 SCC 44 [*PHS*].

104 Adelina Iftene, "Applying Older Prisoner Empirical Data to Test a Novel s. 7 *Charter* Claim" (2017) 40:2 Dal LJ 497 [Iftene, "Section 7"].

105 Correctional Service of Canada, "Interventions to Preserve Life and Prevent Serious Bodily Harm," Commissioner's Directive No. 843 (Ottawa: CSC, 1 August 2017), online: https://www.csc-scc.gc.ca/005/006/843-cd-eng.shtml [CD 843]; Correctional Service of Canada, "Discipline of Inmates," Commissioner's Directive No. 580 (Ottawa: CSC, 26 October 2015), online: https://www.csc-scc.gc.ca/005/006/580-cd-eng.shtml [CD 580]; Correctional Service of Canada, "Administrative Segregation," Commissioner's Directive No. 709 (Ottawa: CSC, 1 August 2017), online: https://www.csc-scc.gc.ca/politiques-et-lois/709-cd-eng.shtml [CD 709].

106 Correctional Service of Canada, Document A-2015-00641 [unpublished letter]. This document and explanations were obtained through an *Access to Information Act* request in May 2016.

107 Correctional Service of Canada, Document A-2015-00640 [unpublished letter]. This document was acquired through an *Access to Information Act* request in May 2016.

108 Correctional Service of Canada, "Food Services," Commissioner's Directive No. 880 (Ottawa: CSC, 21 February 2000) online; https://www.csc-scc.gc.ca/005/006/880-cd-eng.shtml. [CD 880]; Correctional Service of Canada, Standard Operating Practices No. 880-01, "Food Services – Central Feeding" (Ottawa: CSC, 21 February 2000), online: https://www.csc-scc.gc.ca/005/006/880-1-sop-eng.shtml.

availability or lack of medical supplies for those with disabilities due to the prohibitions in the CSC's *National Essential Healthcare Framework*;[109] and the limited medication options for chronic pain as prescribed by the *CSC Drug Formulary*.[110]

When analysing a section 7 claim, a judge will attempt to establish if the conduct at issue, either legislative or administrative, impairs life, liberty, and security of the person. Life, liberty, and security of the person are achieved through the protection of various substantive rights, such as the right to only be found guilty of murder upon a finding of *mens rea* of intent,[111] the right not to be extradited to a country where one risks facing capital punishment,[112] the protection of the security of the person when a risk of death due to lack of certain forms of medical treatment is involved,[113] the right to be free from state-induced stress,[114] and the right to make autonomous choices. Such personal choices have thus far been related to where one could live,[115] what medical treatment[116] to give to one's children, the choice to terminate one's pregnancy,[117] and, ultimately, the option to choose assisted death in certain circumstances.[118] Once the impairment is established, the judge would need to determine if the impairment is in accordance with the principles of fundamental justice. The most common principles utilized in analysing substantive claims have been purpose based (how the purpose of the conduct is connected to the means utilized to gain the result).[119]

In the same piece, I argued that the prison directives and frameworks apply with the force of law, and they should be reviewed under section 7 in the same way that policy-creating legislation is reviewed

---

109   Correctional Service of Canada, *National Essential Healthcare Framework* (Ottawa: CSC, 23 July 2015) [CSC, *Healthcare Framework*]. This document was obtained through an *Access to Information Act* request in April 2016.

110   Correctional Service of Canada, *National Drug Formulary* (Ottawa: CSC, 2013) [CSC, *Formulary*]. This document was obtained through an *Access to Information Act* request in April 2016.

111   *R v Vaillancourt*, [1987] 2 SCR 636, 60 CR (3d) 280; *Martineau No. 2, supra* note 22.

112   *United States v Burns*, 2001 SCC 7.

113   *Chaoulli, supra* note 102; *PHS, supra* note 103.

114   *New Brunswick (Minister of Health and Community Services) v G(J)*, [1999] 3 SCR 46 [*G(J)*]; *Blencoe v British Columbia*, 2000 SCC 44, [2000] 2 SCR 307; *R v DB*, 2008 SCC 25, [2008] 2 SCR 3.

115   *Godbout v Longueuil (City)*, [1997] 3 SCR 844.

116   *R v Parker* (2000), 49 OR (3d) 481, 146 CCC (3d) 193 (Ont CA).

117   *R v Morgentaler*, [1988] 1 SCR 30 (most notably Justice Wilson's concurring opinion).

118   *Carter, supra* note 75.

119   *PHS, supra* note 103; *Bedford, supra* note 74; *Carter, supra* note 75; *R v KRJ*, 2016 SCC 31 [*KRJ*].

currently.[120] Decisions and prison practices should be reviewable as state conduct. Moreover, based on the available empirical data, the breaches of rights caused by legislative policies are not in accordance with the purpose-based principles of fundamental justice, namely arbitrariness, gross disproportionality, and overbreadth.[121] Thus, the state conduct harming older people could and should be reviewed, in the right circumstances, as a potential violation of section 7. In short, the courts must be willing to listen to the evidence and refuse to automatically defer to prison administrators.

Third, section 15 states that "every individual is equal before the law and under the law and has the right to equal protection and equal benefit of the law without discrimination and, in particular, without discrimination based on race, national or ethnic origin, religion, sex, age or mental or physical disability."[122] Section 15 has been interpreted to apply to both direct and indirect discrimination.[123] As such, treating everybody the same does not ensure that section 15 is respected. When the same treatment has disproportionate effects on a certain category of people based on their race, national or ethnic origin, religion, sex, age, or mental or physical disability, the state may take affirmative action for the benefit of the disadvantaged group.[124]

Thus, when the same correctional policies and practices are applied on a one-size-fits-all basis, without consideration for the unique challenges facing aging people, some concerns regarding indirect age-based discrimination may emerge. Failure to provide health services and appropriate infrastructure to accommodate people with health problems disproportionately affects older individuals. Thus, prison policies that impose the need to stand in line for medication pickup or limit the availability of pain medication, medical services, or access to health items, creates an age- and disability-based disadvantage, which is discriminatory against older individuals.

As discussed earlier, section 15 has been inconsistently applied in the prison context,[125] and few section 15 cases in general have been

---

120 Iftene, "Section 7," *supra* note 104; *Great Vancouver Transport Authority v Canadian Federation of Student – British Columbia Component*, 2009 SCC 31 [*GVTA*].

121 Iftene, "Section 7," *supra* note 104.

122 *Charter*, *supra* note 14, s 15.

123 *Andrews v Law Society of British Columbia*, [1989] 1 SCR 1989; *Eldridge v British Columbia (AG)*, [1997] 2 SCR 624 [*Eldridge*]; *Vriend v Alberta*, [1998] 1 SCR 493.

124 *Charter*, *supra* note 14, s 15(2); *Eldridge*, *supra* note 123; *R v Kapp*, 2008 SCC 41 [*Kapp*].

125 See also Campbell, *supra* note 5 at 316; Parkes, "Prisoners' Charter," *supra* note 34 at 660.

successful on the grounds of age.[126] However, coupled with a section 7 or a section 12 challenge, section 15 could prove a useful tool in the search for accommodating conditions of confinement for older individuals.[127]

Once a legislative provision has been found to breach a *Charter* right, the state is given the opportunity, according to section 1 of the *Charter*, to prove the breach was justified by showing that the provision in question had a pressing objective and the means chosen were proportional to that objective. To evaluate the justification provided, courts apply the *Oakes* framework: they first assess the importance of the objective and then inquire into the proportionality of the law. For the latter, courts evaluate if (a) the means chosen are rationally connected to the objective of the law; (b) they are minimally impairing the right in question; and (c) there is proportionality between the deleterious and salutary effects of the law.[128]

Section 1 has often proved to be of limited application for sections 12, 7, and 15. Section 1 essentially allows for an inquiry into competing social interests. Because section 7 (as well as section 12) rights are fundamental, it is difficult to find that competing social interests can override them.[129] In addition, the principle of fundamental justice analysis, an integral part of section 7, partially overlaps with section 1 analysis. *Bedford* held that it will be difficult to justify a law "that runs afoul of the principles of fundamental justice and is thus inherently flawed."[130] Similarly, the last portion of the section 15 framework, inquiring into whether the practice is discriminatory towards the group in question, also overlaps with portions of the section 1 analysis: both involve a balancing exercise between the disadvantage created on a group and the reasons for its existence.

However, more recently, *Carter* and *KRJ* held that there are a limited number of circumstances where the state will be able to provide justification for a section 7 breach. In particular, the principles of fundamental justice analysis do not contain a public good inquiry,[131] while section 1 allows for a "normative and contextual balancing of the interests of

---

126 The only notable cases are *McKinney v University of Guelph*, [1990] 3 SCR 229; *Tetreault-Gadoury v Canada (Employment and Immigration Commission)*, [1991] 2 SCR 22.

127 The availability of evidence of systemic discrimination is particularly important in section 15 cases, even when the challenge is brought in an individualized case. See court comments on this point, e.g, *CBA*, *supra* note 76 at paras 70–85.

128 *Oakes*, *supra* note 32.

129 *Re BC Motor Vehicle Act*, [1985] 2 SCR 486 at 518; *G(J)*, *supra* note 114 at para 99; *Charkaoui v Canada (Citizenship and Immigration)*, 2007 SCC 9 at para 66.

130 *Bedford*, *supra* note 74 at para 96.

131 *Carter*, *supra* note 75 at para 95.

society with those of the groups in question."[132] Thus, the proportionality test in section 1, and in particular the analysis of deleterious versus salutary effects of a law, may be of use to the state.

Section 1 only applies to legislation.[133] Thus, in cases where the senior officials' decisions or prison practices are found to be unconstitutional, Canada will never be able to justify them under section 1. However, considering that the directives and certain prison frameworks are, for all intents and purposes, legislative in effect,[134] the state may attempt a section 1 justification in those cases. It is difficult to predict what the responses of the CSC would be to justify its policies. In responding to the criticism of the Office of the Correctional Investigator (OCI), the CSC often denies that its practices are flawed without providing any concrete justification. When the CSC does provide justifications, these revolve around security concerns and budgetary restrictions. The CSC often offers a blanket justification, stating that, based on its assessment and using the resources at its disposal, its methods were the best to fulfil its mission.[135]

For instance, the CSC has often been criticized for its extended use of administrative segregation and for employing segregation to manage mentally ill prisoners, practices vetted by a host of CDs.[136] The CSC would likely allege that certain individuals cannot be managed in the general population and that, for their own safety and that of other prisoners, they need to be isolated, sometimes for very long periods, whether they are mentally ill or not. While such policies may have a pressing objective (ensuring the safety of the institution), an argument can be made that the means chosen to achieve that goal are not proportionate. On one hand, they do not just minimally impair the rights, and on the other, the salutary effects are not greater than the deleterious ones. This study shows that both administrative and disciplinary segregation are disproportionately used on individuals who are physically and mentally ill. As other studies show, segregation has no therapeutic value and, on the

---

132 *KRJ, supra* note 119 at para 139.

133 *Charter, supra* note 14, s 1.

134 *GVTA, supra* note 120.

135 See e.g. Correctional Service of Canada, "Response of the CSC to the 39th Annual Report of the Correctional Investigator 2011–2012" (Ottawa: CSC, 2012), online: https://www.csc-scc.gc.ca/publications/005007-2801-eng.shtml; Correctional Service of Canada, "Response of the Correctional Service of Canada to the 38th Annual Report of the Correctional Investigator 2010–2011" (Ottawa: CSC, 2011), online: https://www.csc-scc.gc.ca/publications/ci10-11/index-eng.shtml. All responses to the OCI's reports follow the same trend, and they are available at www.csc-css.gc.ca.

136 CD 709, *supra* note 105; CD 843, *supra* note 105; CD 580, *supra* note 105.

contrary, increases mental deterioration and leads to a high rate of suicide attempts.[137] Upon return to the general population, then, these individuals will be even sicker and more unstable.[138] What these people need is access to psychiatric care and treatment, either in the institution, in the regional treatment centre,[139] or in a community hospital. As such, humane and long-term effective options are available. Considering the devastating effects of segregation on the mentally ill, this policy does not minimally impair their rights. Also, because the positive effects (that is, management) are temporary, these individuals may be rendered even more unstable over the long term, as the salutary effects are not proportional to the deleterious ones.

Another policy the CSC may try to justify is its limitation on medical items and pain medication as per the *National Essential Healthcare Framework*[140] and the *National Drug Formulary*.[141] In terms of limiting drugs, the number one justification is likely also security. It often happens that drugs are stolen and trafficked in prison, and the availability of strong narcotics would fuel these practices. However, the study suggested that senior inmates, who are highly affected by these practices, have in fact much shorter lists of disciplinary charges as well as good relations with staff members. For example, only 31 per cent of the prisoners interviewed reported receiving a disciplinary charge after the age of fifty, with only 6 per cent of these being for violent behaviour. On the other hand, only 6.1 per cent reported poor relations with staff members. Thus, for this particular group, a drop in security in favour of holistic palliative care or a more permissive drug policy should not be too difficult to arrange. One could imagine the creation of seniors-only units where security concerns would be lower and a better drug policy could be in place. It cannot be said, then, that a blanket prohibition on needed drugs is only minimally impairing older prisoners' rights.

---

137 Ivan Zinger, Cherami Wichmann, & D.A. Andrews, "The Psychological Effects of 60 Days in Administrative Segregation" (2001) 43:1 Can J Crim 47; Canada, Office of the Correctional Investigator, *Annual Report, 2014–2015* (Ottawa: OCI, 2015) at 25–31, online: http://www.oci-bec.gc.ca/cnt/rpt/pdf/annrpt/annrpt20142015-eng.pdf; Howard Sapers, Correctional Investigator of Canada, *A Preventable Death* (Ottawa: OCI, 2008), online: http://www.oci-bec.gc.ca/cnt/rpt/pdf/oth-aut/oth-aut20080620-eng.pdf.

138 See e.g. Iftene, "Unlocking the Doors," *supra* note 90.

139 Regional treatment centres are CSC institutions where prisoners with acute mental illnesses are being treated. There is one in every region, and most of them are accredited psychiatric facilities. For a general description, see Correctional Service of Canada, "Institutional Profiles," online: https://www.csc-scc.gc.ca/institutions/index-eng.shtml.

140 CSC, *Healthcare Framework*, *supra* note 109.

141 CSC, *Formulary*, *supra* note 110.

Finally, the CSC may offer budgetary restrictions as a potential reason for withholding medical items and drugs, as well as for refusing to allow tailored medical diets. However, it has never been accepted in Canada that the state can save money at the cost of people's direct well-being and safety. A financial justification has only once been accepted under section 1, in a very different context.[142] It is doubtful that any court would justify threats to life and security of the person because the government is facing budgetary restrictions. To conclude, while the state may attempt to justify *prima facia* unconstitutional legislative policies as the best way to ensure security based on the resources available, there are instances when it is unlikely those justifications will be successful. The extreme effects of such polices, at least on older individuals, in addition to the availability of better solutions to achieve the same results, would make such justifications unfeasible.

The Benefit of a Charter Challenge for Older Prisoners

While, historically, *Charter* challenges brought by prisoners have not been considerably more successful than other types of litigation, the current trend is encouraging. With the increase in the availability of empirical data, case law shows that courts are less likely to defer to prison administrators and more likely to investigate prison claims in depth. The fact that *Charter* challenges can be brought directly to a provincial superior court presents its own set of advantages. As noted by the SCC, the provincial courts generally have more expertise both on *Charter* and on criminal justice matters than the Federal Court (and thus are less likely to need to defer to the wisdom of the prison administrators), and they are locally more accessible to prisoners.[143]

That said, bringing forward the type of claim proposed here will not be easy. It will require that prisoners be willing to sue the government and have access to legal advice and support to do so. Litigation is also expensive, and a lot is at stake for such claimants.[144] However, in the absence of other viable options (including legislators and the government not voluntarily addressing such matters) as well as the increase in older prisoners with declining health, such claims will eventually arise. Moreover, courts have allowed for public standing in *Charter* challenges to unconstitutional legislative provisions,[145] and in such cases a prisoner

---

142 *Newfoundland (Treasury Board) v N.A.P.E.*, 2004 SCC 66.

143 *May, supra* note 13 at paras 68, 70.

144 For the barriers faced by prisoner litigants, see Parkes, "Prisoners' Charter," *supra* note 34 at 667.

145 *Canada (AG) v Downtown Eastside Sex Workers United Against Violence Society*, 2012 SCC 45 at para 51; *BCCLA, supra* note 60 at paras 4–7.

claimant would not even be needed.[146] While the views on this avenue are conflicting, public standing may also be allowed for challenges to state conduct,[147] which is a distinct advantage of a *Charter* challenge as opposed to any other type of litigation.

When a *Charter* violation occurs as a result of state conduct, remedies will generally be granted under section 24; when it results from a legislative violation, remedies under section 52 apply.[148] It is sometimes considered that only section 52 remedies have the potential for systemic effects.[149] For instance, a finding that the CD allowing the use of segregation for mentally ill people or the framework banning medical items needed by older people was unconstitutional would force the CSC to redraft these documents. This reform would benefit all individuals affected by these documents.

However, courts have proven that they are able and willing to provide creative remedies under section 24(1) that go beyond the claimant.[150] We can thus imagine how a court may use the opportunity of a *Charter* challenge to prison practices to influence systemic prison change. For example, if the court finds that the decision to limit the hiring of medical personnel is unconstitutional, it may order the CSC to employ more mental health specialists based, for instance, on community standards. Equally, a court may order that the warden cannot impose a blanket prohibition on medical items available according to the framework, or that a pre-established assessment must be in place before people are given

---

146   The test of public standing for issues of broad interest was developed before the *Charter* was enacted in *Thorson v Canada (AG)*, [1975] 1 SCR 138; *Nova Scotia Board of Censors v McNeil*, [1976] 2 SCR 265; *Canada (Minister of Justice) v Borowski*, [1981] 2 SCR 575. The test for public standing in the *Charter* era relied on these three cases and was refined in *Finlay v Canada (Minister of Finance)*, [1986] 2 SCR 607. When a party that has no stake in a matter of public interest brings a challenge to court, the court will need to decide if the plaintiff has standing, that is, if they meet the requirements for public standing. This decision is made using the criteria in the above four cases; see e.g. *CBA, supra* note 76 at paras 20–7.

147   *Chaudhary v Canada (AG)*, 2010 ONSC 6092 at paras 19–25. The judge specifically expressed his uncertainty regarding the application of public standing to cases where section 24 remedies are sought (thus cases where state conduct is at issue); however, in *Conseil-scolaire francophone de la Colombie-Britannique v British Columbia (education)*, 2016 BCSC 1764 at paras 1123–31, the judge allowed public standing for individuals seeking section 24 remedies. Public standing was recently granted for the BC Civil Liberties Association and the John Howard Society by the British Columbia Supreme Court in a prison case challenging the use of segregation.

148   *GVTA, supra* note 120 at para 87.

149   *Ibid* at para 88.

150   The most notable case is *Doucet-Boudreau, supra* note 81.

androgen treatment. As Roach has argued, there is no reason courts cannot grant positive remedies under the *Charter*.[151]

Finally, even if courts are not willing to provide a positive remedy, a mere recognition, either under section 24 or section 52, that the practice or the directive violates *Charter* rights (for example, through a declaration) could go a long way towards pushing the matter onto legislators' tables and forcing discussions that Parliament and the government currently do not appear to be willing to have.

The *Charter* should not be the main remedial mechanism, and, as some have argued,[152] other mechanisms may be better suited to encourage systemic change. However, when a branch of the government operates in the grey area of legality, shaded from oversight, and is only intermittently held accountable, wide access to courts through direct *Charter* challenges must be available. All things considered (cost of litigation, difficulty of producing evidence from behind bars and meeting the high standards imposed by courts for *Charter* analysis, the still-apparent inclination of courts to defer to prison administration and to apply a double standard in prison cases), there is some consensus that, provided empirical evidence can be brought forward, *Charter* cases may be more successful and produce more extensive results than other forms of litigation.

Particularly considering the option of public standing for *Charter* challenges, one can only hope that civil rights groups will take notice of the problems associated with aging in prison and will file a *Charter* claim utilizing the emerging empirical data.

Habeas Corpus

John had heard of *habeas corpus*. He did not exactly know what it entailed, but it did appear that this old writ had a bit of notoriety among prisoners.

> Guys apply for it when they are transferred to higher forms of security. Transfers happen every day by the dozens, for all reasons. Some for good reasons, but mostly as scare tactics, because they can. So I know many guys that took it to court to have their transfers revoked. Some were successful, most of them weren't ... I am not sure if they are more successful now than they were in the '80s. These days I don't socialize as much as I did back then, you see.

---

151 Kent Roach, "The Courts and Medicare: Too Much or Too Little Judicial Activism?" in Colleen Flood, Kent Roach, & Lorne Sossin, *Access to Care, Access to Justice: The Legal Debate over Private Health Insurance in Canada* (Toronto: University of Toronto Press, 2005) at 184–201.

152 See e.g. Berger, *supra* note 73.

Status Quo

The popularity of *habeas corpus* among prisoners is not surprising. First, it is one of the oldest remedies available to incarcerated individuals, an English writ of rights going back to the Magna Carta in England and used since the eighteenth century in Canada.[153] Second, it is now a constitutionally entrenched protection[154] against depriving prisoners of residual liberty through some very common disciplinary and management tools: segregation, transfer to higher security or to the special handling unit (SHU), and refusal of parole. Third, it is a very straightforward, expeditious, and, when successful, effective procedure.

Despite its long history, *habeas corpus* has been applied to cases involving the legality of confinement in strictly limited scenarios. It used to apply to cases in which an individual was illegally detained and sought complete liberty.[155] Its use for prisoners legally incarcerated was marginal.

This state of affairs changed with the entrenchment of *habeas corpus* in the Constitution[156] and, in practice, with a trilogy of three cases decided together by the SCC in 1985.[157] In all three cases (*Cardinal, Miller,* and *Morin*), the prisoners brought applications of *habeas corpus* with *certiorari* in aid to the SCC in order to quash a decision that restricted their residual liberty. As a constitutional remedy, *habeas corpus* could be brought to a provincial superior court. However, according to the *Federal Courts Act, certiorari,* a writ that allows for an administrative decision to be quashed, was to be brought in Federal Court. Nonetheless, the SCC made a number of groundbreaking statements in this trilogy of decisions. First, the SCC confirmed that a superior court can issue a *certiorari* in aid of *habeas corpus,* having concurrent, not conflicting jurisdiction with the Federal Court.[158]

Second, the SCC confirmed that *habeas corpus* can be used by the judge to look beyond the legality of the warrants produced on the return. Thus, even where the individual is not looking for complete liberty but rather release from a more restrictive form of confinement, *habeas corpus*

---

153 For the history of *habeas corpus*, see David Cole & Allan Manson, *Release from Imprisonment: The Law of Sentencing, Parole and Judicial Review* (Toronto: Carswell, 1990) at 82–6 [Cole & Manson].

154 *Charter, supra* note 14, s 10(c).

155 *Re Sproule* (1886), 12 SCR 140; *Goldhar v R,* [1960] SCR 431; *Mitchell v R,* [1976] 2 SCR 570; *R v Miller,* [1985] 2 SCR 613 at 634–6 [*Miller*].

156 *Charter, supra* note 14, s 10(c).

157 *Cardinal v Kent Institution (Director),* [1985] 2 SCR 662; *Morin v National Special Handling Unit Review Committee,* [1985] 2 SCR 662; *Miller, supra* note 155.

158 *Miller, supra* note 155 at 641.

can still apply.[159] For instance, in *Cardinal*, *habeas corpus* with *certiorari* in aid was utilized to quash a decision to detain someone in solitary confinement. In *Miller* and *Morin*, the decisions to transfer the prisoners to the SHU were quashed. Both solitary confinement and transfer to the SHU were deemed "significant reduction in the residual liberty of the inmate."[160] However, the court further stated that it could not apply to "all conditions of confinement" that reduce the residual liberty.[161]

Subsequently, *habeas corpus* was utilized to uphold a *Charter* section 7 right, and relief was granted under section 24(1) of the *Charter*.[162] In *Gamble*, the appellant was convicted under a harsher law, which affected her parole eligibility. The court confirmed the jurisdiction of the superior court to hear *habeas corpus* applications and ruled that *Charter* remedies can be granted based on such application.

Based on the *Miller* trilogy and *Gamble*, Allan Manson summarized[163] the law and scope of *habeas corpus*, which to this day stands as good law, if somewhat refined:

- *Habeas corpus* is the primary tool to challenge the legality of confinement.
- *Habeas corpus* can be issued by a superior court, regardless of the cause of the confinement.
- *Habeas corpus* can include extrinsic evidence as long as there is no attempt to usurp the role of the Court of Appeal (it is not an appeal mechanism).
- Concurrent Federal Court jurisdiction does not preclude *habeas corpus*.
- *Habeas corpus* is available to assert challenges based on *Charter* rights, especially section 7, section 9, and section 12.
- Based on *habeas corpus*, courts can order transfers to a more lenient regime of confinement.
- *Habeas corpus* is commonly used to challenge a transfer to higher security, use of segregation, and the refusal of transfer to lower security, as long as entitlement is shown.
- The application of *habeas corpus* is still limited for assertion of privilege and for conditions of confinement, except when conditions create "a discreet regime which involves a significant reduction in the residual liberty of the inmate."[164]

---

159 *Ibid* at 634–41.
160 *Ibid* at 634.
161 *Ibid* at 641.
162 *R v Gamble*, [1988] 2 SCR 595 [*Gamble*].
163 Cole & Manson, *supra* note 153 at 101–2.
164 *Miller, supra* note 155.

In *Steele*,[165] the SCC decided in favour of a prisoner who brought an application of *habeas corpus* combined with section 12 of the *Charter*. He was labelled a dangerous offender and refused parole for thirty-seven years. The court stated that decisions of the Parole Board of Canada should normally be challenged through judicial review in the Federal Court. However, acknowledging that the test for section 12 is very stringent and that, because of the prisoner's age and health, it is not fair to ask him to apply for judicial review, the court granted, "in this highly unusual circumstance,"[166] Steele's release, based on his *habeas corpus* application. Manson noted that this decision was important because it exemplified how *habeas corpus* can be used to bring forward a *Charter* challenge that by itself would likely not have succeeded.[167] It was also important because it exemplified the flexibility of remedies under section 24(1), which could be granted for both *habeas corpus* and *Charter* challenges. In this case, the court released Steele and imposed conditions for his release. At the time, Manson called attention to the fact that this "instructive example of judicial scrutiny of long term confinement should not be blunted by undue attention to his [the Justice's] remarks about judicial review."[168] In his commentary, Manson argued that the Federal Court lacks the expertise in sentence fitness and criminal justice needed to assess the constitutionality of parole decisions, so it was normal that superior courts be allowed concurrent jurisdiction.[169]

Ironically, for fifteen years, the one sentence from *Steele* to have any real impact was the one stating that a *habeas corpus* application was to be granted on an exceptional basis.[170] In many cases to come,[171] this sentence was used to deny jurisdiction by superior courts based on the rule that prisoner applications should follow the route of the internal grievance procedure and judicial review in Federal Court. Jurisdiction was denied despite criticism that *habeas corpus* was rejected even in

---

165 *Steele v Stony Mountain Institution*, [1990] 2 SCR 1385 [*Steele*].

166 *Ibid* at 1419.

167 Allan Manson et al, *Sentencing and Penal Policy in Canada: Cases, Materials, and Commentary*, 2nd ed (Toronto: Emond Montgomery, 2008) at 1019 [Manson et al].

168 Allan Manson, "The Effects of Steele on *Habeas Corpus* and Indeterminate Sentences" (1991) 80 CR 282 at 285 [Manson, "Steele"].

169 *Ibid*.

170 Debra Parkes, "The 'Great Writ' Reinvigorated? *Habeas Corpus* in Contemporary Canada" (2012) 36:1 Man LJ 351 at 355 [Parkes, "*Habeas Corpus*"].

171 See e.g. *St. Amand v Canada (AG)* (2000), 147 CCC (3d) 48 (Que CA); *Armaly v Canada (Correctional Service)*, 2001 ABCA 280; *Spindler v Milhaven Institution* (2003), 15 CR (6th) 183, 110 CRR (2d) 173 (Ont CA); *Hickey v Canada*, 2003 BCCA 23 [*Hickey*]; *Bernard v Kent Institution*, 2003 BCCA 24.

circumstances not envisioned by *Steele* and that the internal grievance procedure was not an "adequate alternative remedy," as *Steele* required for rejection of a *habeas corpus* application.[172]

The SCC put an end to this trend in *May v Ferndale*[173] on the very basis that Manson invoked fifteen years prior.[174] *May* is one of the most important legal indictments of the internal grievance system[175] and of judicial review in Federal Court. The SCC affirmed the importance of judicial oversight over prison decisions and stated that the concurrent jurisdiction of superior courts by way of *habeas corpus* is essential because the grievance procedure is highly flawed, and superior courts are better placed to hear prison claims than the Federal Court. Prisoners may choose to follow the standard process and first exhaust the grievance procedure and appeal in Federal Court[176] or, if they wish, they may bring a constitutional challenge directly to superior court (such as *habeas corpus*) for the following reasons:

- The prisoners are highly vulnerable individuals, under complete state control, and they are entitled to choice of forum and remedy.
- Provincial courts have more expertise than the Federal Court to hear prison claims, because these often include matters pertaining to sentencing, criminal justice, and *Charter* rights, which are rarely dealt with in the Federal Court.
- *Habeas corpus* offers a considerably faster remedy (it requires only 6 days' notice, as opposed to judicial review, which requires 160 days' notice).
- Provincial courts are locally accessible, which is an important aspect of access to justice.
- *Habeas corpus* is non-discretionary, whereas the judicial review is at the discretion of the Federal Court.
- Once the prisoner shows a restriction of liberty, the burden of proof is on the state to prove that confinement was legal; on judicial review, the burden rests with the claimant to prove that confinement was illegal.[177]

In *May*, based on the *habeas corpus* application, the SCC found that the prison administrators were in breach of their procedural duty of fairness

---

172 Charles Davidson, "Whittling Away at Greatness: The Narrowing of the Availability of *Habeas Corpus*" (2004) 15 CR (6th) 192 at 196–8.

173 *May, supra* note 13.

174 Manson, "Steele," *supra* note 168.

175 *May, supra* note 13 at para 64.

176 *Ibid* at paras 44, 72.

177 *Ibid* at paras 62–70.

when they transferred the prisoner to a higher form of security without explaining to him the reasons and the procedure as required by the *CCRA*.[178] The SCC quashed the transfer order and ordered the return of the applicant to minimum security.

In recent years, the SCC confirmed in *Khela*[179] that *Miller* and *May* are good law and still apply in terms of concurrent jurisdiction of superior courts and the Federal Court. In *Khela*, the application was successful because the CSC was found to be in breach of its duties of procedural fairness according to the *CCRA*[180] regarding the legislative procedural rules for transfer. Though not applicable in this case, the court, *in obiter*,[181] addressed the issue of review of the substantive issues that may arise following a *habeas corpus* application (in this instance it would have been the legality of the reasons for transfer, as opposed to the procedure followed).

Lisa Kerr has documented the debate that took place before the SCC regarding the standard of review a court should use to determine the latter issue.[182] Allan Manson, on behalf of the prisoner, argued that the standard utilized should not call for deference towards prison authorities. A transfer is either legal or not legal; it cannot fall on a spectrum of legality, which deference entails when the administrative reasonableness standard is used. He also pleaded with the court that the *habeas corpus* law be developed separately from the administrative law of judicial review and that new standards be created.[183] Michael Jackson, as counsel for the same party, argued that there is a difference between cutting wardens some slack and installing broad deference towards prison authorities. He asserted that judges may accept the decisions of the administration when they prove to be right, but that automatic deference is misplaced because prison officials have biases and a particular focus. The organization of prisons tends to resist constitutional constraint, and the status of prisoners is defined in relation to managerial roles rather than the larger legal order.[184]

Nonetheless, the SCC imposed a reasonableness standard for the review of the substantive aspects of a matter under *habeas corpus*. It did, however, mention that this standard should not change the nature of

---

178   *Corrections and Conditional Release Act*, SC 1992, c 20, ss 27–8 [*CCRA*].
179   *Mission Institution v Khela*, 2014 SCC 24 [*Khela*].
180   *CCRA*, *supra* note 178, ss 27–8.
181   *In obiter* is a Latin term referring to the parts of a decision that are not relevant to the facts of the case. It does not constitute law, as it is not the legal principle generated by the case, but it has a significant influence over subsequent cases that directly address that issue.
182   Kerr, "Easy Prison Cases," *supra* note 7 at 254–8.
183   *Ibid* at 254.
184   *Ibid* at 258.

the writ and that it does not apply to all the flaws in a decision.[185] It is unclear if this ruling is a restrictive decision for prisoner rights or simply confirms the current status quo of *habeas corpus*. The court does not say to which flaws reasonableness applies and to which it does not.[186] It is also unclear how much deference is owed to administrators under *habeas corpus* or, indeed, considering the constitutional nature of *habeas corpus*, why any deference is owed at all.

Steele[187] is proof that one phrase can throw *habeas corpus* jurisprudence back fifteen years despite the rest of the decision being supportive of enhanced access to justice.[188] In such context, it is of concern that the standard set *in obiter* in *Khela*, despite the general tone of the decision, may also hinder successful *habeas corpus* applications in the future. Indeed, if superior courts are to show the same level of deference as the Federal Court shows upon judicial review based on the reasonableness standard, a significant part of the advantage that *habeas corpus* presents over judicial review[189] is effectively negated.

While constitutional questions were, at one time, answered based on a correctness standard upon judicial review,[190] in 2010 *Doré v Barreau du Québec*[191] asserted that non-legislative state conduct is to be reviewed based on reasonableness, even when it is challenged as unconstitutional. Even though the law of *habeas corpus* has been repeatedly described as different if sometimes of concurrent application from that of judicial review, it is possible that *Khela* is a reinforcement of the deferential attitude of the courts in *Doré*. Nonetheless, *Doré* was largely seen by critics as an anomaly of the jurisprudence, and they questioned whether *Doré* will continue to constitute "good law."[192] Audrey Macklin criticized the decision, questioning the purpose of incorporating the *Charter* in the decision-making process of administrators and tribunals if courts were allowed to simply look at whether or not the *Charter* had been considered and not at how much weight was given to it in the process. She equated

---

185 *Khela, supra* note 179 at para 77.

186 For a criticism of the incoherence of *Khela*, see The Honourable Justice David Stratas, "The Canadian Law of Judicial Review: A Plea for Doctrinal Coherence and Consistency" (2016) 42:1 Queen's LJ 27 at 34 [Stratas].

187 *Steele, supra* note 165.

188 Manson et al, *supra* note 167 at 1019; Parkes, "*Habeas Corpus*," *supra* note 170 at 355.

189 *Miller, supra* note 155 at 105; *Gamble, supra* note 162 at 223; *May, supra* note 13 at paras 62–70.

190 *Dunsmuir v New Brunswick*, 2008 SCC 9.

191 *Doré v Barreau du Québec*, 2012 SCC 12 [*Doré*].

192 See Stratas, *supra* note 186 at 33–4; see also *Loyola High School v Quebec (AG)*, 2015 SCC 12, [2015] 1 SCR 613, where three out of seven SCC judges did not even mention *Doré, supra* note 192, in their minority opinion.

a reasonableness standard with insulation from meaningful scrutiny.[193] She made significant recommendations for rethinking the standard applied,[194] citing David Mullan, and said that "to prevent devaluation of rights and freedoms, there should be recognition that the framework within which deference operates will often, perhaps invariably, need to be different than in the case of judicial review of administrative action that does not affect *Charter* rights and freedoms."[195]

While deference is often explained by the fact that administrators are experts in their field, prison officials are not experts in constitutional law, and "there is simply no basis for presumption that certain officials should receive deference when they exercise their *Charter*-impacting discretion."[196] Since *habeas corpus* is a constitutional, rights-based remedy, often used in combination with a *Charter* challenge, the same critique applies for the use of reasonableness in a *habeas corpus* application.

As was the case in *Steele*, we are once more confronted with a conflicting decision on *habeas corpus* that could be read either as strengthening or restricting prisoner remedies. So far, there has been inconsistency in deciding *habeas corpus* applications post-*Khela*. On one hand, a number of applications have been successful even in situations not traditionally dealt with under the writ, such as challenges to the continuing detention of immigration detainees,[197] being placed in federal as opposed to provincial institutions,[198] classification,[199] and denial of parole.[200]

On the other hand, a significant trend among lower courts has been to take a restrictive approach to *habeas corpus*, often stating that, while the writ has encountered an expansive application in recent years, such applications should not replace judicial review in Federal Court for contesting administrative decisions.[201] For instance, despite the recent *DG*

---

193 Audrey Macklin, "Charter Rights or Charter-Lite? Administrative Discretion and the Charter" (2014) 67:2 SCLR 561 at 584 [Macklin].

194 *Ibid* at 587.

195 David Mullan, "Administrative Tribunals and Judicial Review of *Charter* Issues after *Multani*" (2006) 21 NJCL 127 at 149. See also Mark Walters, "Respecting Deference as Respect: Rights, Reasonableness and Proportionality in Canadian Administrative Law" in Hanna Wilberg & Mark Elliott, eds, *The Scope and Intensity of Judicial Review: Traversing Taggart's Rainbow* (Oxford: Hart Publishing, 2015).

196 Macklin, *supra* note 193 at 576.

197 *Chaudhary v Canada (Minister of Public Safety & Emergency Preparedness)*, 2015 ONCA 700; *Chhina v Canada (Public Safety and Emergency Preparedness)*, 2017 ABCA 248.

198 *Bowden Institution v Khadr*, 2014 ABCA 225.

199 *Gogan v Attorney General*, 2017 NSCA 4.

200 *DG v Bowden Institution*, 2016 ABCA 52.

201 See e.g. *LVR v Mountain Institution (Warden)*, 2016 BCCA 467; *Chambers v Daou*, 2015 BCCA 50.

case, most other courts have supported the previous position[202] that challenges to denials of parole are to be dealt with under the *CCRA* regime and through judicial review in Federal Court. *Khela* stated that two situations can be found where a superior court should decline jurisdiction, one of them being "where the legislature has put in place a complete, comprehensive and expert procedure"[203] [the old exception developed in *Peiroo*[204]]. Some post-*Khela* decisions have stated that the parole regime in *CCRA* is one of those procedures.[205]

Courts have also taken a restrictive approach to *habeas corpus* applications, even where the application was for more typical uses of the writ such as transfers to other institutions, re-classifications,[206] and/or administrative segregation.[207] In other cases, for instance, an application for *habeas corpus* to challenge the result of a criminal proceeding where the relevant appeal period has expired, the claim has also been deemed *prima facia* inadmissible.[208]

The hope is that, in the face of the current criticism of the use of the reasonableness standard for constitutional matters, the history of the *Steele* decision, and the numerous instances and reasons for which *habeas corpus* has been found to be more effective than judicial review in the Federal Court, courts will move away from applying the one sentence in *Khela* that could render *habeas corpus* ineffective as judicial review and wipe out a decade of progress.

Habeas Corpus *Applications by Older Prisoners*

Habeas corpus has proven to be a highly efficient remedy when combined with *Charter* remedies, in particular section 7, section 9, section 12, and

---

202 *R v Graham*, 2011 ONCA 138; *John v Canada (National Parole Board)*, 2011 BCCA 188, leave to appeal to SCC refused, 34309 (1 December 2011).

203 *Khela, supra* note 179 at para 55.

204 *Peiroo v Canada (Minister of Employment and Immigration)* (1989), 69 OR (2d) 253, 1989 CanLII 184 (Ont CA).

205 *Babinski v Canada (AG)*, 2014 ONSC 6493 [*Babinski*]; *R v Latham*, 2016 SKCA 14, leave to appeal to SCC refused, 36947 (8 September 2016) [*Latham*]; *Urbano v Bowden Institution*, 2015 ABQB 279 [*Urbano*]; *Gallant v Springhill Institution*, 2014 NSSC 122 [*Gallant*]; *Little v Canada (AG)*, 2017 ONSC 6282 [*Little*]; *Ewanchuk v Canada (Parole Board)*, 2017 ABCA 145 [*Ewanchuk*].

206 *Ricci c Centre régional de réception*, 2018 QCCA 82; *LVR v Mountain Institution (Warden)*, 2016 BCCA 467; *Horton v Warden (Atlantic Institution)*, 2018 NBQB 5; *Palfrey v Warden (Mission Institution)*, 2015 BCSC 1777.

207 *Badger v Canada (Correctional Service)*, 2017 ABQB 457.

208 *Latham v Canada (AG)*, 2018 ABQB 69.

even section 15.[209] While it has been limited to situations that restrict the residual liberty of prisoners (generally solitary confinement, transfer to higher forms of security, or sometimes denial of parole), *habeas corpus* may also apply to conditions of confinement if they create "a discrete regime which involves a significant reduction in the residual liberty of the inmate."[210] While it may turn out to be quite difficult in light of the current restrictive approach courts have taken post-*Khela*, older prisoners should be able to access this remedy, especially in combination with a *Charter* challenge, in a significant number of situations that excessively restrict their liberty and endanger their health.

For instance, one of the biggest issues that older, disabled individuals encounter, as explained in chapter three, is the difficulty they have in accessing parole, whether under general conditional release or under parole by exception. Because of issues outside their control, older prisoners are often not granted release upon their parole eligibility dates, and issues determinative for their actual risk and their need for services, such as age and health, are not considered.

However, in *Steele*, the court laid down three criteria upon which to assess the claimant's *habeas corpus* application: the prisoner has reached the maximum benefit from imprisonment; more imprisonment will only further impact the prisoner's health; and the prisoner is not an undue risk to society. The court used evidence related to Steele's advanced age and health status in determining these three factors. Based on that evidence, the court ordered Steele's release.[211] In light of *May*, which confirmed that *Steele* is not an exception and that, in fact, prisoners have direct access to apply to superior courts even when there is concurrent jurisdiction with the Federal Court,[212] it is clear that *Steele* is an important precedent for aging prisoners who have done all they personally can to meet the terms of their sentence and have ceased to be a risk to society. First, in combination with a section 12 challenge (right to be free from cruel and unusual treatment or punishment), these individuals could apply for *habeas corpus* when they have been refused parole even though they were housed in prison with deteriorating health and limited access

---

209   *Beaudry v Canada (Commissioner of Corrections)*, [1997] OJ No. 5082 (QL) (CA).
       A challenge was brought by a group of women who were to be transferred to
       Kingston Penitentiary (a male institution) upon the closing of the Prison for
       Women in Kingston. The court stayed the transfer until the section 15 issues were
       resolved. The case never reached the trial phase because the CSC cancelled the
       transfer altogether: Manson et al, *supra* note 168 at 1041.
210   *Miller, supra* note 155.
211   *Steele, supra* note 165.
212   *May, supra* note 13.

to mental health care, pain medication, health items, appropriate infrastructure, and so on. If they have not reached their parole eligibility date, those who are terminally ill or whose health is incompatible with incarceration and are refused compassionate release under section 121 of the *CCRA* could apply for *habeas corpus* on those bases. Under a section 24(1) challenge, similar to *Steele*, the court would be able to order the release of the individual immediately and set the necessary conditions. Legal logic dictates that, based on the difference between judicial review and *habeas corpus* (as set out in *May* and confirmed in *Khela*) and on the emerging empirical evidence showing the inappropriateness of services for the health of older individuals, a *habeas corpus* application should be treated differently from an application for judicial review for the decisions of the parole board (which have largely been unsuccessful). Thus far, however, this logic has been subdued, as mentioned, by recent decisions in which courts have refused to exercise *habeas corpus* jurisdiction in parole matters.[213]

Second, solitary confinement, both administrative and disciplinary, is used to manage mental illness. Many of those interviewed for this book had not discussed their suicidal ideation with mental health professionals for fear of being thrown in isolation. A higher percentage (almost double) of those individuals who reported a mental illness also reported spending time in segregation, as compared to those who did not report a mental illness. One could argue that this further restriction of an individual's liberty is dangerous for their health, in addition to constituting cruel and unusual punishment. Combining a *habeas corpus* application with a *Charter* challenge based on sections 7 and 12 could aid applicants in getting timely release from solitary confinement. Similarly, there have been cases where individuals with dementia were transferred to a higher security institution or section for better management. This type of situation could also be challenged by a *habeas corpus* application in combination with a *Charter* challenge.

Third, some arguments could be made based on conditions of confinement that restrict older individuals' residual liberty. In certain institutions, the infrastructure is not disability-friendly. Prisoners with mobility problems spend most of their time in their rooms, with little access to programs or activities. In most institutions, no safe place is provided for older individuals to exercise, and they are continually bullied by younger prisoners. In three institutions, pills are picked up outdoors, often in bad weather, leading some individuals with disabilities or illnesses to

---

213 *Babinski, supra* note 205; *R v Latham, supra* note 205; *Urbano, supra* note 205; *Gallant, supra* note 205; *Little, supra* note 205; *Ewanchuk, supra* note 205.

simply stop taking their required medication. All of these examples are *de facto* limits to the freedom of prisoners beyond what incarceration entails for most of their peers. The lack of accommodation for the needs of older individuals factually limits their residual liberty. It is hard to think of clearer examples of conditions of confinement that create "a discrete regime which involves a significant reduction in the residual liberty of the inmate."[214] Basically, wherever the lack of accommodation forces an individual to give up something they are fully entitled to and people who do not need accommodation can reasonably enjoy it, an argument could be made that the conditions of confinement have restricted the residual liberty of the individual. Coupled with a section 15 *Charter* challenge (depending on the case, section 7 or section 12 challenges could also be appropriate), such applications should provide fast and flexible remedies for older individuals.

As a *Charter*-entrenched right, section 24(1) remedies can be granted under a *habeas corpus* application. This section allows for flexible and creative remedies, which in the past varied from an order to transfer to minimum security to release with conditions set by the judge. In the past, all *habeas corpus* remedies were limited to the individual, and it would likely be the case in the vast majority of applications brought forward by older individuals. For instance, release on conditional or compassionate release could be ordered, or release from segregation, or transfer to an institution that is more accommodating to the needs of seniors when it comes to infrastructure. However, considering that section 24(1) offers significant discretion to the judge to decide what is an appropriate relief, systemic remedies are not excluded. Faced with evidence that, for instance, few institutions have safe spaces for an older person to exercise, a judge may order the creation of a seniors-only unit or the allocation of separate time slots for aging people to access institutional gyms.

Considering that *habeas corpus* can be brought in superior courts, with all of their advantages over the Federal Court, it is unfortunate that *habeas corpus* is an underused tool (and perhaps for good reason in light of what seems to be the deferential attitude of courts dealing with *habeas corpus* applications). Nonetheless, numerous situations beyond transfer and solitary confinement that significantly limit the liberty of certain individuals by the very nature of unaccommodating institutional design have never been attempted under this writ. *Habeas corpus* would allow for fast transfers to an institution that carries the needed services or could potentially even force institutional authorities to change some

---

214   *Miller, supra* note 155.

of their policies in a manner that allows older individuals to enjoy the same rights as everyone else. Thus, pushing for an expanded application of *habeas corpus* to both traditional and less traditional situations, as *May* and *Khela* seem to mandate, may be worthwhile.

Tort Claims and Damages

> If you want something done you have to sue them. In my forty years here I learned that whenever I have been wronged, anything else but suing them is a waste of time. When you sue them, they rush to give you what you want. They don't want to go to court. (AA, 63, in prison 43 years)

Filing a civil law complaint for personal injury is the most common avenue for obtaining monetary redress for physical and emotional wrongdoings. Such an avenue is ill equipped to address systemic issues, but, in most cases, what complainants want is an acknowledgment that they have been wronged and money to help them recover.

Today, tribunals and courts have the option of ordering complainant compensation as a result of a human rights or *Charter* challenge. However, the classic tort-based claim for damages continues to be the basic avenue and has a considerably wider spectrum of application. In such cases, damages may be granted for wrongs other than human rights violations (which can only be perpetrated by state agents) and without the need to undergo complex human rights analyses. Thus, a plaintiff may be granted monetary compensation as a result of a tort-based complaint when they were victim of an intentional wrongdoing or were hurt by negligent conduct or by a breach of a third party's duty towards the complainant.

Status Quo

There are two types of torts on which basis individuals can sue. The first type, intentional torts, where an individual is harmed by another's intentional action, is recognized by common law as a wrongdoing, such as battery, assault, or false imprisonment. The difficulty with such claims is proving the intention to commit the action and cause the harm that resulted. However, as with all private law claims, the standard to prove intention is relatively low "on a balance of probabilities": it is more likely that the defendant intended to cause the harm through the action prohibited by law.

Such claims are rather straightforward, and they have been moderately successful in the prison context. For instance, prisoners have been successful in cases where they sued for being beaten or assaulted by prison guards,[215] or for being held past their release dates or unjustly kept in segregation (false imprisonment).[216]

In the context of health care for older individuals, intentional torts would be difficult to prove based on the main issues identified by this study. One prisoner I interviewed explained it this way:

> It's not that they purposefully harm us. It's just indifference on their part, for our fate. That's hard to fix. (AB, 53, in prison 9 years)

While the situation may be hard to fix, it is not impossible. The second type of torts under which individuals can sue is torts based in negligence. A remedy may thus be claimed where unintended harm caused by careless conduct occurred. To be successful in such a claim, the plaintiff must prove a set of elements: that the defendant owed them duty of care; that the defendant breached the standard of care by failing to do what a reasonable person of "ordinary intelligence and prudence"[217] would have done in those particular circumstances; that "but for"[218] the action of the plaintiff, the harm would not have occurred; and that the harm thus caused is not too remote.[219]

We could thus imagine numerous situations where harm was brought about to older prisoners by negligent conduct on the part of the CSC or its employees due to delayed medical treatment, unclean pathways, unsafe top bunks, lack of needed medical items, solitary confinement, and other such issues. In all of these situations, prisoners would have to prove that the CSC and/or its employees owed them a duty of care. The test for establishing when duty of care is owed is framed in *Cooper v Hobart*,[220] based on a British case, *Anns v Merton London Borough Council*.[221] The test is now known as the *Anns/Cooper* test. A duty is owed where the harm was

---

215   *Abbott v Canada* (1993), 64 FTR 81, [1993] FCJ No. 673 [*Abbott*]; *Proctor v Canada (AG)*, [2002] OJ No. 350, [2002] OTC 79 (Sup Ct) (motion for summary judgment dismissed, case settled outside court); *British Columbia v Zastowny*, 2008 SCC 4, [2008] 1 SCR 27.

216   *Hermiz v Canada*, 2013 FC 288 (Prothonotary), rev'd 2013 FC 764 [*Hermiz*]; *Hill v British Columbia* (1997), 36 BCLR (3d) 211, 148 DLR (4th) 337 (CA) [*Hill*]; *Brandon v Canada (Correctional Service)* (1996), 131 DLR (4th) 761, 105 FTR 243; *Canada (AG) v McArthur*, 2010 SCC 63, [2010] 3 SCR 626.

217   *Arland v Taylor*, [1955] OR 131 at 142, 3 DLR 358 (CA).

218   *Clements v Clements*, 2012 SCC 32, [2012] 2 SCR 181, rev'g 298 BCCA 56 [*Clements*].

219   *Wright v Davidson* (1992), 64 BCLR (2d) 113, 88 DLR (4th) 698 (CA).

220   *Cooper v Hobart*, 2001 SCC 79, [2001] 3 SCR 537.

221   *Anns v Merton London Borough Council* (1977), [1978] AC 728 (HL (Eng)).

a reasonably foreseeable consequence of the defendant's act, a sufficient relationship of proximity exists between the parties, and no residual policy considerations negated the imposition of a duty. Nonetheless, this test only needs to be undertaken where courts are faced with a novel duty of care claim. Where the type of duty raised falls within a previously recognized category, no test is needed.[222]

In the small number of cases brought forward, courts have already recognized a few types of duty of care owed to prisoners. A first type relates to the prison environment. Similar to the *CCRA*,[223] courts have recognized the duty of correctional systems to provide prisoners with healthy and safe environments. In particular, such a duty includes an obligation to provide safe working conditions.[224] Of the seventeen participants in my study who brought a civil suit against the CSC, half sued on similar grounds.

> I have been working for CORCAN for a while. It's a good job but I work with heavy machinery and one of them did not have the safety feature on and it crushed my hand. The CSC paid me because otherwise I would have gone ahead with the trial. (DD, 62, in prison 5 years)

Supporting other *CCRA* provisions, courts have recognized that the duty to provide a safe environment also includes an obligation on the part of the CSC to protect individuals from their peers and from themselves. Such successful claims were brought by prisoners who were victims of a fire set by other prisoners[225] and by an individual who was severely beaten by a peer after the former reached out to the CSC and asserted that he felt in danger.[226] In other cases, the duty to protect prisoners from harm has been framed as an "obligation to take reasonable steps to intervene and protect the at-risk inmate,"[227] a "duty to keep [the prisoner] safe and ... to promptly come to his rescue,"[228] a duty to "attend to the

---

222 *Mustapha v Culligan of Canada Ltd*, 2008 SCC 27, [2008] 2 SCR 114.

223 *CCRA, supra* note 178, s 70.

224 *Chilton v Canada*, 2008 FC 1047, [2008] 336 FTR 308, leave to appeal to SCC refused, 33705 (16 September 2010) (individual harmed himself while working in a CSC wood shop) [*Chilton*]; *Sarvanis v Canada* (1998), 156 FTR 265, [1998] FCJ No. 1304; aff'd 2002 SCC 28 (the CSC denied liability for an injury suffered by the plaintiff while working in the penitentiary's hay barn, but the SCC dismissed the government's motion for summary judgment).

225 *Williams v New Brunswick* (1985), 66 NBR (2d) 10, 34 CCLT 299 (CA).

226 *Wiebe v Canada (AG)*, 2006 MBCA 159, [2007] 2 WWR 598, rev'g 2006 MBQB 5, leave to appeal to SCC refused, 31860 (10 May 2007).

227 *Carr v Canada*, 2008 FC 1416 at para 23, 339 FTR 50.

228 *Guitare v Canada*, 2002 FCT 1170 at para 1, 224 FTR 272 [*Guitare*].

safety of the inmates,"[229] a "duty to take reasonable care of inmates,"[230] an "obligation to take reasonable steps to protect an inmate from fellow inmates,"[231] a "duty to ensure the safety of the inmates,"[232] an obligation "not to act in a fashion that put the [prisoner] at risk of harm that was reasonably foreseeable,"[233] and a duty to "protect ... from foreseeable risks."[234] Several of the prisoners interviewed for this book spoke about their experiences with making this type of claim.

> When I was in Millhaven, I was working and some guys started a fight. I didn't fight, I was just doing my thing and I got stabbed. CSC refused to do anything about it but then my lawyer said I should sue them because I could get some money. And I did and it was good. (SS, 52, in prison 10 years)

The duty to provide a safe environment has also come up in the context of accommodation. For instance, relying on the CSC's statutory duties[235] and the common law, a court held that second-hand smoke is particularly dangerous for the health of prisoners.[236] The prisoner received compensation, and a ban on smoking was instated. Prisoners interviewed reported some successes in receiving compensation, not only in the context of second-hand smoke but also related to harm occurring due to unsafe sleeping arrangements and unsanitary health clinics.

> I sued them a couple decades ago over the effects of second-hand smoke. It was a big deal back then. The decision prohibiting second-hand smoke had just come out. And I developed asthma while in prison, so I won that case. (TT, 72, in prison 36 years)

---

229   *Chilton v Canada, supra* note 224 at para 55. See also *Miclash v Canada*, 2003 FCT 113, 227 FTR 116.

230   *Scott v Canada*, [1985] FCJ No 35 (QL) (TD).

231   *Coumont v Canada (Correctional Services)* (1994), 77 FTR 253 at para 38, [1994] FCJ No. 655 [*Coumont*]. See also *Hodgin v Canada (Solicitor General)* (1998), 201 NBR (2d) 279, 514 APR 279 (QB).

232   *Légère v Canada* (1999), 159 FTR 87 (TD) at para 5.

233   *Carlson v Canada*, [1998] FCJ No. 733 at para 23 (TD). See also *Wild v Canada (Correctional Services)*, 2004 FC 942, 256 FTR 240; *Bastarache v Canada*, 2003 FC 1463, 243 FTR 274 [*Bastarache*]; *Timm v Canada* (1964), [1965] 1 Ex CR 174 (available on QL); *Iwanicki v Ontario (Minister of Correctional Services)*, 45 WCB (2d) 600, [2000] OTC 181 (Sup Ct) [*Iwanicki*].

234   *Pete v Axworthy*, 2004 BCSC 1337 at para 62, 34 BCLR (4th) 146 [*Pete*]. See also *Russell v Canada*, 2000 BCSC 650 at para 6.

235   *CCRA, supra* note 178, ss 4, 70.

236   *Maljkovich v Canada*, 2005 FC 1398 at para 19, 281 FTR 227 [*Maljkovich*].

I lost my legs [due to amputation] because of an infection while in a CSC hospital. I wanted to sue them but they settled fast. Didn't bring my legs back though. And all these years that have passed, it has been hard to do my time in here without legs. (YY, 51, in prison 13 years)

A second type of recognized duty of care owed to prisoners relates to prison investigations and mandated reports. Thus, courts have held that a duty of care is owed when investigating a disciplinary offence[237] and also a duty to review a segregation order on a timely basis.[238]

A third type, particularly important for older prisoners, is the recognized duty to provide health care in prison,[239] an obligation correspondingly supported by the *CCRA*.[240] In general, the CSC has been held under obligation to ensure effective access to medical services through timely access to health care, adequate record keeping and reporting, and supervision of medical staff.[241] While I have no study examples of individuals who sued because of improper health care, one can imagine that under the current case law and *CCRA* standards, a prisoner may bring claims that tardive health care and lack of access to medication and medical items are depriving them of access to substantive health care.

In addition, an advantage of tort claims is that a prisoner can sue both the individual who caused the harm through their action (that is, a prison staff member) and the CSC. A prison service will be vicariously liable for the torts of its employees as long as those acts are sufficiently connected to their employment, in the sense that the job creates or enhances the potential risk of tortious conduct.[242] This connection is particularly likely to be true in prisons where friction and confrontation, coupled with the opportunity for abuse of power, are inherent in the enterprise. There are numerous cases in which prison staff members have been found negligent and the correctional institution found to be vicariously liable.[243]

---

237 *Hermiz, supra* note 216.

238 *Hill, supra* note 216 at para 17.

239 *Lipcsei v Central Saanich (District)* (1995), 8 BCLR (3d) 325, [1995] 7 WWR 582 (SC) [*Lipcsei*]; *Lavoie v Canada*, [2008] OJ No 4564 (QL) at para 13 (Sup Ct) [*Lavoie*]; *British Columbia (AG) v Astaforoff* (1983), 54 BCLR 309, 6 CCC (3d) 498 (CA); *R v Hall* (1996), 45 Alta LR (3d) 166, [1997] 4 WWR 390.

240 *CCRA, supra* note 178, s 80.

241 Adelina Iftene, Lyn Hansen, & Allan Manson, "Tort Claims and Canadian Prisoners" (2014) 39:2 Queen's LJ 655 at 663 [Iftene, Hansen, & Manson].

242 *Bazley v Curry*, [1999] 2 SCR 534, 174 DLR (4th) 145.

243 See *Benard v Canada*, 2003 FCT 41, 2003 CFPI 41; *Lavoie, supra* note 239; *Lipcsei, supra* note 239; *Geary v Alberta (Edmonton Remand Centre)*, 2004 ABQB 19, 25 Alta LR (4th) 231.

In at least two cases, a breach of the standard of care was found when prison guards failed to send a prisoner whose condition had visibly deteriorated to a doctor.[244] A breach was also found when a prisoner who had been shot by a guard failed to receive medical treatment.[245]

Surprisingly, however, the CSC has not been held vicariously liable for the negligence of health care practitioners. In *Braun Estate v Vaughan*, the Manitoba Court of Appeal held that a hospital's duty is not displaced or altered because its doctors are independent contractors.[246] In 1997, in *Oswald v Canada*, the Federal Court rejected this view, holding that, even though a surgeon was liable for failing to exercise appropriate professional judgement, the CSC had nonetheless fulfilled its duty "by arranging for services of qualified members of the medical and dental professions."[247] Considering the high level of direction and control that the CSC exercises over all of its employees, including contractors, this decision runs afoul of the decision rendered in situations where the employer is in a better position than the employee to guard against risk, allocate costs, and insure against loss.[248] Thus, *Oswald* is a curious and unfortunate decision: it hints at the existence of a double standard between prison and non-prison tort cases.

Limitation of Negligence-Based Action for Prisoners

Despite the recognition of numerous types of duty of care owed to prisoners, fewer successful negligence-based cases have taken place than might be expected. Considering the existing case law and the testimonials of those interviewed for this book, one can identify a number of factors behind this phenomena.

THE DOUBLE STANDARD

Establishing that a duty of care is owed to the prisoner is mandatory but not sufficient for a successful claim. The plaintiff must also prove that that duty was breached or that the actions of the defendant fell short of the standard of care owed. The standard of care is dictated by what

---

244   *Steele, supra* note 165; *Lipcsei, supra* note 239.

245   *Abbott, supra* note 215.

246   *Braun Estate v Vaughan* (2000), 145 Man R (2d) 35 at para 44, [2000] 3 WWR 465 (CA).

247   *Oswald v Canada* (1997), 126 FTR 281, [1997] FCJ No. 203.

248   *Douglas v Kinger*, 2008 ONCA 452, [2008] 57 CCLT (3d) 15, leave to appeal to SCC refused, 32787 (11 December 2008); *Lewis (Guardian ad litem of) v British Columbia*, [1997] 3 SCR 1145, [1998] 5 WWR 732.

a reasonable person would have done in similar circumstances. When clear standards have been established by policy documents or legislation, this step is easier to assess, and the claims are more likely to be successful. For instance, the standard of care was breached when a guard prematurely opened the gates, resulting in a prisoner being assaulted by some of his peers.[249]

However, when the standard cannot clearly be found in provisions, the analysis becomes complicated, and courts tend to defer to the expertise of prison administrators. In a situation where a prisoner was assaulted in a corner of the yard that was not monitored by video cameras, the court held that the standard of care was met.[250] Similarly, where an individual who was known to be suicidal, with documented acute mental illness, was left unsupervised in his cell and subsequently committed suicide, the court held that the standard of care was met.[251] As well, even though duty to provide timely medical care is recognized, instances occurred in which medical assistance was delayed, resulting in serious consequences for the prisoners, including serious injury and death. In these cases also, the court decided that the standard of care had not been breached.[252]

This trend is concerning, given that the lack of access to emergency care is well documented both in this book and in other places. I have argued elsewhere that not considering repeated failure to provide emergency care to prisoners as breaching any standard of care leads to an unreasonably low standard of care for prison matters.[253] The double standard for prisoners is even more apparent when prison cases are compared to non-prison cases. For instance, medical personnel owe prisoners a well-established duty of care akin to that owed to any other patient.[254] However, cases in which the negligence of prison doctors was

---

249 *Guitare, supra* note 228.

250 *Hamilton v Canada*, [2001] OTC 617 (available on QL) (Sup Ct J).

251 *Rhora v Ontario*, [2004] OTC 651 (available on QL) (Sup Ct J).

252 See *Swayze v Dafoe*, [2002] OTC 699, 116 ACWS (3d) 781 (Sup Ct). (Swayze ingested drugs and choked on his vomit. The officers met delays in transporting him from his cell to the hospital because they required additional guards, as he was a very large individual, and he died en route); *Corner v Canada* (2002), [2002] OJ No. 4887 (QL) (Ont Sup Ct J) (the prisoner was attacked in the yard of a maximum security facility and stabbed from behind, and he alleged that he did not receive medical care immediately); *Bastarache, supra* note 233 (the prisoner was hit over the head by another prisoner with a metal bar, and he did not receive medical attention until the following day, when the correctional officer sent him for medical treatment after noticing blood on his bedding).

253 Iftene, Hansen, & Manson, *supra* note 241 at 678.

254 See *ter Neuzen v Korn*, [1995] 3 SCR 674, 127 DLR (4th) 577; *White v Turner* (1981), 31 OR (2d) 773, 120 DLR (3d) 269 (H Ct J), aff'd (1982), 47 OR (2d) 764, 12 DLR (4th) 319 (CA).

asserted were not resolved in the same way as those reported to have happened in non-prison contexts. In a number of prison cases, the court concluded – without explaining the established standard of care – that no evidence showed the medical worker to have failed to act in accordance with the standard of practice.[255]

Similarly, the causation analysis seemed to impose lower obligations on correctional services than on other plaintiffs. When the standard of care is breached, the action must be proven to have caused the injury. In other words, "but for" the action,[256] the injury would not have occurred. *Coumont v Canada* held that, even if a certain part of an institution had a history of stabbings, the officials' failure to supervise that place did not amount to a breach and was not ultimately the cause of the plaintiff's stabbing.[257] Similarly, *Iwanicki v Canada* held that, even if the prison had fallen below the standard of care by giving razors to prisoners, the breach was not found to be causally linked to the stabbing of the plaintiff with a razor.[258] By requiring the plaintiff to show a clear connection between the standard of care breach and the attack, the court arguably went beyond the robust and pragmatic approach endorsed in *Clements* – an approach that would obviously have led to a finding of liability on these facts, as the injury would not have occurred "but for" the prison's negligence in providing razors.[259]

In another controversial case, *Hickey v Canada*,[260] an HIV-positive prisoner claimed damages for the negligence of a prison doctor when he was given an overdose of medication and developed a peripheral neuropathy, a condition not inherent in HIV-positive people. The court held that the plaintiff could not prove a causal relationship, as HIV itself might also cause the condition in question. Conflicting medical evidence was presented on this point; to make the causal connection, the prisoner would have had to bring additional expert evidence not readily available. The court in *Sutherland v Canada* imposed a similarly high threshold, finding that causation was not established because the prisoner was unable to prove that the delay in providing medical care was linked to the deterioration of his ulcer condition.[261] Arguably, this burden was too

---

255 See *Pete, supra* note 234; *Vittis v Younger,* 1990 Carswell BC 2550 (SC); *Ewert v Marshall,* 2009 BCSC 762; *Gawich v Klar,* 2010 ONSC 4972.

256 The "but for" test was framed in *Snell v Farell,* [1990] 2 SCR 311 [*Snell*], and confirmed in *Clements, supra* note 218.

257 *Coumont, supra* note 231.

258 *Iwanicki, supra* note 233.

259 *Clements, supra* note 218.

260 *Hickey, supra* note 171.

261 *Sutherland, supra* note 29.

heavy – calling for scientific proof that went well beyond the "robust and pragmatic" approach to the "but for" test, as set out in *Snell v Farrell*[262] and endorsed in *Clements*.[263] Thus, aside from imposing a higher threshold than for cases brought by non-prisoners, courts requested medical evidence specifically deemed unnecessary in other cases, which was particularly difficult to obtain for people behind bars.

EXPANSION TO NOVEL DUTIES OF CARE

Elsewhere, a set of colleagues and I discussed the need for courts to recognize a duty to provide adequate conditions of confinement to prisoners.[264] The duty to provide a safe environment is unduly restrictive; it refers mostly to the safety of premises, the provisions of necessities of living, and the protection of individuals from harm inflicted by others or by themselves. It does not include the duty to provide a decent standard of living, the lack of which often leads to significant harm. At best, in cases involving the standard of living, there is uncertainty as to where the obligation falls under the duty to provide a safe environment. There is evidence that when such uncertainty exists, courts interpret the duty narrowly and require the creation of a novel duty of care in the new fact situation.[265]

It would not be difficult to establish proximity between the prisoner and the correctional service, evidence of which would be needed for a new duty to be recognized. However, the *Anns/Cooper* analysis required for a novel duty also involves concepts such as conflicting obligations of the defendant (especially to public safety) and policy considerations. The CSC may easily argue that accommodation issues pertaining to older people are policy and not operational decisions. It may also argue that, in making such decisions, it needs to consider public safety, and thus courts are not in a position to decide on such duties. In such circumstances, courts tend to defer to governmental discretion and are generally loath to interfere with the government's balancing of competing concerns. This tendency is especially the case where allocation of resources is at stake.[266]

---

262 *Snell*, *supra* note 256.
263 *Clements*, *supra* note 218.
264 Iftene, Hansen, & Manson, *supra* note 241 at 675–80.
265 *Paxton v Ramji*, 2008 ONCA 697, 299 DLR (4th) 614, Feldman J, leave to appeal to SCC refused, 32929 (23 April 2009).
266 *Mitchell v Ontario* (2004), 71 OR (3d) 571, 188 OAC 385; *R v Imperial Tobacco Canada Ltd*, 2011 SCC 42 at para 95.

SETTLING, ACCESS TO LEGAL AID, AND REPERCUSSIONS

Aside from the difficulties that courts themselves have in deciding on a claim brought forward by a prisoner, either by being unreasonably lenient on the government when conducting their analysis or highly deferential to the government's expertise, prisoners also encounter barriers that precede a judicial hearing.

First, litigation is expensive. Unlike an administrative claim, bringing the government to court requires legal knowledge and, for most prisoners, legal representation. Legal aid is often not available for this type of prison litigation. Frequently, people with very serious concerns are unable to proceed because they lack the resources to do so.

> I fall on ice every single year. Sometimes I get up and move, otherwise I twist an ankle or a wrist. There are guys here who broke bones on ice. If I were to sue them every time I fell on ice that they did not clean properly, well, those would be a lot of trials. But that's complicated. You need a lawyer and all. (AG, 54, in prison 12 years)

Second, as with the administrative grievance procedure, repercussions are attached to suing.

> Everyone here says that if you fight them they will say you are not rehabilitated. When you have a short bid like me, better do your time and get out as fast as possible. (AI, 56, in prison 1.5 years)
> The money you get, it's really not worth the hassle. They [the officers] treat you like shit afterwards. (AY, 55, in prison 6 years)

Third, even for those with a significant claim who bring themselves to sue, the CSC often tries to settle the matter out of court. Unlike the Canadian Human Rights Tribunal (CHRT), however, where the settlement agreement is presided over by the Canadian Human Rights Commission (CHRC) in an attempt to ensure a fair deal, no supervision takes place in a tort-based action. If the prisoner is unrepresented, the government can get them to settle for a fraction of what the claimant would get in court. Nevertheless, the imbalance of power, the prohibitive cost of proceeding, the lack of legal knowledge, and the prisoner's need for money leads, more often than not, to a settlement.[267]

While a settlement provides individuals with the benefit of compensation, it has two main shortcomings. First, as argued, there is the running risk that the claimant will be pressured into accepting a bad deal.

---

267 Iftene, Hansen, & Manson, *supra* note 241 at 681.

Second, a settlement prevents the establishment of a precedent, or a novel duty of care, given that settlements are made discreetly and lack judicial authority. For instance, in the past, double bunking was not found to be in breach of the duty to a safe environment. Double bunking was a policy matter.[268] However, one of the study participants who reported having fallen from the top bunk and suing the government did receive a settlement. This outcome would not have happened had he not had a solid chance of winning a formal legal case. Nonetheless, the only legal precedent is the one asserting that double bunking is not part of the CSC's duty of care. That fact alone will deter individuals from bringing similar claims forward in the future.

> Last year I fell off my top bunk. There was no bar-handle or anything and I often get dizzy. I actually hurt my shoulder very badly and I now have limited mobility in it. I sued and CSC settled almost immediately. I got some money. (AH, 51, in prison 2 years)

Where To?

Private tort claims are poorly equipped to bring about systemic change. By nature, damages are meant to fix a past wrongdoing through monetary compensation, a short-term solution that does not prevent future harm from occurring. Administrative and human rights–based actions are considerably better equipped for the latter.

Nonetheless, tort actions are some of the most common types of suits, in part because the standard of proof, as well as the type and the amount of evidence needed, are the lowest required from all the legal actions. In addition, tort actions still empower the claimant by recognizing the wrong and awarding money that may help them move forward. Furthermore, repeated tort claims, or tort-based class actions (where a group of people claims damages), may lead in time to institutional reform, as different agencies might find it cheaper to change than to continue to pay damages. For instance, the tort suit over second-hand smoking[269] led to a complete smoking ban in all correctional institutions.

Thus, access to civil law courts is an integral part of prisoners' access to justice and to their avenues of pressing for change. Prisoners should have equal access to this judicial avenue, particularly because they live in an environment where they are charges of someone else who has complete control over their environment, health care, and safety. In the context

---

268 *Savard v Canada*, 2003 FCT 683 at para 21, 235 FTR 168.
269 *Maljkovich, supra* note 236.

of older prisoners, the ability to sue for damages is particularly useful. As courts have already recognized duties of care owed to prisoners, older prisoners should be able to bring forward a host of claims. An unsafe environment and insufficient access to medical care in accordance with the needs of an aging individual is what often led to significant injury among those who participated in the research for this book. John may attempt to claim that he developed diabetes due to years of improper eating, or that his ulcer is continuously infected because he lacks daily access to a nurse. Others may claim that they were left with significant physical damage due to failure to immediately treat heart attacks, or that their medical conditions worsened due to the obligation to stand in line outdoors to pick up their medications. They may claim that they are in pain due to strict limitations on narcotics, or that they underwent emotional stress by exposure to incompatible, younger, and violent cellmates.

The promotion of individual rights in prison and old-age reform must include better access to courts. I will separately address the issue of access to legal aid in the next section, as it is a common issue for all types of actions. However, for tort-based actions specifically, courts will need to do a significant check of their biases. Perhaps training on prison issues and access to justice should be mandated for all judges. The pattern of holding correctional services at a lower standard and asking for more evidence from prisoners than from other similarly situated plaintiffs reinforces the historical deference of courts towards the government. Based on tort law, such deference is not justified and leads to limiting prisoner access to the most basic form of judicial redress. Hopefully, in a time where increased reflection is given to prisoners' rights and prison *Charter* challenges are flourishing, civil law courts will follow suit and reassess the manner in which they apply the law to prisoner claims.

Practical Barriers to Accessing Justice

Can't they just give us a law student or something to help me with my will? (AP, 79, in prison 4 years)

When John started his sentence, the *CCRA* was not yet in force. Many prisoners' rights did not exist even on paper, and the internal grievance procedure was radically different, barely functional, in fact. *Martineau* had recognized the duty of the administrators to act fairly towards prisoners,[270] but that was the extent of prisoner protection. *Habeas corpus*

---

270   *Martineau No. 2, supra* note 22.

was in place, but the decisions that recognized the concurrent jurisdiction of *habeas corpus* and judicial review in the Federal Court were still to come. The *Charter* was in its early days and yet to produce any litigation that would serve prisoners. So how did John find out about all the changes in the law that could benefit him?

> Word of mouth. You see what others are doing. You ask people who have been in here longer than you have. Who else would tell us?

John conceded that certain changes had occurred. For instance, with the enforcement of the *CCRA*, the Office of the Correctional Investigator's phone number appeared next to the prison phones and was free to call. If an individual did not know what the OCI did, they just asked their peers. Now it was common knowledge in prison: everyone had heard about the OCI. Also, a poster of the *Charter* was posted on institution walls. Inmate committees would sometimes inform people who asked about various pieces of legislation.

> And there are the libraries. We have a law section, so we can go check that one out. It generally has laws and such. But you need to know how to use those books. Most time when I needed it I'd just ask a guy in here who was more knowledgeable. In here you know who these guys are, and you try to keep friendly in case you ever need them to help. We also had internet back in the day. We were allowed computers and we were able to check the internet in the library. It was easier. Now we can't do that, so it's only the library left.

Compared to some others, John was in a good position. He spoke English as a first language and could read and write. While not well educated, he had completed school up to the tenth grade. He could read and understand the law, knew to ask his peers questions, and read the pamphlets about prisoner rights that were sometimes distributed in the different prisons in which he'd served time.

> Ultimately you learn because you have to. When you have been in for as long as I have, it's your house. You learn the rules to your house.

At no time in the course of his incarceration has John used the services of a lawyer. He knows he could have a lawyer with him at disciplinary hearings and parole hearings, but he says he does not have that kind of money, and he does not think it would do any good. He knows some people have lawyers, but most of those he knows do not. Like most other interviewees, John knew about the Prison Law Clinic at Queen's

University, which sends students in to help provide legal advice, and he knew about the complaint system with the OCI. He did not know about any other publicly funded service he could access for information or representation if he needed it.

> I don't know. Some people ask for lawyers all the time. They call all the toll-free numbers we have. We are offenders, we don't get anything. You want something done, you have to do it yourself. Unless you are rich. If you are rich you get all the lawyers you want. Some guys in here are. But most are like me. We just do what we can ourselves.

Eric did not care much about any legal services or legal information. He was a well-educated man and had a good understanding of the justice system. In the two years he had been in prison, he had learned the ropes and knew what was needed to survive behind bars. But he was not interested in using the law library or in having the advice of a lawyer for his parole hearing.

> I am sick. I don't have strength for this. I just want to get out to my wife. I am so worried about her. I don't want to upset anyone. I didn't want to take a lawyer with me to the parole hearing because this would upset them. I just want to get out.

Legal Needs of Older Prisoners

Fear of repercussions for seeking formal legal advice was widespread. It seemed the sicker an individual was, and the less well educated, the more reluctant they were to contact lawyers, write complaint letters, and ask staff members for basic legal information. They simply did not want to be seen as "trouble-makers." The fear of antagonizing authorities is a significant barrier to prisoners seeking to enforce their rights or even understanding what their rights are.

> I don't want any trouble. It's all good. I don't need anything. I don't have problems with anyone. (AD, 74, in prison 5 years)

There were, of course, a significant number of individuals who had challenged, attempted to challenge, or would have liked to challenge the system by demanding their rights. Long-term prisoners and repeat offenders were likely to be more assertive in this regard than individuals incarcerated for the first time in old age and serving shorter terms. Short-term prisoners looked ahead to their parole dates and just wanted to navigate the prison system as smoothly and quickly as possible. Those serving long sentences in general had a history of fighting for their rights. On one hand, prison was their home, and they tried to make life bearable. One the other hand, years of incarceration and what they perceived as injustices suffered in prison made them less concerned about upsetting individuals or the system.

> Reality is it doesn't matter what you do or what you don't do. We are nothing to them, they just don't care. If you want something you have to force them to give it to you. They don't give you anything unless you sue them. (AO, 57, in prison 20 years)

To sue "them," however, is easier said than done. Even if courts were more willing to hear prisoner claims, getting to court is a struggle. First, access to legal information is a significant problem. A number of the institutions visited had poorly staffed law libraries with outdated books. In none of the institutions was there a librarian able to help prisoners conduct legal research or at least advise them as to what to read or how to read a legal book.

> I went into the law library once, but I don't even know where to start. It's not like there is a book on prisoners' rights and how they apply exactly. It would be useful if someone could direct us to what to read depending on the problem we have. (AL, 50, in prison 6 years)

Many prisoners need significantly less complex descriptions of rights and mechanisms than a law book to claim their rights. The CSC itself, and agencies like the John Howard and the Elizabeth Fry Societies, produce and distribute pamphlets describing in simple words the options prisoners have and what they are entitled to. However, the distribution of pamphlets is sporadic, the level of detail varies, and sometimes people in special units, like segregation, protective custody, and mental health units, do not have access to them at all. Also, out of the 197 people I interviewed, three were illiterate. There were likely significantly more in this situation, since the recruitment took place via letters, which an isolated, illiterate person would not have been able to read. Also, two of the people interviewed needed a translator since they spoke neither English nor French. Reading posters, pamphlets, or law books is a significant problem.

> It is very difficult for me in here because I don't speak the language and I don't understand the law of this country. They don't offer any language

courses. You have to take English with everyone else, but it's high school English for native speakers. I just sit there and don't understand anything. And we need a crash course on Canadian law. It's so different from Chinese law! And I am mistreated so much but I can't even complain because I can't write a complaint in English. (AQ, 51, in prison 2 years)

I can sign my name. That's pretty much it. And people talk about your letter so I knew what it was. But I don't like people to know that I can't read and write. I keep it to myself as much as possible. It's embarrassing. (QQ, 63, in prison 8 years)

Information sessions on rights or on how to ask for something are not widely available. In the assessment unit, individuals are supposed to undergo an orientation about the basics of prison life within the first week. Of the seventeen individuals I interviewed in that unit, over half had been there for three weeks or more (though the prescribed duration for assessment is a maximum of four weeks), and they were yet to undergo an orientation. It is thus not surprising that orientation on the law is basically not available at all.

Well no. They don't ask if you need anything, and they don't give you the tools to make their life more difficult. That would be a lot to expect from them. They don't want people to sue them or complain. (HH, 64, in prison 16 years)

It would be useful to have someone teach us how to fill in a complaint, you know, what is worth wasting time with, stuff like that. Not even how to sue someone, but just to fill out some paperwork within the institution. (DD, 52, in prison 5 years)

The need to have someone explain the law to them and distribute some legal advice was acute. First, people needed help with internal documents and documentation on prison matters – grievances, parole, disciplinary hearings, and so on. Second, they needed help with general law matters, such as family and custody disputes, writing of a will, filing for bankruptcy, and other such issues.

Well I am so worried because I might die soon, and I want to leave my things in order. I don't have much but I want to have it all in a will. And I have seen what happens if you just write a will on a piece of paper. You die, the guards throw it away. Nothing comes of it. Can't they just send a law student every few weeks to help us prisoners write our wills and deposit them at the law school until we die? (AP, 79, in prison 5 years)

Third, prisoners who want to file a tort claim, *habeas corpus* and/or *Charter* challenges, or a judicial review application in the Federal Court need advice.

> I want to appeal the decision on my grievance. I do a lot of reading in the library. But without internet it's hard. There are so many rules on how to do this. I know other people do it all the time. It would just be useful to have someone look over the paperwork and see if it is ok. You know? Nothing much, just look over it, or say what is missing. (AL, 50, in prison 6 years)

One in five prisoners asked me for a publicly funded service. They needed a lawyer to help them with a disciplinary problem, to file a challenge, or to appeal their case.

> I want to sue them [for damages] but it costs money. I can't afford a lawyer and the prison law clinic doesn't help with that. I tried. (FF, 52, in prison 6 years)
>
> Do you know some lawyer that could give me some advice pro bono? No, not the prison law clinic. Those guys didn't even return my calls. (AE, 57, in prison 17 years)

The issue of access to lawyers and legal information was not the purpose of my study. It was simply incidental to age-related issues, and it occurred in the context of the discussion on the options older people have to ask for accommodation for their needs. Even so, the high need for legal advice and access to affordable lawyers was clear, and it turned out to be a significant barrier to prisoner access to better accommodation and release.

In 2002, the Department of Justice (DOJ) undertook a research project into the availability of legal aid to federally incarcerated individuals.[271] At the time, the DOJ listed the unmet legal needs of prisoners, which were more or less acute depending on the province: access to legal information and properly stocked libraries, access to advice and representation for civil suits (generally pertaining to access to medical care, diets, and visitation), access to advice and representation for suits for increased liberties, lack of information on resources available, funding for appeals

---

271 Canada, Department of Justice, *Study of the Legal Services Provided to Penitentiary Inmates by Legal Aid Plans and Clinics in Canada,* Legal Research Series (Ottawa: DOJ, 2002), online: https://www.justice.gc.ca/eng/rp-pr/csj-sjc/ccs-ajc/rr03_la10-rr03_aj10/rr03_la10.pdf [DOJ].

from correctional decisions, and prison law–related issues in general (disciplinary hearing, parole, challenges to segregation, and so on).[272] The report noted that the need was even more acute for vulnerable groups such as people with mental illnesses, Aboriginal groups, and women, as well as for those with little to no education or poor language skills.[273]

Fifteen years later, the findings of the DOJ report remain valid. Older individuals are a vulnerable group with a host of special needs: many are mentally ill, almost one in four is Aboriginal, some are illiterate or come from outside of Canada, and many have very little education. Self-representation or filing legal documents is difficult for anybody, but it is particularly hard on individuals in such life circumstances. In addition, many older prisoners, especially after spending thirty years in prison, are poor and cannot afford to pay for legal advice.[274]

In such a context, it is particularly difficult to see how prisoners can make their needs known and assert their rights. Lack of physical access to courts, together with the factors tackled in the previous chapters, explains the relatively poorly developed prison jurisprudence, the still prevalent discomfort of judges with prison matters, and the very slow improvement of conditions of confinement, as well as the failure to accommodate vulnerable groups whose numbers are increasing in step with broader demographic shifts in society. When discussing the Arbour Report and its recommendation for increased court scrutiny in prison matters, Manson criticized Arbour for failing to acknowledge that most of the issues discussed in the report would not have been brought forward to courts because of lack of adequate funding. In Manson's words, "courts have the power to enforce compliance with the rule of law, but there will be no enforcement if issues are not placed before them carefully and effectively by an adequately funded counsel."[275] Thus, the issue of prison reform through courts as a last resort mechanism goes beyond – otherwise very important – aspects pertaining to the standards applied by courts in prison matters and their deference to prison administrators. Ultimately, courts can refine their view on prison matters and take a stronger stance on pushing the law through the prison gates if they familiarize themselves with prison problems, evaluate evidence pertaining to

---

272   *Ibid* at 24–7.

273   *Ibid* at 3.

274   On the lack of availability of legal resources for prisoners, see Parkes, "Prisoners' Charter," *supra* note 34 at 667; Parkes & Pate, *supra* note 1 at 276; Debra Parkes et al, "Listening to Their Voices: Women Prisoners and Access to Justice in Manitoba" (2008) 26 Windsor YB Access Just 85 [Parkes et al]; DOJ, *supra* note 271; Manson, "Scrutiny," *supra* note 5 at 326.

275   Manson, "Scrutiny," *supra* note 5 at 326.

prison issues, and understand the context in its practical dimension. This change cannot happen if cases do not make it to the courts on a regular basis, raising a diversity of pertinent issues through a diversity of legal actions that on paper are available to prisoners. Without lawyers, courts will either never be confronted with certain cases or will be confronted with self-represented litigants, bringing forward poorly argued motions. The likelihood, then, of securing groundbreaking decisions that lead to systemic change and improve prisoner rights is very small.

Publicly Funded Legal Services for Prisoners

Each province has a legal aid system that is provincially funded and offers a limited number of legal services to poor individuals who meet certain financial criteria (either through staff lawyers, through certificates, or by working with members of the private bar). All legal aid centres offer services in the area of criminal law defence and family law, with some of them providing services related to immigration, workers' compensation, unemployment insurance, income security, and automobile insurance.

If the prisoner's needs fall under one of these categories, then they are eligible to apply for funding, which is granted at the discretion of the legal aid organization in the province. Specific prison law needs are not covered by legal aid plans and generally are not available to prisoners. In *Howard*, the SCC extended the constitutionally protected right to counsel to disciplinary hearings. Thus, an individual is allowed to be represented both at a disciplinary and a parole hearing because their residual liberty is at risk.[276] However, they are not entitled to legal aid–funded lawyers for these hearings. An SCC decision in 1999 stated, based on the BC legal aid statute, that BC prisoners are entitled to legal aid for disciplinary hearings that could affect their liberty.[277] Because the decision was not based on the *Charter*, however, it was not of federal application. When funding to the Prisoners' Legal Services clinic was discontinued, the right was moot and could no longer be applied.[278]

The DOJ noted in its 2002 report that only Ontario offers regular services for liberty issues, especially for parole, and other jurisdictions offer infrequent certificates for such matters. The DOJ pointed out that many of the specific prison law issues, such as loss of residual liberty and other rights, have drastic consequences as serious as non-prison matters routinely covered by legal aid plans, and still public funding is

---

276 *Howard, supra* note 24.
277 *Winters v Legal Services Society*, [1999] 3 SCR 160.
278 Parkes, "Prisoners' Charter," *supra* note 34 at 667.

not available.[279] In provinces like Ontario and Manitoba, however, certain civil claims for institutional mistreatment, assaults and injuries, and medical or dental malpractice may be covered on a case-by-case basis. Finally, for *Charter* or *habeas corpus* applications, legal aid funding is not usually available.[280]

At one time, there was a specialized clinic in BC, Prisoners' Legal Services, which was intended to assist with prison matters surrounding issues like human rights and health care. Its funding was cut in 2006, and the clinic was replaced by a non-profit society called West Coast Prison Justice Society (WCPJS),[281] a minimally provincially funded clinic for *Charter*-related prisoner services.[282] The clinic still operates under the name "Prisoners' Legal Services" (PLS), and, despite funding struggles, it has done some significant work in advancing prisoners' rights.[283] The clinic has a number of staff members, including lawyers, paralegals, and some community advocates. It provides legal aid assistance to federal and provincial prisoners in BC on issues that affect their liberty rights under section 7 of the *Charter*, including segregation/separate confinement, enhanced supervision placement, disciplinary hearings, sentence calculation, transfers, parole applications, parole suspension, and detention hearings. The clinic can also provide some assistance for conditions of confinement, human rights, and health care issues. Services range from summary advice to legal representation at hearings by an in-house or referral lawyer.[284]

Ontario has a Prison Law Clinic, affiliated with Queen's University and partially funded by Legal Aid Ontario.[285] The Prison Law Clinic serves the federal penitentiaries in South-East Ontario (the seven penitentiaries at which I conducted my interviews; two Ontario penitentiaries, including the one for women, are not covered by the clinic's jurisdiction). The clinic offers representation and advice at disciplinary and parole hearings, deals with institutional matters (such as writing letters on behalf of clients, grievances, human rights complaints, and offers opinions on clients' issues), and is currently engaged in some limited litigation

---

279   DOJ, *supra* note 271 at 3.
280   *Ibid* at 22–4.
281   West Coast Prison Justice Society, online: https://prisonjustice.org.
282   Parkes et al, *supra* note 274 at 117.
283   See, for instance, the discussion presented in the previous chapter on the Canadian Human Rights Commission and Tribunal and on the work PLS has done in advancing claims before the commission and the tribunal.
284   Private correspondence with Jennifer Metcalfe, executive director at Prisoners' Legal Services (23 January 2018).
285   Queen's Prison Law Clinic, online: https://queenslawclinics.ca/prison-law.

(to address some disciplinary court concerns and systemic issues of prisoners).[286] Most services are offered through law students who receive credits for their clinic work and are supervised by staff lawyers. In addition, Legal Aid Ontario has a Prison Law Advisory Committee[287] and, in 2016, began a four-year strategy to develop services for incarcerated individuals. It also has a Test Case branch, which aims to fund novel prison claims, be they *Charter* or civil claims.[288] Finally, in 2008, the Law Foundation of Ontario, together with the Canadian Association of Elizabeth Fry Societies and the Faculty of Law at the University of Ottawa, created a pilot project to develop a manual for law students to provide legal advice to federally sentenced women prisoners via a toll-free telephone line.[289]

The services available in Ontario mean that the prisoners I interviewed are in the best position in the country to access publicly funded legal advice and representation. Aside from Ontario and BC, none of the other provinces has a clinic specifically devoted to prison matters. But still, many of the needs of those I spoke to in Ontario prisons are not being met. In 2014, when most of the interviews for this book took place, many of the prisoners were unhappy with the Prison Law Clinic at Queen's. Because of the overwhelming number of requests, help with disciplinary hearings and parole was scarce; many of their requests for advice on different institutional matters were dismissed as not sufficiently important; and representation for litigation, including *Charter* challenges, was not available. Until recently, any kind of systemic issue was outside the jurisdiction of the Prison Law Clinic.

Some legal aid clinics offer sporadic support for prisoners challenging systemic problems. For instance, Legal Aid Manitoba funded some ad-hoc cases through its Public Interest Law Centre (PILC). One case challenged the systemic discrimination against provincially incarcerated women: lack of access to Aboriginal spirituality and culture, inadequate opportunities to meet with lawyers, and other such issues. It concluded with a mediated settlement. PILC was also involved in *Sauvé*, in support of the voting rights of prisoners in Stony Mountain Institution.[290]

---

286 Private correspondence with Kathy Ferrara, staff lawyer and director at the Queen's Prison Law Clinic (15 March 2017).

287 Legal Aid Ontario, "Board Advisory Committees," online: http://www.legalaid.on.ca/en/publications/board-advisory-committees.asp.

288 Legal Aid Ontario, "LAO's Prison Law Test Case Strategy," online: http://www.legalaid.on.ca/en/info/testcases-prison-law.asp.

289 Parkes et al, *supra* note 274 at 118.

290 *Ibid* at 116–17.

Until 2006, an organization called the Court Challenges Program (CCP) funded litigation of public interest brought forward by poor people. The litigation funded was mostly limited to equality claims. The CCP funded litigation on same sex marriages, violence and discrimination against women, national security and impact on racialized communities, systemic discrimination against African-Canadian communities, and other similar issues. It also funded *Sauvé*, the prison case that sought the introduction of the right to vote in federal prisons.[291] The CCP was a good program for disadvantaged groups who sought systemic change. In 2006, the program was cut by the Conservative government with the understanding that it was not logical to fund people intent on suing the government in opposition to its policies.[292] This reasoning failed to acknowledge that public interest litigation works to enrich the institutional framework of the democratic system.[293] In 2017, the Liberal government resurrected the program, with funding of $5 million annually. While a portion of this money will be dedicated to equality cases, the rest will be used to expand services to the protection of other *Charter* rights.[294] This fund could prove useful for prisoners seeking reform.

Where To?

To summarize, prisoners are entitled to retain lawyers to assist them with matters affecting their residual liberty rights in prison. They are entitled to sue the government based on breaches of correctional law in Federal Court, to bring *Charter* and *habeas corpus* applications in Federal Court, and to sue prison administration or other inmates for damages. They are equally entitled to help with other legal matters, such as family problems, advance directives, wills, and property and tax issues, and to secure legal advice and access the law library. Nonetheless, the lack of adequate, readily available legal information and the lack of legal aid funding make all of these rights illusory.[295]

---

291 Bhabha, *supra* note 2 at 160.
292 Court Challenges Program of Canada, online: https://www.canada.ca/en/canadian-heritage/services/funding/court-challenges-program.html.
293 Bhabha, *supra* note 2 at 160.
294 Daniel Leblanc, "Liberals Revive Funding for Groups That Take Government to Court," *The Globe and Mail* (7 February 2017), online: https://www.theglobeandmail.com/news/politics/liberals-restore-and-expand-court-challenges-program/article33924559/; Carissima Mathen & Kyle Kirkup, "Defending the Court Challenges Program," *Policy Options* (22 February 2017), online: http://policyoptions.irpp.org/magazines/february-2017/defending-the-court-challenges-program.
295 On this matter, see also Parkes & Pate, *supra* note 1 at 275.

More generally, aside from the constitutionally protected right to counsel in the criminal law context, the SCC recognized a right to publicly funded counsel in the civil context. On the circumstances of the case, the court allowed for legal aid for parents in a custody battle under section 7 of the *Charter*. While it is comforting to know that the *Charter* does not only provide for legal assistance in criminal contexts, this ruling is of limited utility considering that it is circumscribed to the facts in the case. In 2006, the Canadian Bar Association (CBA) brought a *Charter* challenge to the lack of civil legal aid for poor people. While the court of appeal acknowledged that the matter is important, it refused to grant the CBA public standing in the case and dismissed the motion.[296]

Such constitutional protection would go a long way to assist prisoners who are trying to deal with civil legal matters. What would be truly helpful, though, would be the constitutional protection of the right to legal aid where prisoners' rights are impacted.[297] The type of legal action chosen should not matter; rather, the important issue would be what the action seeks to protect and its remedial potential. If it is clear that prisoners are vulnerable without court intervention, and equally clear that court intervention cannot happen without financial legal assistance, the right to legal aid should be as protected as the *Charter* rights themselves, otherwise those rights are meaningless in the prison context.

In terms of available services, prisoners need advice regarding both prison-specific issues (grievances, disciplinary issues, and parole) and *habeas corpus* or *Charter* challenges that they may want to file to protect their rights. More should be invested in specialized clinics like the ones in Ontario and BC, both from university and legal aid programs. The university programs are particularly useful: they do not require as many staff lawyers; they rely on students who are not and do not expect to be paid; and they build expertise in a new generation of lawyers. Such clinics should be considered by all law schools as part of their clinical practice, especially as prison law is the one area in which no other program or community clinic offers services. Not only would such clinics provide a unique legal service, but they would also offer students the opportunity to specialize in this area of law, an opportunity most do not have due to a lack of articling positions in the field of prison law.

You know ... things do not have to be complicated. If someone could come in one day a couple times a month and provide some minimal advice. What

---

296   *CBA, supra* note 76.
297   See also Parkes & Pate, *supra* note 1 at 275.

tribunal should I contact, how to fill the grievance, if I should fight the charge. Just minimal, it would be so useful. (AP, 79, in prison 5 years)

Basically, a "duty counsel" who could be a student and would provide bimonthly advice based on a schedule in the area of the law school's jurisdiction is easy to envision. It would also remove a lot of pressure from the local legal aid, which would receive fewer applications for representation and advice.

In addition, community legal clinics, currently funded by legal aid organizations, should consider spreading their services to detention centres in their jurisdiction. Most community clinics offer a limited number of services due to funding restrictions. However, they are meant to serve everyone in their jurisdiction.[298] At the moment, this mandate means everyone except prisoners. Though prisoners are not excluded *per se*, access to these clinics is difficult if not impossible for incarcerated individuals: many prisoners do not know about their services; staff lawyers are not trained in the prison system; and communication between clinics and prisoners is difficult to establish. At a Rural Justice Legal Forum in January 2017, I was surprised to find that the majority of community clinics would like to extend their services to prisoners. However, the staff lawyers pointed out that they do not know how to reach prisoners; they have difficulty establishing contacts within institutions; and it is challenging to actually gain access to prisons in order to determine exactly what the needs are. It would be useful if legal aid organizations would secure basic training for community clinics to deal with such matters. Such training would enable community clinics to address matters of general interest in prisons, such as will writing, family problems, financial advice, bankruptcy, issue certificates for human rights challenges, and so on. Even if the clinics did not handle prison-specific issues, this service would still be of considerable help to prisoners and would require extending the practice to other areas of law than those clinics are already undertaking.

I don't need a criminal lawyer. I need a tax lawyer. Otherwise, the minute I get out I will be sent right back in for my tax situation. (AG, 63, in prison 12 years)

Prisoner access needs to be made a priority for the new Court Challenges Program. The human rights issues in prison are systemic and

---

298 On community legal clinics, see e.g. Legal Aid Ontario, "Community Legal Clinics," online: http://www.legalaid.on.ca/en/contact/contact.asp?type=cl; Buhler, *supra* note 3.

often do not fall under areas benefiting from statutory or constitutionally protected legal aid rights (criminal, quasi-criminal, civil). While the program cannot and should not replace a properly functioning legal aid system for prisoners that would cover a number of areas of the law, it would be a significant complement with the potential to address a broad range of issues (and thus would probably solve many individual complaints that would otherwise fall on the shoulders of legal aid). Before the CCP was cut, the Elizabeth Fry Society proposed the creation of a Prisoner Court Challenges Program, modelled on the general CCP and working with clinics across the country, which would help individuals and groups who do not have the resources to vindicate their rights in court.[299] Perhaps it is time to reinforce this recommendation now that the Court Challenges Program has been recently reopened. If a Prison Court Challenges Program cannot be created, at least a portion of the annual funding for the CCP should be dedicated to prison litigation, which would go a long way towards fixing significant systemic problems such as that of accommodation for older people.

Finally, other than access to publicly funded advice and representation, a wide variety of services could be introduced, which are basic, cheap, and would have a significant impact. For instance, law libraries should be better stocked by seeking donations from university libraries, professors, and law students. The librarian should receive special training in working with legal materials, or a law librarian position could be created for a prisoner to occupy. This person could act as a peer mentor for those seeking legal information. Legal orientation sessions, with support from community or specialized clinics as well as not-for-profit organizations, should take place on a monthly basis in every institution. Organizations like Community Legal Education Ontario, which creates materials and sites for the dissemination of legal information,[300] should ensure that their printed materials are reaching detention centres. Last but not least, a comprehensive and up-to-date list of all legal resources should be made available in the library.

In 2002, the DOJ listed the consequences of continuing to ignore the legal needs of prisoners: delays in grievances, inaccessible programs, lack of timely conditional release, excessive time in segregation before transfer, overuse of force, use of force on mentally ill prisoners, excessive use of restraints, failure to adequately investigate prisoners' complaints, failure to investigate injuries and self-harm incidents, sexual harassment

---

299 Parkes & Pate, *supra* note 1 at 276–7; Parkes, "Prisoners' Charter," *supra* note 34 at 667.
300 Community Legal Education Ontario, online: https://www.cleo.on.ca/en.

of female prisoners, female prisoners housed in male institutions, and other prison issues.[301] Given that change is rarely undertaken voluntarily by the CSC, lack of legal aid may also mean an absence of systemic reform to account for the demographic changes in the prison population and to bolster the general respect for prisoner rights.

Conclusion

Sustainable reform cannot be undertaken without rigorous judicial oversight. The correctional system is an enterprise with its own duties and goals that sometimes trump other considerations. Ensuring that these duties and goals are achieved in the larger constitutional framework must be done by courts that benefit from guarantees of impartiality and independence.

Thus, when a novel correctional problem requiring extensive reform is identified, the benefit of legal action to push for reform, to ensure that reform is conducted in accordance with the law, and, ultimately, to force a conversation between the state branches that should undertake this reform in the first place cannot be neglected. In Canada, prisoners' rights are guaranteed both by the Constitution and by statutes, and prisoners should have access to the same remedial mechanism as everyone else. Unfortunately, legal history has shown that when prisoners challenge the actions of their incarcerators, either through judicial review or a *Charter* challenge or apply for damages, they are treated as second class citizens, legal standards are often loosened, and courts often defer to the expertise of the incarcerators.

With the rise of prison activists and the increase in prison research, the time has never been better for courts to utilize the available evidence, acknowledge their responsibility to supervise the quality and not just the quantity of the sentences they impose, and hold prison administrators accountable for breaches of the law just as they would for any other defendant. In most situations, courts step in when dialogue between parties ceases to exist, as a last resort mechanism. In prison settings, the role of the courts goes beyond that of arbitrating a dispute and offering relief to the harmed party. In the prison setting, courts are a last resort mechanism for a conversation that has not yet been initiated and is now overdue: a conversation about reform and the legality of conditions for vulnerable prisoners.

---

301 DOJ, *supra* note 271 at 28.

An integral part of the right to seek vindication in courts is prisoner access to those courts. By a simple syllogism, if no institutional reform and respect for the rule of law in prison can happen without court intervention[302] and if prisoners do not have access to courts without legal aid because they are poor and undereducated,[303] then no reform and respect for the rule of law in prison can be achieved without adequate prisoner legal aid. This issue goes beyond older prisoners (though it affects them particularly acutely) and beyond general carceral issues. It is an issue that speaks to the quality of our democracy.

---

302   Arbour Report, *supra* note 4; Parkes, "Prisoners' Charter," *supra* note 34; Parkes & Pate, *supra* note 1.
303   Manson, "Scrutiny," *supra* note 5; Parkes & Pate, *supra* note 1.

Chapter Seven

Conclusion

When I began this study in 2012, the population of inmates over fifty years old in the federal correctional system was about 15 per cent of the total prison population.[1] The Office of the Correctional Investigator (OCI) predicts that this number will continue to increase in the next decade.[2] In 2017, the number had reached 25 per cent and was continuing to grow.[3] At the end of 2018, the Correctional Service of Canada (CSC) had developed a policy framework addressing some of the issues raised by older prisoners. At the time of writing (March 2019), the policy was not publicly available.[4] The OCI has strengthened its efforts to push for reform for age-related matters behind bars;[5] at the time of writing, it had just released a report, together with the Canadian Human Rights Commission, on a systemic investigation into aging and elderly prisoners.[6] Legal Aid Ontario has made it part of their prison law test case strategy

1 Canada, Office of the Correctional Investigator, *Annual Report, 2010–2011* (Ottawa: OCI, 2011) at 14, online: http://www.oci-bec.gc.ca/cnt/rpt/pdf/annrpt/annrpt20102011-eng.pdf.

2 *Ibid.*

3 Canada, Office of the Correctional Investigator, *Annual Report, 2015–2016* (Ottawa: OCI, 2016): http://www.oci-bec.gc.ca/cnt/rpt/pdf/annrpt/annrpt20152016-eng.pdf.

4 Correctional Service of Canada, "Response to the Office of the Correctional Investigator's Report – Aging and Dying in Prison: An Investigation into the Experiences of Older Individuals in Federal Custody – February 2019" (Ottawa: CSC, 2019), online: https://www.csc-scc.gc.ca/publications/005007-1509-en.shtml.

5 See Canada, Office of the Correctional Investigator, *Annual Report, 2016–2017* (Ottawa: OCI, 2017), online: http://www.oci-bec.gc.ca/cnt/rpt/pdf/annrpt/annrpt20162017-eng.pdf.

6 Canada, Office of the Correctional Investigator & Canadian Human Rights Commission, *Aging and Dying in Prison: An Investigation into the Experiences of Older Individuals in Federal Custody* (Ottawa, OCI, 2019), online: http://www.oci-bec.gc.ca/cnt/rpt/pdf/oth-aut/oth-aut20190228-eng.pdf.

to fund challenges to the lack of medical services for elderly individuals. In terms of prisoners' rights, some moderate success has been recorded,[7] indicating perhaps a willingness on behalf of courts to give increased consideration to prisoner litigation.

Yet, for those I interviewed, change is yet to happen on the ground. What happened to John and Eric after they left the interview room? I do not know, as I could not follow up with the participants. Let's take a look at their chances.[8]

Most of the participants in this study will eventually be released, though the majority face many years of incarceration before that happens and will live in the same conditions described in this book, their health declining before they are finally released on parole. As they age, the number of those who report that they are affected by mental illnesses will likely increase. The number of people reporting dementia will likely double among the sample.

None of the participants will likely be compassionately released, no matter how sick they are. Recent CSC data show that, in 2015–2016, forty people across the country applied for compassionate release. Consistent with this study, none of these applications was successful. The three people who applied and were granted parole by exception were not released because there was nowhere for them to go (that is, no beds were available for them in the community).[9]

It is unlikely that any of those released on regular parole will ever re-offend. Nonetheless, based on the trend illustrated by this study, almost half of those released in old age will return to prison for breaches of administrative conditions. A return to prison often occurs because older prisoners are inappropriately prepared for release following years of incarceration and lack crucial support. As one study participant put it, "the struggle, the punishment, starts after you have been released on parole. That's the hard part for people like us."

---

7 See e.g. *British Columbia Civil Liberties Association v Canada (AG)*, 2018 BCSC 62.

8 This prediction is informed by the numbers from this study and from other studies: Anthony N. Doob, Cheryl Marie Webster, & Allan Manson, "Zombie Parole: The Withering of Conditional Release in Canada" (2014) 61 Crim LQ 301 at 304; Canada, Office of the Correctional Investigator, *Deaths in Custody* (Ottawa: OCI, 28 February 2007), online: http://www.oci-bec.gc.ca/cnt/rpt/pdf/oth-aut/oth-aut20070228-eng. pdf; Canada, Office of the Correctional Investigator, *A Three Year Review of Federal Inmate Suicides (2011–2014)* (Ottawa: OCI, 10 September 2014), online: http://www.oci-bec. gc.ca/cnt/rpt/pdf/oth-aut/oth-aut20140910-eng.pdf; and by the latest CSC report on death and dying in custody: Correctional Service of Canada, *Annual Report on Deaths in Custody 2015–2016*, Report No. SR 17-02 (Ottawa: CSC, November 2017), online: https:// www.csc-scc.gc.ca/research/092/005008-3010-en.pdf [CSC, *Deaths in Custody 2015–2016*].

9 CSC, *Deaths in Custody 2015–2016, supra* note 8 at 19.

Those who do manage to stay out will struggle with finding treatment for their addictions, mental health problems, and a host of chronic problems. Many will have family relationships broken by time and distance, more so than by crime. With little support and struggling with illness, many will depend on limited state support and die impoverished.

About two or three will die in prison, most likely from cancer. One or two might die of a heart attack that will have taken authorities over an hour to attempt to address. The likelihood of this prognosis is confirmed by the latest report on death and dying in prison. In 2015–2016, cancer was the leading natural cause of death, accounting for 40 per cent of all cases. Cardiovascular diseases were the second most common cause of death at 33 per cent of the total.[10]

One or two inmates will commit suicide. Because of their calm, non-belligerent, and non-threatening attitude overall, it is unlikely that any of those in the sample will die as a result of homicide (though there is always a possibility of being in the wrong place at the wrong time, especially at higher forms of security). They will, nonetheless, continue to face abuse from peers and staff, humiliation, threats, beatings, and theft, which will slowly but surely eat away at their self-esteem, self-worth, and sanity.

So, what are the chances the participants in this study will be released in a timely manner, their families intact, still healthy and sufficiently well off to live out their lives in a fulfilling way? Out of 200, we can expect this outcome will be the case for only a small handful.

This book is an attempt to inform and challenge. The issues discussed here point to systemic problems that, despite the decades-long fight of scholars, lawyers, and activists, continue to afflict the correctional environment: inadequate health care behind bars; disciplinary responses to medical conditions; the overwhelming use of solitary confinement; difficulties with accessing parole; inadequate preparation for release and a lack of community support once released; a deficient internal grievance process; an often deferential stance of courts, and especially of the Federal Court, towards prison administrators' decisions; and an overall difficulty for prisoners to access any kind of courts and tribunals due to lack of access to lawyers and legal advice.

While the issues discussed in this book are not new, the lens is. These systemic problems were presented through the perspective of a high-needs group of individuals who are likely experiencing the shortcomings of the system in a more acute manner than the mainstream population: individuals reaching old age behind bars.

---

10 *Ibid* at 12.

The data from 197 interviews with older prisoners not only reaffirmed these long-standing issues, but also put a new spin and sense of urgency on the need to address them. Aging is linked to a significant increase in the number of chronic and acute medical conditions, terminal illnesses and death, mental decline, and loss of family support. Aging is also associated with a decline in the risk of misbehaviour in prison and of reoffending once released. Coupled with the inability of the system to address the medical and social needs of older individuals, the risk decline calls into question the need for continued incarceration and points to an enhanced obligation to prioritize release, appropriate planning for release, and community support. Furthermore, when individuals do not receive the care they need and continue to languish in prisons under conditions that contribute to their physical and mental decline, the access to legal recourse is key, not only for their well-being but also for the well-being and validity of our system of rights. While progress has been registered in terms of the affirmation of prisoners' rights and their access to legal remedies, I argued in this book that such progress is still a far cry from the protection a holder of rights – whoever they may be – is entitled to.

Thus, through the lens of the experiences of older incarcerated individuals, I set out to address two issues in this book. First, I looked to establish the "what": What problems does the demographic shift bring to prisons? What legal obligations do these problems trigger? What can we do to improve the status quo? Second, I addressed the "how": How can we reform our release system and institutions of confinement to better meet the needs of this new wave of elderly individuals and, implicitly, of some of the other, lower-needs prisoners? How can we make the CSC undertake the needed reforms? How can reforms be imposed? How can prisoners challenge the lack of accommodation? How can prisoners obtain redress when the lack of accommodation is deteriorating their health or killing them? How can we improve access to justice and ensure meaningful change for these individuals?

Building on work previously conducted by Canadian scholars and activists, as well as on court rulings, I argued that, despite the new sense of urgency installed by the demographic shift, change does not come naturally behind prison bars. Despite a fairly robust legislative framework, a *Charter of Rights*, and an oversight mechanism, the CSC remains an intransigent institution that rarely undertakes reform or implements external recommendations willingly. In such a context, the need to improve prisoner access to administrative and legal recourse is key. I reviewed a number of avenues that should work in tandem to ensure the legitimacy of the penal system and the protection of prisoner rights.

First, the independent oversight of the correctional system must be bolstered. While the OCI is a progressive institution that has led to reform behind bars, it needs more teeth in order to keep the CSC on its legal track. The need for Canada to ratify the UN *Optional Protocol to the Convention against Torture* (OPCAT) and thus ensure a two-tier oversight mechanism in its correctional facilities is crucial; ratification would be a testimony to the country's commitment to human rights. The OCI would continue to operate within this framework, but with renewed strength given by the international training, advice, and resources it could access.

Second, prisoners do not have access to an impartial and effective grievance mechanism. In the current grievance system, the CSC is both the accused and the judge. Despite being the governmental agency second only to the police in terms of the use of force, the CSC is the only agency that does not have a grievance system that benefits from independent adjudication.[11] The concerns raised by this process are all the more serious since, as a general rule, prisoners do not have access to courts until they have exhausted the internal grievance process.

Third, access to courts is difficult for prisoners in a number of ways. Courts have historically been unwilling to overturn prison administrative decisions and have shown enhanced deference towards their "expertise." While there have been changes brought about by an increase in the number of *Charter* challenges and by empirical data on the effects of the carceral regime on individuals, courts continue to apply a double standard when the complainant is a prisoner. Thus, *Charter* challenges have been of limited success; *habeas corpus* applications continue to be dealt with by courts in a restrictive manner; and torts claims are often settled out of court. In addition, human rights tribunals, struggling across the board with backlogs and the ability to oversee the implementation of their decisions, have been little utilized by prisoners. Yet, tribunals and especially courts, with their guarantees of impartiality and independence, remain some of the best venues for claiming rights and requesting remedies that may change the face of the carceral regime. In such a context, building prison expertise in courts and tribunals is essential if we are to see more successful cases that result in changes behind bars. For that to happen, more cases need to make it to court, with better evidence and stronger representation. This necessity points to another type of systemic problem: prisoners' significant lack of access to procedural justice such as legal information, legal advice and representation, and legal aid services in general.

---

11   Jeremy Patrick, "Creating a Federal Inmate Grievance Tribunal" (2006) 48:2 CJCCJ 287 at 288.

As mentioned, while this issue is not a novel one, the demographic shift and the increase in the number of people dying in prisons after long, inadequately addressed illnesses add a renewed sense of urgency to reform. Working from the interview data, contextualized by participants' lived experiences, and building on previous work, I sought solutions for such reform in the last chapters of this book. These solutions are not all encompassing, and much more will need to be done to fix a broken system. But they may constitute a significant step forward, not only in protecting older prisoners but also in consolidating the status of incarcerated individuals as holders of substantive rights in general.

As a society faced with a growing problem, we need to adapt and make changes. When these changes do not come naturally, we need to involve the government, Parliament, and the courts in a conversation. When this conversation fails to happen, we must bring the matter to the courts, as the strongest protectors of our rights and the last resort mechanism that can force change. If courts refuse to get involved in a substantive manner, a void is created. Like a domino effect, lack of access to courts leads to ineffective prison oversight, which leads to lack of reforms, which leads to lack of accommodation, which leads to denial of rights, which leads to pain and suffering, which leads to broken individuals, which leads to longer prison terms, which leads to a greater demand on taxpayer money, less healthy and stable released individuals, and a big dent in our humanity, our democracy, and our inclusive society.

Index

CPSIA information can be obtained
at www.ICGtesting.com
Printed in the USA
LVHW092049241019
635287LV00002B/2/P